Peace, Politics & Economics in Asia

Pergamon Titles of Related Interest

Alsudairy et al.   Five War Zones: The Views of Local Military Leaders

Barnett   Beyond War: Japan's Concept of Comprehensive National Security

Hanks   American Sea Power & Global Strategy

Joes   From the Barrel of a Gun: Armies Revolutions

Matthews & Brown   Assessing the Vietnam War

Palmer   Westward Watch: The United States & the Changing Western Pacific

Research Institute for Peace and Security, Tokyo   Asian Security 1987

Yoder   The Conduct of American Foreign Policy Since World War II

Related Journal

(Free specimen copy available on request)

Defense Analysis

Peace, Politics & Economics in Asia
The Challenge to Cooperate

Edited by

Robert A. Scalapino

and

Masataka Kosaka

Published in cooperation with
the Security Conference on Asia and the Pacific,
Marina del Rey, California

PERGAMON-BRASSEY'S
INTERNATIONAL DEFENSE PUBLISHERS
(a member of the Pergamon Group)

WASHINGTON · NEW YORK · LONDON · OXFORD · BEIJING
FRANKFURT · SÃO PAULO · SYDNEY · TOKYO · TORONTO

LP

U.S.A. (Editorial)	Pergamon-Brassey's International Defense Publishers, 8000 Westpark Drive, Fourth Floor, McLean, Virginia 22102, U.S.A.
(Orders)	Pergamon Press, Maxwell House, Fairview Park, Elmsford, New York 10523, U.S.A.
U.K. (Editorial)	Brassey's Defence Publishers, 24 Gray's Inn Road, London WC1X 8HR
(Orders)	Brassey's Defence Publishers, Headington Hill Hall, Oxford OX3 0BW, England
PEOPLE'S REPUBLIC OF CHINA	Pergamon Press, Room 4037, Qianmen Hotel, Beijing, People's Republic of China
FEDERAL REPUBLIC OF GERMANY	Pergamon Press, Hammerweg 6, D-6242 Kronberg, Federal Republic of Germany
BRAZIL	Pergamon Editora, Rua Eça de Queiros, 346, CEP 04011, Paraiso, São Paulo, Brazil
AUSTRALIA	Pergamon-Brassey's Defence Publishers, P.O. Box 544, Potts Point, N.S.W. 2011, Australia
JAPAN	Pergamon Press, 8th Floor, Matsuoka Central Building, 1–7–1 Nishishinjuku, Shinjuku-ku, Tokyo 160, Japan
CANADA	Pergamon Press Canada, Suite No. 271, 253 College Street, Toronto, Ontario, Canada M5T 1R5

First edition 1988

Library of Congress Cataloging in Publication Data
Peace, politics & economics in Asia: the challenge to
cooperate [edited] by Robert A. Scalapino and Masataka
Kosaka.
1. East Asia—Politics and government. 2. Asia,
Southeastern—Politics and government. 3. East Asia—
Economic conditions. 4. Asia, Southeastern—Economic
conditions. I. Scalapino, Robert A. II. Kosaka, Masataka,
1934–   . III. Title: Peace, politics, and economics in Asia.
DS518.1.P44 1988   87-25840

British Library Cataloguing in Publication Data
Peace, politics and economics in Asia: the
challenge to cooperate.—(A SeCAP publication).
1. Asia—Economic integration
I. Scalapino, Robert A.   II. Kosaka, Masataka
III. Series
337.1'5   HC412
ISBN 0-08-035961-2

*Printed in Great Britain by
Hazell Watson & Viney Limited
Member of BPCC plc
Aylesbury Bucks*

Contents

SECTION ONE. Strategic Issues

SECTION TWO. Economic Issues

4. *The Roots of Stability: The Economies of Northeast and Southeast Asia*   65
by Lawrence B. Krause

5. *Future Prospects for Economic Cooperation in Asia and the Pacific Region*   87
by Ryokichi Hirono

SECTION THREE. Political Issues

6. *Domestic Developments Affecting Stability and Regional Relationships in Northeast Asia*   107
by William H. Gleysteen, Jr.

7. *Korea: A Tricycle in Transition*   122
by Hongkoo Lee

viii   *Contents*

List of Tables

List of Illustrations

Preface

This volume is dedicated to Richard L. Sneider (1922–1986)—public servant, scholar, and founding member of SeCAP (the Security Conference on Asia and the Pacific).

Dick Sneider was an outstanding member of that generation of Americans drawn into the affairs of Asia by World War II; and his productive career spanned four decades during which the United States became thoroughly enmeshed in the political development and economic growth of the region. Indeed, Mr. Sneider's career included major contributions to one of the most successful phases of U.S. foreign policy in a region once distant and esoteric to most Americans, yet now central to America's interests abroad.

Mr. Sneider's wartime training as a Japanese language officer led to his participation in the post-war occupation in Okinawa and Tokyo. This early experience served him well in his foreign service career, where he specialized in Japanese affairs, ultimately serving as principal negotiator for the Okinawan Reversion negotiations.

Dick Sneider's analytical strengths were developed through graduate training in Soviet and Japanese affairs at Columbia University and they found immediate practical application in the State Department. In the summer of 1950, he developed unique background on the Korean Communist movement—information that enabled the U.S. government to respond to the shock of war on the Korean Peninsula. His understanding of Korean affairs ultimately led to the culmination of his official career as ambassador to the Republic of Korea (1974–1978).

Mr. Sneider was unique among foreign service officers in his ability to bridge the worlds of politics and scholarship, practical affairs and analysis. Upon his retirement from the foreign service in the late 1970s, he returned to Columbia to teach and write and to engage in business consulting. At the same time, he sustained his foreign policy interest by helping to organize SeCAP as a vehicle for promoting discussion of international political, security, and economic issues among Asians and Americans.

This volume, one of Dick Sneider's last professional projects, reflects the full scope of his interests and concerns, covering security and political developments in the region as well as prospects for regional economic cooperation. Indeed, the theme of this volume—the challenge of regional

cooperation—and Dick Sneider's skill in helping to bring together a
diverse group of Asians and Americans to assess prospects for regional
cooperation are meaningful tributes to Sneider's lifelong contributions to
Asian–American relations.

Dick Sneider was a friend and professional colleague of great
accomplishment, insight, and intensity. In dedicating this volume to his
memory, we express both our personal affection for him as an individual
and our recognition of all that he contributed to the advancement of America's relations with Asia.

Acknowledgments

The authors want to express their appreciation for the invaluable support and assistance provided by a number of institutions and individuals in the publication of this volume.

Financial support for the August 1985 SeCAP conference on "Opportunities and Constraints on Asian Regional Cooperation," which was the initial source of the papers in this volume, was provided by grants from the U.S.–Japan Foundation, the Olin Foundation and the United States Information Agency.

In preparing the manuscript, Brigadier (ret.) Kenneth Hunt provided timely and important editorial assistance. We are indebted to Masashi Nishihara, Akihiko Tanaka, Hajime Izumi, Ms. Chieko Kitagawa Otsuru and Michiko Suzuki for indispensable assistance in making the necessary arrangements for the conference and to Ms. Dorothy Diamond and Masashi Nishihara for their invaluable care in organizing and supervising revision of the papers for publication. The Japanese language version of this book has been published by Ningen-no-Kagaku Sha.

Editors' Note

We have grouped the essays that follow into sections that explore various facets of the broad subject with which our workshop was concerned, seeking to provide a logical sequence. The opening section deals with strategic issues affecting cooperation, with the broad context provided by Masashi Nishihara and a treatment of key strategic issues set forth by Robert Scalapino. There follows a section presenting an overview of economic conditions in the Asian-Pacific region and prospects for economic cooperation, contained in essays by Lawrence Krause and Ryokichi Hirono. A third division probes the critical question of political stability, another factor with major implications for the type and degree of cooperation possible. A regional treatment is provided by William Gleysteen, with special problem areas analyzed by Hongkoo Lee, Jesus Estanislao, and Sukhumbhand Paribatra. Our studies conclude with the contribution of Evelyn Colbert on the prospects for regional cooperation in Southeast Asia and Richard Sneider's survey of potentialities for the Asian-Pacific area as a whole.

ROBERT A. SCALAPINO and MASATAKA KOSAKA

1

Introduction

by Robert A. Scalapino and Masataka Kosaka

When one reflects upon the travails undergone in the course of building and maintaining the European Economic Community and the North Atlantic Treaty Organization, pessimism with respect to the creation of a genuinely regional structure in East Asia seems warranted. In far greater degree than Western Europe, East Asia represents a mosaic of states differing in culture, stage of economic development, and political-economic institutions. Historic animosities project themselves into the present, even between societies that share common interests. And unlike the situation with respect to the two Germanies, the divided states of Asia have no international sanction. Together with contested boundaries, they remain festering sores, potentially malignant.

It is thus natural that cooperation in Asia, whether economic, political or strategic, has been heavily bilateral rather than multilateral in structure. To an extensive degree, moreover, it has gravitated around the two major nations whose power and influence have been projected throughout the region, namely, the United States and the Soviet Union. Since the end of World War II, these two nations fashioned alliances in East Asia, ties that combined economic assistance, political bonds, and military support. These alliances were relatively exclusive in nature, demanding firm commitments on the part of both parties. The heavier burdens rested upon the dominant party to the alliance, the returns being mainly strategic in nature. Some weak linkages combining bilateral alliances were forged, but always, the effectiveness of such linkages was dependent upon the initiatives (and pressures) of the principal power, either the U.S. or the USSR.

Since this was the case, trends in the fortunes of the two "superpowers" in Asia and shifts in their respective foreign policies affected not only the balance of power throughout the region, but the foreign policies of virtually all of the East Asian states. In the years immediately after 1945, events were shaped by the outcome of the twentieth century's second global conflict. While horribly wounded and only a regional power at most, the Soviet Union—determined to create an effective buffer against future incursions—projected itself both west and east on the Eurasian continent. In Asia, the alliances with China and North Korea, in addition to the long-standing tie with Outer Mongolia, provided the USSR with a presence in

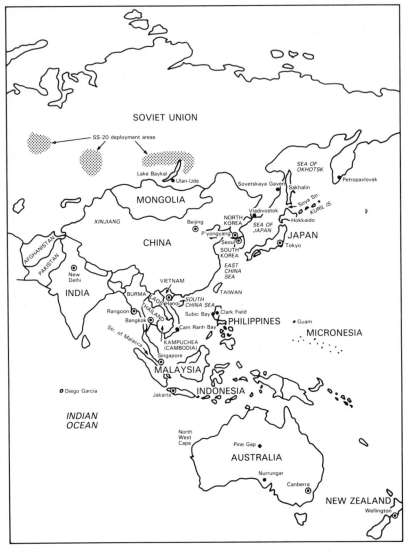

FIG. 1.1. The Soviet Far East, Asia, and the Western Pacific.

Northeast Asia greater than that ever previously attained by Russia. Soviet gains were not without cost. Considering the devastation suffered by the Soviet Union and the impoverished condition of its people, Soviet economic assistance to Asian allies represented a great sacrifice. Military aid was also substantial, although Russian leaders resolutely refused to commit Soviet manpower, except for a few aviators, to the Asian conflicts that ensued. They preferred to enable Asians to fight Americans.

In earlier years, it was customary in the West to speak of "the Communist Camp" versus the "Free World." Indeed, Moscow sought in every way possible to forge tight ideological, economic, and strategic bonds among the nations—new and old—under its banners. In contrast to Eastern Europe, however, Soviet alliances in Asia retained a substantial degree of separateness despite some linkages. In part, this was a product of history. The Chinese Communists came to recognize Outer Mongolia as an independent entity reluctantly, as had their predecessors in power. North Korea represented another region historically within the Chinese sphere of influence, a fact that manifested itself in the North Korean factional divisions that reached a climax in the years immediately after the Korean War.

Although its voice was muted in the years of the Sino-Soviet alliance, China's reassertion of its "legitimate rights" as the center of the Asian world was inevitable when conditions—its own and others—permitted. The Sino–Soviet cooperation that emerged in the face of a common enemy and the exigencies that followed a lengthy, destructive war had their underside in the competition that progressively came to the fore as Chinese self-confidence rubbed against Russian defensiveness. Enmity came more quickly than anyone had imagined possible. Now, having assessed the cost of unalleviated hostility, both China and the USSR are seeking a relationship that enables reduction of tension and some degree of normalcy so that pressing domestic needs can be given greater attention. Precisely what mix of competition and cooperation will evolve in Sino–Soviet relations cannot presently be predicted. Neither end of the continuum is likely to prevail. War or alliance seem remote possibilities today. Most plausible, at least in the near term, is a cautious normalcy, calculating rather than trustful.

Meanwhile, the Soviet alliance with North Korea also confronted serious difficulties after the initial postwar years. At first, the Democratic People's Republic of Korea was a true Soviet satellite, a condition that undoubtedly grated upon the xenophobic, nationalistic Koreans, including Kim Il-song, whom the Russians had placed in power. The Korean War and the Sino–Soviet split that occurred shortly thereafter provided the opportunity for the shrimp to swim between rival whales with greater flexibility. Yet in recent years, after generally tilting toward China, North Korean leaders have accepted Soviet overtures. Moscow's economic assis-

tance has become more important as the North Korean economy has run
into difficulties. Military aid, although doled out somewhat carefully, is
equally welcome. In exchange, the Russians now get greater political support and, more importantly, privileges that include overflights and port
visits for military ships. In addition to the strategic gains, these privileges
signify the return of the Soviet Union to the Korean peninsula in a more
impressive manner. Moscow was visibly unhappy about earlier Chinese
primacy and about its exclusion from the negotiations of recent years
involving China and the United States as well as the two Koreas. To be a
part of the decisionmaking process in all major regions, in Soviet eyes, is
an essential factor in one's status as a global power, particularly in a region
as vital to Soviet national interests as Northeast Asia. In important
measure, increased assistance to Pyongyang is also a response to the
perceived strategic entente now encompassing the United States, Japan,
and South Korea.

Yet the Russians know that there are limits to the new Soviet–North
Korean relationship. Pyongyang cannot afford to alienate China by
embracing Moscow too closely; nor are its natural instincts in that direction. Even now, the Chinese are showing signs of growing unhappiness
with the new Soviet–North Korean relationship. It has not been possible
to link North Korea closely with the East European-Soviet economic orbit
(COMECON) despite Pyongyang's need for modern technology and its
recent decision to turn outward for such purposes. If finances and politics
permitted, North Korea would choose Japan as its leading trading partner
and source of technology. Soviet leaders must also be careful lest they
damage the prospects for improved Sino–Soviet relations by appearing to
pose yet another threat on China's borders. The essays by William Gleysteen, Hongkoo Lee and this author provide additional perspectives and
details on current political-strategic relations in Northeast Asia.

Building cooperative relations between the Soviet bloc and southern
Asia has proven equally complex. The Soviet alliance with Vietnam ranks
today with the Soviet–Mongolian alliance as the most comprehensive
Soviet tie outside the European theater. Massive economic and military
aid has enabled Hanoi to continue its campaign to establish hegemony
over Indochina in the face of substantial opposition from various neighbors. The benefits to both parties comprising the Soviet–Vietnamese
alliance have been substantial; so have the costs. The USSR now has a
presence in Southeast Asia, and it is closely connected with the foremost
military power of the region. By the same token, the fact that it underwrites
Vietnamese expansion complicates its relations both with the ASEAN
community and with China. Moreover, it is difficult to see how this particular bilateral relation can be broadened to take on a cooperative regional
character. If the economic and political regional bonds it so badly needs
are to be developed, Vietnam must overcome a confrontational image

insofar as most of the Southeast Asian states are concerned, and abandon the arrogance that marks its international behavior. Sooner or later, moreover, Hanoi's leaders must confront the issue of relations with China, since the present level of hostility exacts an extremely heavy price. Perhaps a neutral Cambodia can be fashioned, providing a partial answer, but no such solution appears on the immediate horizon. Intransigence now dominates the scene, clouding the prospects for cooperation outside the prevailing political-military lines. Sukhumbhand Paribatra provides his own views on the Cambodian problem in this volume, in an essay that sets forth alternatives and their possible consequences.

In South Asia, the bilateral ties to which the USSR is a party have taken two forms: those with Afghanistan, a state once fiercely independent, now reduced to the position of client state; and those with India, representing what Soviet leaders rightly view as their most successful bilateral relationship in Asia. The latter tie has endured through regime change because diverse Indian leaders have perceived it to have served India's national interests in both security and developmental terms. Whether that will be true in the future remains to be seen. Meanwhile, this particular Soviet bilateral relation has greater opportunity than others of lending itself to regional and international linkages. India now takes a leading role in the recently established organization labeled South Asian Association for Regional Cooperation (SAARC), and while SAARC has as yet very limited substantive meaning, it represents a forum for airing issues of consequence to the states that coexist on or alongside the Indian subcontinent. India is also in a position to counter anti-Soviet moves in the so-called Non-Aligned Conference.

However, despite these bilateral ties and its periodic calls for Asian collective security and other forms of regional cooperation, the Soviet Union is acutely aware of the fact that its image in Asia is generally negative. More important, it has taken virtually no part in the dynamic East Asian economic revolution of the last several decades. Thus, General Secretary Mikhail Gorbachev sought to signal a new course for Soviet Asian policies in his Vladivostok speech of July 28, 1986. With his primary appeal directed at China, Gorbachev indicated that the Soviet Union was prepared to negotiate upon specific grievances, wanted to subordinate revolution to peace and development, and desired to join in both global and regional efforts toward economic cooperation.

The response from Asians at this point has been cautious, but a willingness to await Soviet actions and a further unfolding of Soviet policies has generally been exhibited. Two critical variables will heavily influence the long-term results of the new Soviet approach: the outcome of economic reform efforts within the USSR itself and the evaluation by each Pacific-Asian state of its own national interests as these relate to Soviet overtures. Whatever the outcome, we are witnessing the beginning of a serious effort

on the part of the USSR to strengthen its position in Asia by adding
economic and political increments to what has been an overwhelmingly
military policy. Its dilemma is how to effect this improvement without
abandoning those strategic and political gains of recent years it does not
wish to jeopardize. The strategic gains are set forth in the initial essay of
this volume contributed by Masashi Nishihara.

In the years following World War II, the United States has also cultivated numerous bilateral ties in Asia. Washington's initial hope was that
China would play a key role throughout the region on behalf of democracy
and stability, but events dictated otherwise. Thus, in a very brief period
of time, Japan was elevated from the status of enemy to that of ally, albeit
an ally of dramatically unequal rank in the initial period. After American-
sponsored reform came American aid, enabling Japan to commence its
march to economic power. There followed in quick succession a firm
security linkage. U.S. policies, to be sure, were not the sole source of the
events that were to unfold. Japan's success has also been a product of
its culture, a lengthy experience with modernization, and governmental
policies well-conceived in terms of the then prevailing needs and capacities
of Japanese society and those of the world. One of the present challenges
is whether the latter asset, enormously important in terms of its past contributions, can be maintained in the future.

The bilateral ties between the United States and Japan have become the
most intense and comprehensive experienced by either nation in its history. For this very reason, tensions and opportunities vie with each other
at this stage in the evolution of the U.S.–Japan relationship as Lawrence
Krause indicates in his essay. With Japan's emergence as a global economic
power came the economic challenge to the United States at roughly the
same time that the Soviet Union was presenting a military challenge. The
United States has lost its competitiveness in certain industries previously
considered critical to its economic and military strength. The threat continues to spread. The blame to be assigned is hotly debated. Suffice it to
say that faults lie on both sides. Meanwhile, two opposite trends intensify.
On the one hand, economic nationalism—long a central factor in Japanese
policies, receding slowly amid reluctance—has reasserted itself on the
American front. It promises to be a prominent issue in both nations,
especially in the United States, in the period immediately ahead. At the
same time, we are witnessing the rapid and continuous growth of interdependence, as the two economies become ever more intertwined. No
development augurs greater potential—and risks—for the future.

As we shall soon note, the issues troubling U.S.–Japan economic
relations are increasingly multilateral in character. Just as the health of the
U.S. and Japanese economies is crucial to the future of the entire Pacific-
Asian region, so the policies of the NICs (newly industrializing countries)
and the less developed states are vital in determining the extent of cooper-

ation versus conflicts in the economic sphere. The central issues are rendered more complex because of the radically different developmental stages at which these societies find themselves today. Economic nationalism, however, whatever justifications are advanced in its favor by emerging states, can only make more difficult the task of maintaining or developing open economic policies on the part of the advanced industrial nations.

Important though it has been, the U.S. alliance with Japan is but one of a number of such ties created after 1945. The initial American emphasis was upon those nations that lay off the shores of the Asian continent, since one persuasive strategic theory held that Communist expansion could best be contained by creating an island cordon sanitaire along the perimeters of the Asian mainland, thereby relying upon U.S. air and sea power and avoiding the commitment of land armies to the vast, populous continent. Thus, strategic ties were strengthened with the Philippines, Australia, and, after 1950, with the Republic of China on Taiwan. As in the case of Soviet bilateral alliances, moreover, the United States attended closely to the economic and political aspects of these relationships. Indeed, American aid was vastly larger in quantity and more generous in terms than that of the USSR to its allies.

For the most part, the ties remained bilateral, however, since economic and political conditions did not lend themselves to extensive multilateralism. The United States served as the vortex around which others positioned themselves. In the strategic arena, a later foray was made into multilateralism via SEATO (Southeast Asia Treaty Organization), but this effort had limited success apart from strengthening the American commitment to the region.

SEATO, however, illustrated a dilemma, which had been present for U.S. policymakers since the outset of the postwar era, that encompassed Thailand as well as the Philippines. Given the economic, political, and strategic considerations involved, could the Asian continent be separated from the offshore states? Was the island cordon sanitaire thesis sound? This issue had first been raised in acute form in Northeast Asia. As a result of World War II, the United States had inherited a commitment to South Korea for which it was ill-prepared. The difficulties of molding the Republic of Korea into a democratic polity in short order soon became obvious. Indeed, in considerable measure, democracy and development appeared to be in conflict. In any case, as an ex-colony, Korea was not in a position to build upon a lengthy experiment with economic development, as in the case of Japan. The extent to which these problems as well as the troubled American occupation that failed to resolve them, contributed to the U.S. decision to withdraw militarily from South Korea in 1949 can be debated. However, there can be no doubt that the military withdrawal and the authoritative American statements accompanying it misled the Communists into believing that the United States would not defend South Korea.

A similar scenario unfolded in the course of the events that ended with large-scale American participation in the Vietnam War. As the United States wrestled with very basic political-strategic issues, it sent decidedly unclear signals for others to interpret.

Today, the issue of continental versus island commitments that plagued American strategists for several decades is less germane due to the changing political-strategic configuration of Asia and the revolutionary developments in military technology. The 1969 Guam Declaration, however, is still broadly operative in establishing the limits upon and conditions of American military cooperation with Asian allies. The stress is upon auxiliary assistance, with the primary responsibility resting with the threatened country. American aid, moreover, is to take the form principally of air and sea power. It is clear, however, that American strategic commitments, limited although they may be, make no discrimination at present between mainland and island nations. Yet the character of the security relationship varies considerably among the many bilateral ties currently in existence. With Japan and South Korea, separate commitments extend to joint defense plans and military exercises. With the Philippines, despite intensifying domestic debate, U.S. bases remain a critical factor in juxtaposition to the growing Soviet presence in Southeast Asia. With virtually all of the ASEAN states, the United States has some type of strategic relation, even if it extends only to arms transfer. Highly limited assistance even flows to the Khmer noncommunist guerrillas in their struggle against Hanoi. In the South Pacific, security agreements are now in effect between the United States and certain of the newly independent regions of Micronesia. But ANZUS is now only an Australian–United States alliance (AUS) as a result of the decision of New Zealand's Labour government to prohibit U.S. ships carrying nuclear weapons from visitings its ports; hence, one of the few genuinely multilateral strategic agreements has lapsed. Finally, a low-level strategic tie with the PRC has evolved, still embryonic and to be tested. This development, moreover, has occurred despite the continued sale of military weaponry and technology to Taiwan.

In *The Soviet Far East Military Buildup*, published under the aegis of the Security Conference on Asia and the Pacific, the same group that organized the sessions from which these essays have emerged—the two editors, Richard Solomon and Masataka Kosaka—set forth what they considered to be the appropriate military responses to the recent Soviet military buildup in the region. Summarized, these are:

The United States should maintain an effective but low-visibility nuclear retaliatory force in Asia.

The United States and allied governments should pursue measures to ensure the survivability of that force.

U.S. allies should maintain sufficiently strong conventional forces to counter nonnuclear Soviet threats.

Arms control negotiation should be one aspect of a comprehensive response to the Soviet nuclear challenge.[1]

As has already been implied, post-1945 Asia has never been divided neatly into two camps. In addition to the fluidity that existed within each so-called "camp," a number of states—virtually all of them ex-colonies—proclaimed themselves independent from either major power center. Originally, they identified themselves as "neutralists." Later, the standard term was to become "nonaligned nations," and various organizations or groups have emerged under this designation, the most prominent being the Non-Aligned Conference, global in its scope. While the term "nonalignment" has considerable political advantage for certain nations, it has always been largely mythical and never more so than at present. If there are any truly nonaligned states in Asia, they do not go beyond Burma, which dropped out of the Non-Aligned Confernce precisely because the states making up that conference were not nonaligned.

In reality, two overarching trends render past and present descriptions of economic, political, and strategic relations between and among Pacific-Asian states increasingly obsolete. On the one hand, as I have indicated in other writings, the broad trend globally is from alliance to alignment. Postwar alliances reflected a relationship relatively exclusive and one in which the major party had extensive, fixed obligations, security and economic in nature, whereas the minor party reciprocated by swearing political allegiance or, in broader terms, loyalty. At present, bilateral and multilateral relations have become more porous. The major party, explicitly or implicitly, defines its obligations as partial and contingent upon the attitudes and actions of its partner(s). The minor party insists upon the right to take separate, sometimes opposing stances in the political realm, and in other ways to manifest a greater degree of independence.

The second broad trend is the rapid growth of regional and global interdependence in all economic, political, and strategic realms. This central fact has compelled virtually every state to find a meaningful cluster—that is, a group of states or an order that serves its needs. Even a hermit like North Korea has now begun to realize that the path of autarky is the route to obsolescence. Thus, the nonaligned states, virtually without exception, tilt economically toward that order in which the Soviet Union plays the dominant role or that order in which Japan and the United States currently exercise a condominium. Politically, also, there are few if any states that practice equidistance. The leaders of a large majority of the authoritarian-pluralist states of Asia find themselves forced to experiment with greater openness, whatever their reservations. In only a very few states can the citizenry be isolated from the political currents flowing in the external world, and while those currents are decidedly diverse, the present trend appears to be in the direction of greater popular participation in the political process. Even among Leninist states, where the political system is much closer to that of the USSR than to that of Japan and the West, if the economic and strategic pulls are in the latter direction, an ideological-political challenge follows, as is currently the case with China. The long-term implications of this development have yet to be tested.

If political "self-sufficiency" has become increasingly difficult, such a stance with respect to security interests is virtually impossible. Thus, it is natural that we have witnessed some seemingly curious strategic align-ments, cutting across "natural" ideological and political lines: the Soviet–Indian and U.S.–PRC connections being two current examples.

In sum, we are in the midst of a great transitional era not only with respect to relations between and among the major powers but with respect to all bilateral ties. Neither bipolarism nor bilateralism is disappearing. To suggest, as some have done, that multipolarism is taking the place of U.S.–USSR predominance is at least premature and probably inaccurate as a prognosis of the era immediately ahead, especially in a strategic sense. Nor is bilateralism a spent force. It will continue to possess both power and validity in certain contexts, for certain reasons. Yet developments in Asia demonstrate that in a tentative, cautious way, most governments are reaching out, sometimes without being fully conscious of their actions, seeking ways to supplement if not to supplant old forms of interstate relations.

The soft regionalism now emerging in Northeast Asia is a case in point. I use the term "soft regionalism" to indicate that it is a regionalism without formal structure. Yet, with Japan having served as the primary initial catalyst, a steadily expanding and deepening network of economic ties among the Northeast Asian states has developed. These ties have cut across political lines. Witness the growing trade between China and Taiwan, China and South Korea, Japan and North Korea, and Japan and China. It takes political as well as economic forms. Summitry between the leaders of the region—potentially including Gorbachev—has been undertaken or is in the offing. Conversations have encompassed such thorny issues as those relating to the divided states. Various leaders—among them Deng and Nakasone—have served as middlemen, conveying messages across political lines. Even unobtrusive security ties have emerged in reciprocal visits by defense officials, the sharing of intelligence information, and plans that encompass some Japanese responsibility for regional security. On all of these fronts, especially the latter, extreme caution must be taken. The land mines are numerous, reflective of ancient and recent history. It may be less easy in Asia than in West Europe to overcome the legacy of the past, but the process is unevenly enroute.

In Southeast Asia, as Evelyn Colbert points out, two hostile groups presently confront each other; however, each, in its own way, constitutes a group and not merely a congeries of wholly separate states. Vietnam is seeking to create an integrated Indochina under its aegis. Whether it succeeds or fails, it must put military power out front, now and for the foreseeable future. Not without reason, one Vietnamese leader privately defined his nation as "the Prussia of Southeast Asia." The ASEAN community rests upon voluntarism. Hence, its structure is looser, its decisions more subject to individual idiosyncrasies and varying perceptions of national interests. For these and other reasons, ASEAN has few economic accomplishments to its credit. It is rather the political-strategic realm where the five now six, since the 1984 inclusion of Brunei, nations of Southeast Asia have made a collective mark. From a highly separatist, even confrontational, past, leaders have come to know each other, with a new atmosphere created. They have discovered, moreover, that their united voices can make a difference to larger states, whereas individual voices can easily be ignored.

ASEAN, however, is not in itself a sufficient vehicle to resolve the economic problems confronting its members. As Lawrence Krause indicates in his broadly gauged essay on the East Asian economies, virtually all of the ASEAN members face serious economic challenges at present. Previous economic strategies appear to need revision, yet the appropriate remedial measures remain elusive. The export-oriented strategy faces growing obstacles as an increasing number of nations concentrate upon the markets of the United States and Western Europe, evoking defensive measures in response. Current prices discourage an emphasis upon the further development of energy and primary products at present. Yet import-substitution policies are frequently uneconomic, especially when they have very limited rationale in terms of indigenous resources.

Economic uncertainties make more difficult the political transition that is taking place in a number of these societies. The recent political scene in the Philippines is well sketched in the essay in this volume by Jesus Estanislao. In most cases, however, the states of Southeast Asia can be defined as authoritarian-pluralist in nature. A political structure that is in some degree restrictive presides over a society in which social and economic institutions have a considerable degree of independence. Such societies always contain a sizable quotient of instability, since tension develops between the more traditional polity and the rapidly changing socioeconomic environment over which it wields power.

These conditions apply not only to a majority of the ASEAN states but to South Korea and Taiwan, as William Gleysteen and Hongkoo Lee indicate in their contributions. Generally, the pressures upon the leaders of such societies are to evolve toward greater political openness—a result in part of the emergence of a better-educated, more affluent citizenry, the byproduct of rapid economic growth. Such pressures also result from the increasing flow of ideas across cultural and political boundaries, another type of interdependence that has rapidly unfolded, as we have already noted.

In sum, it seems clear that we are at a stage of history demanding the development of new and expanded forms of interaction across national boundaries. To stand still is to move backward, and the threat of moving backward into various forms of protectionist, autarkic policies is very real. Nor is this merely a threat among advanced, industrial societies; it is an omnipresent possibility in the developing world. Economic policies in this direction would inevitably have political consequences unpleasant to contemplate. Fortunately, we need not start from ground zero with regard to internationalism in the Pacific-Asian region. Richard Sneider and Ryok-ichi Hirono outline some of the institutions and organizations that have pioneered in bringing peoples and states together. As Sneider makes clear, it is not necessary (and not possible) to require a highly structured, formal organization of the European Economic Community (EEC) type at this point in time. There is a wide range of means, private as well as official, whereby economic and social problems common to most states of the region can be studied, with recommendations advanced.

The twenty-first century seems likely to be an era when regionalism—that intermediate level between nationalism and globalism—makes major advances. It will not be an exclusive development, but the economic and political logic behind such a trend is overwhelming. In preparing for this era, it might be useful to suggest measures and perspectives, political and economic, that would help to support a more harmonious, cooperative relationship among nations, and one that will speak to the primary concerns of every state—security and development. Some of the proposals outlined below have been advanced, either directly or by implication, in the essays that follow.

1. **Only occasionally can one nation impose its values or system upon another, and the effort to do so is generally costly and often counterproductive. At the same time, the political compatibility or incompatibility of two or more nations will have an influence upon the degree of cooperation possible, especially if one of the nations is the United States.** It can be argued, of course, that the USSR has successfully imposed its system upon a number of states peripheral to it. But this has required a great—and continuous—military presence, at least in the case of Eastern Europe. And the Asian Communist states may sleep in the same ideological bed as the Russians, but they have different dreams. The United States has also sought to impose a Western-style democratic system upon societies at times when its presence has been massive. But the results have been decidedly mixed, and even for Japan, where indigenous conditions permitted a successful experimentation with democracy in the course of the second effort, the system works rather differently than in America. Thus, history suggests that when one nation seeks to engage in social engineering in another nation, the hazards are many. This fact poses an especially painful dilemma for the United States since the American people have

long insisted that U.S. foreign policy should have moral foundations, and thus issues like human rights become important when assistance or commitments are contemplated. But every U.S. administration has had to temper its moral judgments with its strategic concerns, recognizing that no perfect or final solutions to this basic issue are likely to be found.

2. **It is wise to assume that irrespective of their ideological commitments, all nation-states today will behave rather similarly, with elitist perceptions of national interest paramount in policy decisions.** The ideological quotient in foreign policies, never as overpowering as some observers imagined, has declined. If one seeks to discern the current and future political-strategic policies of the Soviet Union and China by turning to the works of Lenin or Mao, he is ill-advised. It would be better to read Machiavelli or, even more appropriately, some of the modern treatises on nationalism and balance-of-power politics. Ideology cannot be wholly discarded, nor can tradition and culture. They play supportive roles, but they are not the principal elements. Both policy makers and citizens must take care not to be unduly influenced by rhetoric, thereby missing the substance of the policies—whether of friend or foe.

3. **Much of Asia is in political transition, but the prospects for systemic change of a political nature are less than in many other regions.** The most fragile Asian societies are the authoritarian-pluralist states, where tensions grow between a relatively traditional polity and a dynamic socioeconomic revolution. Continuing instability in these societies is highly probable, and they require the type of special assistance in economic and cultural terms that states like the United States and Japan should be prepared to provide. Yet few if any of these societies will become states of the Leninist type, on the one hand, or Western-style democracies on the other. The broad trend within them is toward greater political openness, though retreats and periodic immobility are to be expected. Yet in political terms, dominant party systems are more likely than alternations in power through elections, with the primary issue being whether such systems permit political openness or are sustained by an extensive quotient of coercion. In any case, the challenge for nations like the United States and Japan is to work out a relationship with such societies that encourages economic development and social pluralism, with the hope that the type of political evolution that proceeds within such a context will increasingly underwrite the humanistic and political values associated with free societies.

4. **In an age when the broad movement is from alliance to alignment, close consultation between and among aligned nations and the acceptance of differences are essential elements to any international order.** The mechanisms for official consultation have generally been expanded. However, the private networks that should buttress and expand such con-

sultations remain extremely weak. It is in this area that major new efforts should be made by the United States, Japan, and their Pacific friends.

5. **In the middle to long term, all Pacific–Asian states should be encouraged to participate in regional economic development, through whatever instrumentalities are at hand.** Isolation or autarky generally results not only in economic backwardness but in political extremism. Clearly, participants in the economic order must accept minimal responsibilities of both an economic and political nature. Boycotts and other forms of exclusion, however, rarely serve their purpose over a long period. As already indicated, this does not mean that economic assistance should be given without conditions, political and security as well as economic. Aid is a privilege, not a right. But generally speaking, the marketplace should be open, in every sense of the term.

6. **Rather than seeking to create a Pacific-wide economic organization of a formal type, an effort not feasible at present or for the foreseeable future, regional economic cooperation should be advanced through existing mechanisms and the expansion of private and semi-official bodies such as the Pacific Economic Cooperation Conference.** There is room for a great deal of creativity in developing a more intensive dialogue and a broader agenda for such unofficial groups, with the fruit of their efforts fed into governmental channels in the form of studies and proposals.

7. **It is appropriate that most assistance be forwarded through such agencies as the World Bank and the Asian Development Bank.** These organizations are removed from single-nation biases and interests. Their recommendations can be more easily advanced without charges of imperialism or the type of angry repercussions that result when an outside nation requests painful policies as a condition of aid.

8. **The two major economic powers, the United States and Japan, must step up the tempo of structural change at home.** Japan is required to develop truly internationalist attitudes and policies, and both nations must realize that with power goes responsibility—domestic, regional, and global. A serious recession in these two states has immediate reverberations throughout the world. Neither nation can live comfortably with international economic anarchy. Under such conditions, security everywhere is placed in greater jeopardy. Hence, the United States must deflate its economy, improve productivity, and resist protectionism. Japan must reflate its economy, expanding its domestic market; increase its social services; relax the remaining barriers to trade and investment, and pursue an enlarged international assistance program. Both nations must keep on the frontiers of the high technology and service industries.

9. **The so-called newly industrializing countries and the other developing societies of this region have their own obligations with respect to trade, technology transfer, and investment policies.** The United States

and Japan, along with most other advanced industrial nations, depend heavily upon their private sectors in advancing any international economic program. If conditions are not propitious for private investment and other types of private economic intercourse, sustained economic assistance will be severely constrained. A recognition of this fact now seems to be growing throughout Asia, but the various following barriers persist:

* extensive corruption,
* excessive bureaucratic red tape,
* restraints on profit repatriation,
* protracted import-substitution strategies, and
* other ultra-nationalist economic practices.

The age of minimally supervised largesse from "wealthy nations" to "poor nations," if it ever existed, is over. If a healthy international economic environment is to be created, the cooperation of all parties concerned is essential.

The opportunities for regional cooperation—one might also say the necessities for such cooperation—are rising. They can be realized more fully and more rapidly as the nations of the region order their domestic and foreign policies so they take into consideration the needs of neighbors. Whatever detours lie ahead, however, one can predict with some confidence the emergence of a dynamic set of interrelations, at a level between the single nation-state and the global community, in the decades ahead. There are no reasonable alternatives.

NOTE

1. Richard H. Solomon and Masataka Kosaka, eds., *The Soviet Far East Military Buildup–Nuclear Dilemmas and Asian Security* (Dover, Mass.: Auburn House Publishing Company, 1986).

ONE

Strategic Issues

2

The Strategic Balance in Southeast Asia

by Masashi Nishihara

In the mid-1980s, as the Soviet Union increases its naval and air force deployments in Indochina and the South China Sea, Southeast Asia presents new dimensions for the global Soviet–American rivalry. The region has long had a low priority for Soviet foreign policymakers. Until the end of the Vietnam War in 1975, Moscow had had little diplomatic and military success there, but the Sino–Vietnamese conflict that surfaced around 1977 gave the Soviets an opportunity to strengthen their military foothold in Vietnam, thus "encircling" China from the south and posing a potential threat to U.S. bases in the Philippines. Soviet military power can now be used to intimidate the noncommunist Southeast Asian states and force them to accommodate themselves to the new reality.

Southeast Asia has today become an important arena in which the two superpowers confront each other with their overseas air and naval bases— Subic Bay and Clark Field for the United States and Cam Ranh Bay and Da Nang for the Soviet Union—only some 1,300 kilometers (810 nautical miles) apart, across the South China Sea. Because all the regional nations have a stake in secure sea lines of communication, the geostrategic importance of the South China Sea is obvious. With security cooperation between the Soviet Union and Vietnam increasing and with growing uncertainty about the political stability of the Philippines and the tenure of American bases there, there is a danger that the strategic balance of power may shift in the Soviets' favor. Dimitri Simes has suggested that Gorbachev "is less interested in diplomacy than in creating 'objective realities' that will force America to become more accommodating."[1]

There are a number of key strategic issues on which Moscow can focus in an attempt to achieve such objective realities in Southeast Asia today. They include:

- how the balance between the Soviet–Vietnamese alliance and a coalition of the United States, Japan, South Korea, the ASEAN nations, Australia and New Zealand may be affected by the evolution of the U.S.–Soviet military balance in the South China Sea;
- how improved Sino–Soviet relations are likely to affect Vietnam's external policies;
- how Kampuchea will affect international relations; and
- how Soviet policies may influence the positions taken by the ASEAN nations, especially Thailand and the Philippines.

U.S.–SOVIET RIVALRY ACROSS THE SOUTH CHINA SEA

The principal Soviet objectives in Southeast Asia seem to be to strengthen the alliance with Vietnam and consolidate the access to Da Nang and Cam Ranh Bay, in order to expand Soviet influence and to reduce that of the United States and China; to improve relations with China so as to reduce border tensions, at the same time weakening China's relations with the United States, Japan, and other noncommunist Asian nations; and to improve relations with the ASEAN states and weaken the ties between those states and China, Japan and the United States. This can be detected explicitly and implicitly from many sources, including Gorbachev's well-known Vladivostok speech of July 28, 1986.

The main dividend that Moscow has obtained for its support of Hanoi in the Vietnam War and in the subsequent Vietnamese conflict with China is access to the military facilities in Da Nang and Cam Ranh Bay, which were left behind by the United States. The Soviet presence there is impressive: 25 to 30 naval ships including surface combatants, attack and cruise missile submarines, and naval auxiliaries; 8 TU-95 *Bear* long-range reconnaissance aircraft; 16 TU-16 *Badger* medium-range bombers; and a squadron of MiG-23 fighters.[2] Soviet military personnel in Vietnam average 7,000, plus some 2,500 military advisers with the Vietnamese forces.[3] An electronic monitoring station has been established in Da Nang and an air field near Phnom Penh has reportedly been extended to provide a 3,000-meter runway. The Soviet Union is also using the ports of Kompong Som and Ream for military purposes.[4] Also, there are about 200 military advisers in Kampuchea and 500 in Laos.[5]

This military presence in Vietnam has given the Soviet Union the capability to project power throughout Southeast Asia and into the Indian Ocean. In 1975 the Soviet Pacific fleet had to operate largely from Vladivostok, whereas now it can monitor U.S. operations in the South China Sea

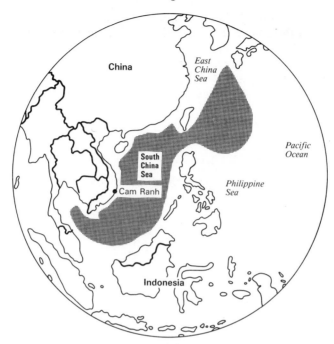

FIG. 2.1. Soviet *BEAR* operating area
Source: U.S. Department of Defense, *Soviet Military Power*, 1985, p. 130.

and extend its own area of operations and influence into the Indian and
Pacific Oceans. From Cam Ranh Bay, Soviet forces can "strike U.S. military units and bases in the Pacific as well as interdict sea lines of communication in the South China Sea."[6]

Cam Ranh and Da Nang are Moscow's largest military facilities outside
the Warsaw Pact. Until 1984, they were considered to be of a temporary
nature; U.S. Assistant Secretary of Defense Richard Armitage, for
instance, saying in mid-1984 that most Soviet assets, such as a floating
drydock and refuel and repair facilities, were removable. He added, "They
have built their own installations, but they have not taken over any large
compounds that we built there. They have their own little sections. They
still have a sandbag-type appearance."[7] However, in his Annual Report
to the Congress, Secretary of Defense Caspar Weinberger in early 1985
declared that "the Soviets continue to develop their naval basing facilities
worldwide, and they have established a naval, air, logistics and operations
base at Cam Ranh Bay."[8] In October 1985 a Thai military source claimed
that the Soviets had built a fuel storage tank and were constructing a new
air control tower in Cam Ranh Bay.[9] Later that year a Pentagon source
was quoted as reporting the construction of a power station and a seventh
dock and that Soviet forces were there to stay.

FIG. 2.2. Soviet TU-16/*BADGER* Combat Radius from Cam Ranh Airfield.
Source: U.S. Department of Defense, *Soviet Military Power*, 1985, p. 130.

This Soviet presence is a challenge to the U.S. bases in the Philippines and gives coverage over a wide area beyond Southeast Asia. TU-95 *Bear* and TU-16 *Badger* have an unrefueled combat radius of 8,300 km (5,200 nm) and 3,100 km (1,940 nm), respectively.[10] They can be augmented by *Backfire* long-range bombers deployed in the Soviet Far East, with an unrefueled combat radius of about 5,500 km (3,440 nm). If *Backfire* bombers were deployed in Vietnam or, indeed, in Afghanistan, they would be a potential threat to the U.S. forces at Diego Garcia in the Indian Ocean. Also able to reach the Southeast Asian region are over 160 SS-20 intermediate-range nuclear missiles with a range of 5,000 km (3,130 nm) based in the Soviet Far East.[11]

Some attention should perhaps also be paid to the possibility of military cooperation between the Soviet Union, North Korea, and Vietnam. In August 1985, Geydar Aliyev, first deputy premier and a Politburo member, visited North Korea—the highest-ranking official to do so in five years. Vitaly Vorotnikov, another Politburo member, went to Hanoi for the fortieth anniversary of socialist Vietnam, after which Vietnamese Defense Minister Van Tien Dung visited Moscow, "reaffirming the overall cooperation between the forces of the two nations," and then for the first time toured the Soviet Far East.[12] The subsequent overflights of North

Korean territory by Soviet military aircraft en route from Vladivostok to Vietnam suggest close cooperation among the three powers.

There are, of course, some weaknesses in the Soviet position. In any hostilities, Soviet forces in Vietnam could be easily isolated by U.S. forces from Okinawa, Guam, Subic Bay and Clark Field, as well as from Hawaii; these could interdict Soviet sea lanes and air routes between Vladivostok and Cam Ranh Bay. Furthermore, the MiG-23 fighters in Vietnam are primarily for air defense, not ground attack. With a combat radius of about 1,300 km (810 nm), they could barely reach the U.S. bases in the Philippines, although they could reach Bangkok easily enough. They could be opposed by superior U.S. F-15s (825 km) and F-16s (925 km) stationed in the Philippines, and F-16s are soon to be purchased by the Royal Thai Air Force and perhaps also by the Singaporean Air Force. The United States has other powerful forces in the theater, which include B-52 bombers (8,000 km), aircraft carriers, and submarines.

The U.S.–Soviet regional military balance could further be affected by the military capabilities developed by the littoral states. Most of the ASEAN nations are modernizing and increasing the size of their naval and air forces. In the ten years since 1976, the total naval strength of the five ASEAN nations has grown from 89,800 to 110,650 men and that of their air forces from 94,000 to 102,000. Over the same period, the personnel of Vietnam's naval and air force increased from 3,000 to 12,000 and from 12,000 to 15,000, respectively.[13] Needless to say, the ASEAN nations' armed forces are uneven in size, and not all of them would be committed in any hostilities with Vietnam. Yet, just two U.S. allies alone, Thailand and the Philippines, now have combined naval and air strengths of 60,200 and 59,900 respectively, easily outnumbering their Vietnamese counterparts. The ASEAN navies and air forces are also superior to those of Vietnam in terms of the number of frigates, fast attack vessels, petrol boats, and combat aircraft. The overall balance favors the American side.

The situation in the South China Sea is, however, also complicated by overlapping territorial claims being made by most of the littoral states of Vietnam, China, Taiwan, the Philippines, Malaysia, Indonesia, Kampuchea, and Thailand. There are potentially rich marine and seabed resources at stake, including oil, natural gas, tin, hydrocarbons, and fisheries.[14] In recent years, some nations have taken military action to demonstrate or preserve their rights. China, claiming both the Paracel and Spratly Islands, has occupied almost all of the Paracels, while Vietnam, making the same claim, controls probably six of the Spratlys. The Philippines control eight islets in the Spratlys. In June 1983, Malaysia took over Commodore Reef—Terumbu—another Spratly islet. So far the highest tension has been between China and Vietnam. Vietnam has strongly condemned China for giving permission for a U.S. oil company to prospect for offshore oil near Hainan Island. Vietnam succeeded in March 1985, with Soviet help, in striking oil off Vung Tau in southern Vietnam.[15]

When Soviet naval forces practiced landing operations off Haiphong in April 1984, Hanoi probably wanted this to convey a message to Beijing that the Soviet–Vietnamese alliance would work against China's territorial claims. Thus the China factor complicates the military balance in the South China Sea.

POWER PLAY OVER VIETNAM

In Vietnam, the Soviet Union has a dominant position in all fields—political, economic, and military. Moscow's substantial economic and military aid have forced Vietnam to be a member of "the socialist community," a term used here to denote an anti-China group. Hanoi strongly supports Moscow on major global issues, particularly those affecting U.S.–Soviet relations, such as nuclear concerns and regional conflicts. Soviet military aid to Vietnam alone is estimated at over $5 billion from 1978 through 1984 and economic aid of over $4 billion through 1983.[16]

The Soviet–Vietnamese Treaty of Friendship and Cooperation, signed in November 1978, represented little more than a marriage of convenience for the two nations. In January 1979, with Soviet support, Hanoi overthrew the Pol Pot regime in Phnom Penh (just as Indira Gandhi's government in India crushed East Pakistan in 1971 shortly after signing a similar treaty with the Soviet Union). The resulting Soviet access to military facilities in Vietnam, challenging the U.S. position in the Western Pacific, had a politico-psychological impact upon the ASEAN nations. The Soviet Union also gained substantially from the post-1975 Vietnamese efforts in driving the Chinese from Vietnam. It supported the installation of a pro-Hanoi regime in Phnom Penh, since this meant the elimination of Chinese influence in Kampuchea. As long as the Sino–Soviet rift continued, Moscow and Hanoi shared the goal of countering Chinese power in the region.

Thus, there is reason to suspect that the Sino–Soviet reconciliation that has been in process for the last past few years has been a source of concern to Hanoi. After China's Twelfth Party Congress in September 1982, Beijing modified its Soviet policy and began to respond to President Brezhnev's call for normalized relations, which had been made that year in his Tashkent speech of March 24. This had an immediate effect on Vietnam's attitudes toward the Soviet Union and China. Half a year earlier, the Fifth Party Congress of Vietnam had reaffirmed its anti-China and pro-Soviet line,[17] but in October 1982, soon after China's shift, Truong Chinh, president of the Council of State, visited Moscow and, apparently in a meeting with Brezhnev, expressed his hope that Moscow-Hanoi links would not be jeopardized by new Soviet relations with China.

The Soviet move to improve relations with China was, it has been said, made partly to reduce border tensions and partly to try to weaken Sino-American relations. As it continued, it made Hanoi nervous. In December 1984, Soviet Deputy Premier Ivan Arkhipov visited Beijing, concluding a five-year economic cooperation agreement. In his March 11, 1985, inaugural speech before the Party Central Committee, newly-appointed General Secretary Gorbachev declared, "We would like to see a serious improvement in relations with the People's Republic of China and believe that, given reciprocity, this is quite possible."[18] China's Deputy Premier Li Peng, in Moscow for Chernenko's funeral, welcomed it.[19] In early July, Deputy Premier Yao Yilin was scheduled to go to Moscow—probably to warn the Soviet leaders against further rapprochement with Beijing—just after Vietnam Party Secretary Le Duan and another group returned from the Soviet Union. In a joint declaration of June 28, Le Duan endorsed the Soviet attempt at reconciliation with China, but only in return for Moscow's full support of Vietnam's new five-year economic plan (1986–1990).

Sino–Soviet relations may have improved, but not at the expense of Soviet–Vietnamese relations. Since mid-1985, Hanoi has toned down its criticism of China, but Beijing continues to condemn Vietnam and intends to "bleed it white."[20] Vietnam is economically in a serious condition; in mid-1985 its external debt soared to $6.7 billion, of which $5.1 billion was owed to the Soviet Union and the Eastern Bloc. Its foreign exchange reserves were down to just $17 million, enough to cover the import of commodities for only three days.[21] It needs Soviet help in all fields, but as long as it is aligned with the Soviet Union it cannot improve relations with China.

Sino-Soviet rapprochement also presents Washington with a dilemma. President Reagan warned China in May 1985 that the United States would lower the level of technology to be transferred should China move closer toward the Soviet Union. But strained Sino–Soviet relations might mean closer Soviet–Vietnamese ties. Both parties at the Moscow–Hanoi summit in late June had probably agreed that if Vietnam made a concession to American interests on the issue of the 2,400 missing American servicemen, Washington might become slightly less hostile to the Heng Samrin government and perhaps would even try to persuade ASEAN to water down its stand condemning the Soviet and Vietnamese roles over Kampuchea. On July 7, soon after Le Duan's visit to Moscow, Hanoi informed Washington, through Indonesia, that it would soon release the remains of 26 American servicemen missing in action. This gesture must have been timed for the ASEAN Foreign Ministers' Conference and its Post-Ministerial Meeting, which U.S. Secretary of State George Shultz was to attend. Hanoi might also have seen it as a sort of "U.S. card" to warn Moscow against moving too fast with a rapprochement with China.[22]

In offering to settle the MIA (missing in action) issue "in two years," Hanoi also proposed that Washington should set up a liaison office in Hanoi, as it had in Beijing between 1971 and 1979. Washington showed no interest in establishing such an office, but in subsequent months it did begin to increase contacts with Hanoi. In November an American search team was sent to Vietnam; a group of over 100 U.S. businessmen made an unprecedented visit there in October; and in December the first U.S. tourist group went to Vietnam.[23] Such developments may bring about less hostile relations, but it is difficult to foresee full normalization in the near future. The United States will not contemplate full relations while Vietnam maintains its military occupation of Kampuchea.

POWER PLAY OVER KAMPUCHEA

For both Moscow and Beijing, the question of who should control Kampuchea is an important one, but for different reasons. For Beijing, it is less a matter of national security than of national prestige. For Moscow, it is a step in the establishment of its sphere of influence in Southeast Asia. It is important for Washington, too, because if Vietnam should fully control Kampuchea this would adversely affect the national security of its ally, Thailand, and might help to further the Soviet expansionist policy. Since the United States had chosen to maintain a low-key profile over Indochina until early in 1985, the balance of power over Kampuchea has been maintained on the one side by the Vietnamese and Heng Samrim forces supported by Soviet military aid and, on the other, by the coalition of anti-Vietnamese resistance forces—the Coalition Government of Democratic Kampuchea (CGDK), with military assistance from China and, to a very limited extent, from one or two ASEAN nations. Of course, U.S. military support to Thailand has helped to give ASEAN relative self-confidence.

This basic international balance changed slightly after early 1985, when the Vietnamese forces waged a large-scale offensive against the Khmer resistance groups. The Vietnamese offensive, unchecked by a second "punitive war" by China, compelled ASEAN to request U.S. military aid, even more strongly than before, for the noncommunist Khmer resistance groups. The ASEAN move came out of the Special Foreign Ministers' Conference held in Bangkok on February 11 and 12. And as a result of it, Washington gradually modified its position. In July Congress responded to the request by committing $5 million of economic and military aid to the Sihanouk and Son Sann groups.[24] The ASEAN Post-Ministerial Meeting in Kuala Lumpur in July also called for a larger American role in bringing about a negotiated settlement of the Kampuchean question. Increased U.S.–Vietnamese contacts since July 1985 over MIAs might provide Washington with an opportunity to influence Hanoi's policy towards Kampuchea, but it would still be in American interests to encourage ASEAN to play the leading role. As Secretary of State Shultz said in Kuala Lumpur on July 12: "We are looking at ways, consistent with your leading role, in which we might provide more support, and will consult with you."[25]

In the meantime, the United States has moved quietly to increase contacts with Laos, taking it off the "enemy list" and thus making it eligible for economic aid. The two capitals also decided to elevate the level of their diplomatic representation to that of full ambassador. In late September, Vice Foreign Minister Soulivong Prasithdeth became the first Communist official from Indochina to visit the U.S. State Department since 1975.[26] In December, U.S. Assistant Secretary of State for East Asia and Pacific Affairs Paul Wolfowitz went to Vientiane and Hanoi for consultations over issues of mutual concern.

As noted already, improved Sino–Soviet relations have encouraged Hanoi to tone down its criticism of China, particularly after the Gorbachev-Le Duan meeting in late June. The earlier attitude was exemplified by an article in *Vietnam Courier*, an official Vietnamese publication, in January 1985, that declared that "China's expansionist and hegemonist policy constitutes the most permanent, direct, lasting and dangerous threat to them [Southeast Asian nations]."[27] But the communiqué issued on August 16 by the foreign ministers of the three Indochinese countries stressed "their goodwill in their relations with the People's Republic of China."[28] In September, General Van Tien Dung issued the Order of the Day on the occasion of Vietnam's Fortieth National Day, in which he referred to the need to "defeat . . . the enemy's land-grabbing war at our border and their multi-faceted war of sabotage" but carefully avoided naming China.[29]

China, however, has not changed its policy toward Vietnam, though there were some events that might have suggested a move toward rapprochement. For example, in August 1985 a Vietnamese external trade delegation went to Beijing to prepare for Vietnamese participation in an Asia-Pacific regional trade fair. But one month later, in September, the Chinese government denied a rumor regarding secret negotiations with Vietnam for rapprochement. That same month, Beijing apparently put pressure on Pol Pot to resign as the commander of the Khmer Rouge forces, presumably to improve the international image of the Khmer Rouge as the date of the United Nations General Assembly approached. In December, Deng Xiaoping invited the three top leaders of the CGDK— Sihanouk, Son Sann, and Khieu Samphan—to Beijing and gave them "unconditional support."[30]

It is most unlikely that China would reduce its support for the CGDK while the Soviet Union continues to aid Vietnam's military operations, since this would allow a settlement of the Kampuchean issue on Hanoi's terms, something quite unacceptable to Beijing. The reverse is more likely, namely, reduced Soviet aid and increased Chinese aid in Kampuchea. The question of who should control Kampuchea is more important for China than for the Soviet Union. But as long as Vietnam thinks that time is on its side and as long as the Soviet Union judges that supporting Vietnam is a convenient way of expanding its influence in Southeast Asia, Moscow will not reduce its military aid to Vietnam in the near future. Also, a second punitive war by China cannot be ruled out, especially if Beijing thinks this would not jeopardize its relations with Moscow. Conflict in Kampuchea is likely to continue, as are strained Sino–Vietnamese relations.

Yet, there is a small possibility, perhaps wishful, that the Soviet Union might reduce its military assistance for Vietnam's Kampuchean operations if Moscow gave greater priority to a détente with China and ASEAN. If this were the case, Moscow might compel Hanoi to accept a negotiated settlement in Kampuchea without accomplishing the full international recognition of the Heng Samrin government that Hanoi wants. China might then be induced to limit its military support to the CGDK, which might lead to a lower level of conflict and to the improvement of Sino–Vietnamese relations. This last scenario, if ever realized, would also be acceptable to the United States and Japan, as well as to ASEAN.

Japan shares an interest with the United States, ASEAN, and China in restraining Soviet influence in Southeast Asia. Unlike the United States, Japan has diplomatic relations with Vietnam, but its influence over Hanoi appears limited, for the Vietnamese regard Japan as unsympathetic to their cause in Kampuchea. Japan's decision to freeze its economic aid to Vietnam has also hindered the development of the Vietnamese economy. Since "hawkish" Nakasone became prime minister in late 1982, Hanoi has been condemning "the revival of Japanese militarism" and the "emergence of a Washington–Tokyo–Seoul military axis." An article in the *Vietnam Courier* of September 1985, for instance, said that "considering Japan as its mainstay in the Far East, the United States is promoting the rearmament of this country [Japan] and encouraging the revival of Japanese militarism and expansionism."[31]

Japan considers ASEAN more important than Indochina both in terms of trade and investment and of political and strategic goals. Its policy of supporting the ASEAN stand on Kampuchea has worked so far to its general diplomatic advantage, although it has narrowed the options for restoring cordial, if not close, relations with Hanoi. The thaw in Sino–Soviet relations might lead Vietnam to seek closer relations with Japan as well as with the United States. If so, Tokyo might be able to play a larger diplomatic role than before, perhaps leading to a lessening of conflict in Kampuchea.

AN INCREASING SOVIET PRESENCE IN THE ASEAN AREA?

The Soviet Union's role is limited in the ASEAN area, not only because of its high-handed behavior, which annoys the ASEAN capitals, but also because there is insignificant trade between ASEAN states and the Soviet bloc. However, the more serious reason for Moscow's circumscribed role lies in its military presence in Indochina and its support of Vietnam's military occupation of Kampuchea. On February 6, 1985, each ASEAN government except Brunei concurrently summoned its Soviet ambassador to the Foreign Ministry and requested that Moscow play a constructive role in the region by withdrawing military aid to Hanoi and by promoting the peace and stability of Southeast Asia.[32] The Soviet Union flatly declined to stop the military assistance, which shows how far apart the Soviet Union and the ASEAN countries still stand. On the other hand, in the wake of the Vietnamese offensive in Kampuchea, China's defense minister flew to Thailand to reaffirm its support of Thailand's security.

This situation accords with China's interests so far, for it is important to Beijing to contain Soviet influence. China has a more influential presence in the ASEAN region. The highest-ranking Soviet government official to visit the ASEAN capitals in recent years was Mikhail Kapitsa, deputy foreign minister, whereas China has sent much higher-ranking officials, including President Li Xiannian, Premier Zhao Ziyang, Defense Minister Zhang Aiping, and Foreign Minister Wu Xueqian. Only in March 1987 did Foreign Minister Schevardnadze tour Thailand and Indonesia. Singapore's former Deputy Premier Goh Keng Swee has been invited by the Chinese government as a senior adviser on economic management. In July 1985, Beijing finally succeeded in opening direct trade with Indonesia, which had broken off diplomatic relations with China in 1967.

There is reason to suspect, however, that the Soviet Union under Gorbachev has changed tactics and once again wants to compete with China in Asia. In 1985, the competition was evident in many fields. Japanese and American trade protectionist measures, from which many of the ASEAN countries are suffering, have given additional scope for Soviet attempts at diplomatic and economic penetration.

Since 1982, the Soviet Union has been recruiting 60 to 70 Thai students each year for studies in the Soviet Union. During the first half of 1985, the pace of recruitment was quickened, as the Soviets started to recruit young students in the Thai countryside. This alarmed the Thai authorities, which in November of that year restricted the number of students and their fields of specialization.[33] Moscow also invites Southeast Asian scholars for international conferences held in the Soviet Union.

There is no public evidence that Moscow was involved in the internal affairs of the Philippines, as, for example, in the form of clandestine assistance to anti-Marcos opposition forces, for labor strikes, campaigns against U.S. bases, or even for the fast-growing New People's Army (NPA), the armed communist subversive forces. However, in May 1985 two Soviet party leaders, Boris Ponomarev, a Politburo candidate member, and Ivan Kovalenko, deputy chief of the International Department of the Party, met Felicismo Macapagal, general secretary of the Philippine Communist Party (PKP) at the Kremlin.[34] In February 1986 a PKP delegation was also invited to the Twenty-seventh Soviet Party Congress held in Moscow. There is some speculation that the Soviets are already penetrating economic, cultural and sports activities in the Philippines. In mid-1985, the Soviet ambassador in Manila and Labor Minister Blas Ople, who was also Chairman of the Philippine–Soviet Friendship Association, discussed an arrangement for Philippine workers to work for Siberian development.

According to Thai government sources, some of those Thai Communist insurgents who split from the Chinese-controlled Communist Party of Thailand (CPT) have since been trained and aided by Laotians and Vietnamese agents in Laos with Soviet help.[35] Soviet organizations in Bangkok, such as the embassy, trade mission offices, news agencies, *Aeroflot*, and the like, are also active in covert intelligence-gathering activities. An agent of GRU (Soviet military intelligence), working in the Bangkok office of the Soviet trade representative, was arrested and deported in May 1983. It was reported at the time that there were 52 such agents operating in Thailand.[36]

Moscow will find it difficult to compete with China in the area of military ties with Thailand. In late February 1985 a Chinese naval delegation, led by the deputy commander in chief, visited Bangkok, and two weeks later, when President Li Xiannian visited there, the deputy chief of staff of the PLA accompanied him. No such high-ranking Soviet leaders have ever been to Thailand.

On October 17, 1985, an ASEAN Economic Ministers' Conference held in Bangkok responded bitterly to the attempt by the U.S. Congress to pass protectionist legislation and threatened to retaliate. A regional textile association also threatened to stop importing U.S. cotton, to the value of some $500 million annually, and to switch to Chinese cotton.[37] Taking these strains to ASEAN–U.S. relations as an opportunity, Soviet Commerce Minister Yashenko Ivanovich went to Bangkok in late October, holding meetings with government and business leaders. He expressed the Soviet government's interest in importing Thai textiles excluded by quotas from the United States. His visit attracted much attention in the Bangkok media, although he failed to establish a Soviet–Thai Friendship Association. Following him, Soviet Vice Premier Yakov Ryabov visited Jakarta and Kuala Lumpur, discussing an expansion of trade.[38] His visit to Indonesia must have been prompted by Indonesia's decision to have direct trade with China, mentioned earlier, thus offering competition.

The Soviet Union has also attempted to court Manila. Imelda Marcos was particularly active in promoting Philippine–Soviet relations, being awarded a medal for her contribution in the field in July 1984 by the Soviet ambassador. She was the only leader in noncommunist Southeast Asia to meet with Gorbachev when she attended Chernenko's funeral in March 1985. In August that year, the Soviet Union also gave President Ferdinand Marcos a medal in recognition of his special contribution to the victory of the Allied Powers in World War II over Japanese militarism.[39] In February 1986, the newly appointed Soviet ambassador—anxious to present his credentials to the Philippine government—was the only ambassador to attend Marcos's presidential reelection ceremony.

As the political situation in the Philippines continued to be volatile, Moscow appeared to be looking for an opportunity to intervene. In January 1984, Defense Minister Ponce Enrile disclosed that the Soviet government had several times asked Manila for permission to make naval port calls.[40] In April of that year, the first secretary of the Soviet Embassy in Manila, giving a lecture to the Philippine Foreign Service Institute, said that the Soviet Union had full confidence in President Marcos's anti-nuclear policy; that the nuclear missiles deployed in the Soviet Far East were not targeted at the Philippines; that Vietnam would not pose a threat to the Philippines; and that the possibility for economic cooperation between ASEAN and COMECON should be explored.[41]

Obviously, the Soviet objective is to weaken U.S.–Philippine ties. In his Vladivostok speech in July 1986, Gorbachev suggested that Moscow would reciprocate if the United States should abandon its military presence in the Philippines. His government's approach to the new Aquino government has been rather cautious, but in August 1986 a Soviet parliamentary delegation intimidated the Filipinos, warning that there was no guarantee that in a crisis the Soviets would not wage a nuclear attack against the Philippines because the U.S. bases are "a dangerous factor." Moscow is likely to support the anti-nuclear clause—a Southeast Asian Nuclear-Free Zone idea—contained in the Philippine Constitution adopted in February 1987. They are also likely to support future campaigns against the U.S. bases in the Philippines, another attempt to exploit the possible differences between Washington and Manila.

PROSPECTS

Many uncertain factors discourage predictions about the course of U.S.–Soviet relations. If they improve, however, the Soviet Union is still unlikely to slow down the pace of its military build-up in the Western Pacific. The United States has to accommodate itself to this objective reality. The fast growth of Soviet force deployments in the region, which may perhaps link the forces of North Korea and Vietnam, calls for the

United States to strengthen multilateral ties with the ASEAN states, as well as with its Pacific allies of Japan, South Korea, Australia, and New Zealand.

Despite its impressive military display, the Soviet Union still faces many political and economic difficulties in Asia. Its relations with China and the Southeast Asian nations are extremely complicated, and it is forced to seek contradictory objectives in the region. On the one hand, some military forces based in Cam Ranh Bay and Da Nang will make a show of force in the form of reconnaissance flights, naval maneuvers and requests for naval port calls. On the other hand, while intimidating, Moscow will also seek to present itself as an attractive trading partner. The Soviets have now expressed interest in joining several regional economic organizations, such as the Pacific Economic Cooperation Conference (PECC) and the Asian Development Bank. Moscow may respond to Beijing by promoting better relations, but is not likely to do so by conceding to Chinese demands for reduced Soviet forces in the border areas.

China has so far played a positive role in maintaining the balance of power in Southeast Asia by supporting Thailand and the Khmer resistance groups. But the historical distrust entertained by some states in ASEAN, particularly Malaysia and Indonesia, restrict the scope of China's maneuverability. Beijing cannot expect to have substantial support from ASEAN countries for its Asian diplomacy.

Although Japan's relations with Vietnam are important for the security of its sea lanes passing through the South China Sea, Tokyo has little choice but to side with ASEAN when relations between Vietnam and ASEAN are strained. The self-denial of a military role by Japan limits the range of its policy options; however, through its support of China's economic development and ASEAN's strategic interests, it has exerted some political influence over the Kampuchean issue. Its foreign policy conduct will continue to be low-key in the foreseeable future, although it is gradually becoming more visible.

It is the United States that can meet the Soviet military challenge and regional security needs most effectively, while Japan can supplement the American role by promoting regional stability through diplomatic and economic activities. For some time to come, Kampuchea and the Philippines are likely to remain as the two most visible security concerns in Southeast Asia, with neither offering clear prospects for early solution. The United States should seek closer coordination between the Manila Pact and the Five-Power Defense Arrangement (FPDA). The United States can initiate the process to establish a coordinating body for the two. The former pact covers the American security commitments to Thailand and the Philippines, with Britain, Australia, and New Zealand as additional signatories. These last three nations are also members of FDPA, together with Malaysia and Singapore. Washington should find ways to settle the current trade frictions with Asian countries, so as to minimize their adverse impact on regional political stability. The United States and like-minded nations should continue their patient and careful efforts to maintain a favorable strategic balance in the region.

NOTES

1. Dimitri K. Simes, "Beware Optimism about Gorbachev," *New York Times*, July 21, 1985, the Week in Review.
2. Department of Defense (DoD), *Soviet Military Power 1985* (Washington, D.C.: Government Printing Office), p. 131.
3. International Institute for Strategic Studies (IISS), *The Military Balance, 1985–1986* (London: IISS, 1985), p. 30.
4. *Sankei Shinbun*, December 31, 1985, morning edition.
5. IISS, *The Military Balance, 1985–1986*, p. 30.
6. DoD, *Soviet Military Power 1985*, p. 118. See also "The Soviets Test the Waters," *Newsweek* May 20, 1985: 12–16.
7. Nayan Chanda, "The Uneasy Alliance," *Far Eastern Economic Review* (September 6, 1984): 41.
8. *Annual Report to the Congress Fiscal Year 1986*, Washington, D.C., p. 19.
9. *Sankei*, October 25, 1985, morning edition.
10. DoD, *Soviet Military Power 1985*, pp. 34, 51.
11. Consult, for instance, Richard Solomon and Masataka Kosaka, eds., *The Soviet Far East Military Buildup: Nuclear Dilemmas and Asian Security* (Dover, Mass: Auburn House Publishers, 1986).
12. *Tōnan Ajia Geppō* (Tokyo, September 1985), pp. 19–20.
13. Computed from IISS, *The Military Balance 1985–1986*.
14. See, for instance, Lim Joo-jock. *Geo-strategy and the South China Sea Basin* (Singapore: Singapore University Press, 1979).
15. Tran Quan Ngoc, "Offshore Oil Exploration at Vung Tau," *Vietnam Courier* (October 1985): 18–19.
16. DoD, *Soviet Military Power 1985*, p. 131.
17. Gorbachev led the Soviet delegation at the Fifth Party Congress in 1982.
18. *Soviet Military Review*, no. 4 (Moscow, 1985), p. 7.
19. "Chinese, Soviet Leaders Seek Closer Relations," *Beijing Review* (March 25, 1985): 6.
20. Xue Mouhong, "Hanoi Must Be Pressured Out of Kampuchea," *Beijing Review* (December 23, 1985): 15–16.
21. *Tōnan Ajia Geppō* (September 1985), p. 13.
22. Richard Nations, "Hanoi's MIAs Card," *Far Eastern Economic Review* (July 18, 1985): 15–16.
23. *Sankei*, December 17, 1985, evening edition.
24. "Cambodia; A New U.S. Role?," *Newsweek* (July 22, 1983): 18–19.
25. Secretary of State George Shultz, "U.S. Joins ASEAN in Quest for Peace, Prosperity," speech presented at the American Embassy in Tokyo, *Official Text*, no. 55, (July 25, 1985), p. 7.
26. *Far Eastern Economic Review* (October 10, 1985); *Sankei*, December 3, 1985, morning edition.
27. Nguyen Huu Chinh, "The Great Powers and Southeast Asia," *Vietnam Courier* (January 1985): 15.
28. *Vietnam Courier* (September 1985): 3.
29. *Vietnam Courier* (October 1985): 4, 9.
30. "China Backs Kampuchean Leaders," *Beijing Review* (December 23, 1985): 7.
31. "Burning Problems of Asia and the Pacific," *Vietnam Courier* (September 1985): 15–16.
32. *Tōnan Ajia Geppō* (February 1985), p. 153.
33. *Sankei*, November 29, 1985, morning edition.
34. *Tōnan Ajia Geppō* (May 1985), p. 109.
35. *Far Eastern Economic Review* (November 8, 1984): 11.

36. *Tōnan Ajia Yōran 1984*, section on Thailand, p. 53.
37. *Sankei*, October 29, 1985, morning edition.
38. *Asahi Shinbun*, October 23, 1985, morning edition.
39. *Sankei*, August 9, 1985, morning edition.
40. *Tōnan Ajia Geppō* (January 1985), p. 102. A more detailed analysis of the domestic political situation is not attempted here, since this is covered in chapter 8.
41. *Tōnan Ajia Geppō* (April 1984), p. 96.
42. President Ronald Reagan, "U.S. Policy in the Pacific Island Region," *Department of State Bulletin* (August 1984), p. 64. See also "America's Wobbly Kingpin," *Newsweek* (May 20, 1985): 14.

3

Key Strategic Issues in Northeast Asia: Sino–Soviet Relations and Developments on the Korean Peninsula

by Robert A. Scalapino

Global politics have entered a period of increasing fluidity with reverberations among both major and minor states. In Northeast Asia, alterations in two relationships are of special importance. What do the recent improvements in Sino–Soviet relations portend? And does the dialogue between North and South Korea augur a more peaceful future for the Korean Peninsula? Intercontinental as well as regional politics will be influenced by the course of developments in these matters. The objective here is to explore recent trends, assess alternative scenarios, and analyze their implications for other nations.

FROM COLD WAR TO TENSION REDUCTION: TRENDS IN SINO–SOVIET RELATIONS

At the end of the 1960s, China found itself in a highly disadvantageous international position. Beijing's foreign policies were in a shambles as a result of the excesses of the so-called Cultural Revolution. Conflict with the Soviet Union loomed up as a possibility, with the 1969 Ussuri River incident symbolic of the gravity of the situation. Yet relations with the

United States were only marginally better, with unacknowledged yet real confrontation taking place in North Vietnam and with Beijing's rhetoric remaining intensely anti-American.

China's political commitment was to global revolution (against Marxist revisionists as well as bourgeois democrats) on behalf of the Third World. Yet, in fact, China was readily in a position to assist only one revolution— that in Vietnam—and Chinese policies had managed to alienate many Third World nations. In any case, the Third World was in no position to meet China's two basic needs: development and security. Meanwhile, China could neither negotiate nor fight with its primary opponent, the Soviet Union, from a position of strength.[1]

Fortunately for China, pragmatism prevailed over ideology. Mao was forced to recognize the precarious nature of the Chinese position, and a new Chinese foreign policy was fashioned. The key to that new policy was a major change in relations with the United States. The United States was in a position to advance or retard China's reentry into the international community, its economic and political ties with the so-called Second World, and even its relations with a number of so-called Third World states. In addition, it was the only countervailing power to the Soviet Union, thus, the only nation that could directly or indirectly strengthen China's strategic position vis-à-vis the USSR.

The United States was receptive to China's turn toward détente for its own reasons. Thus, for the first time in several decades, the interests of the American and Chinese governments coincided sufficiently to underwrite the normalization process of the 1970s. Would this process advance from détente to strategic alliance? The issue was controversial in both nations, but the trend was in that direction by the late 1970s. China's leaders on various occasions had called for a global united front against Soviet hegemonism. In the United States, at the same time, the demand came from certain quarters to build a strategic relationship with China against the Soviet Union, especially after the Soviet invasion of Afghanistan. Concrete steps, moreover, were taken to implement such a policy.

With the advent of the 1980s, however, Chinese foreign policy underwent another shift of substantial proportions. The calls for a global united front against the USSR ceased. Chinese leaders now defined their policy as one of nonalignment, with criticisms directed toward both "superpowers." China's political place, it was asserted, was with the Third World, with a "principled stand" being taken against hegemonism, war, and other economic and social evils perpetrated against weak states. In rhetoric, there was much that was reminiscent of the 1960s, but policies betrayed important differences from the earlier period. The commitment to turn outward for purposes of economic development, together with China's continuing concerns with respect to its security, dictated a policy of tilted nonalignment, with the tilt toward Japan and the West, particularly the United States. Overwhelmingly, students and researchers—more than 90 percent devoting themselves to science and technology—went to the United States and other advanced industrial societies. Loans, investments and joint ventures were solicited from the same sources. In the fields of China's highest priorities, energy and telecommunications, the preferences were especially pronounced. Meanwhile, a low-level strategic relationship—timid and tentative—also got under way. Notwithstanding these developments, however, the decibel level of anti-U.S. criticism rose, as will be noted.

Fundamentally, China's new foreign policy was in accordance with its national interests. If the nation's resources were to be devoted primarily to economic development and the prodigious tasks involved in modernization tackled effectively, China needed a low-cost, low-risk foreign policy. Beijing could ill afford a crash program of military modernization unless it wanted to jeopardize other aspects of its modernization plans. Yet it could justify a low priority for the military only if it could demonstrate a lessened risk to China's security. The interest in reducing tension with the Soviet Union relates fundamentally to these considerations.

The parallels in recent Chinese policies toward the Soviet Union and earlier policies toward the United States are, in certain respects, striking. As in the case of the shift in Chinese policy toward the United States after 1969, the critical initiative for the change in Sino–Soviet relations came from Beijing, not Moscow, although both the United States and the USSR had earlier signaled a desire for improved relations. Moreover, in neither case did the solicited party make any significant concessions to obtain a new Chinese policy. The PRC had long taken the position that there could be no improvement in Sino–U.S. relations unless and until the Taiwan issue was "settled," yet negotiations were opened without it being resolved. Indeed, while American concessions were made on the Taiwan question—over time, major concessions—it remains unsettled today. In the course of the movement toward normalization, moreover, Chinese leaders indicated at various times that they were prepared to downgrade the Taiwan issue, treating it as "secondary," and were willing to be patient, allowing time to resolve a problem "bequeathed by history." Meanwhile, progress was made in economic and cultural relations, and when formal diplomatic ties were established, the Taiwan issue was once again compromised, with Chinese leaders cognizant of the fact that American sales of weapons to Taiwan would continue.[2]

The similarities in the pattern of recent Sino–Soviet relations cannot be missed. The Chinese broke off earlier negotiations with the Soviet Union after the Russian invasion of Afghanistan. Subsequently, they listed "three obstacles"—Soviet military assistance to Vietnam, the Soviet occupation of Afghanistan, and the presence of Soviet troops in Outer Mongolia and around China's borders—as critical impediments to any improvement in

Sino–Soviet relations. Yet negotiations were reopened without solutions to these issues, or even indications of a Soviet willingness to compromise on them. And the lack of progress in resolving them (until recently) has not prevented progress in economic and cultural relations. The Chinese continued to refer to the three obstacles as barriers to normal Sino–Soviet relations, but they did not allow these obstacles to block steps toward normalization. As yet, moreover, despite the significant overtures made by Gorbachev in mid-1986 and unlike the United States with respect to Taiwan, the Soviet Union has made no major concessions on the political-strategic front. Earlier, Soviet spokesmen insisted that Sino–Soviet negotiations could deal only with issues between the two countries, not with those involving a third party, thereby ruling out discussions on two and one-half of the three obstacles.[3] Gorbachev has now asserted that mutual force reductions on the Sino–Soviet border might be arranged, including reductions in Soviet troops in Outer Mongolia, signaling a Soviet willingness to consider some alterations in force dispositions but not those that would likely affect the strategic balance.

Initial Soviet negotiations with China on political and strategic issues followed a predictable pattern, one seen earlier in discussions with Japan and other Asian nations. Soviet spokesmen call for very general "confidence-building" measures, such as agreements on peace, friendship, and non-aggression, while bypassing the specific issues in contention.[4] Thus, in the seven rounds of "consultations" between representatives of the two governments up to late 1985, the Chinese reported no results with respect to the three obstacles.

The official Chinese position on present and future Sino–Soviet relations has generally been optimistic. In a message at the time of Konstantin Chernenko's death, issued on March 11, 1985, a Chinese Ministry of Foreign Affairs spokesman said, 'In the past year, ties between China and the Soviet Union increased significantly in all spheres. We hope that this positive trend in Sino–Soviet relations will further develop."[5] The new Soviet leader, Mikhail Gorbachev, responded in kind: 'We would like a serious improvement of relations with the Chinese People's Republic and believe that, given reciprocity, this is quite possible."[6]

While official contacts were resumed in 1982, Sino–Soviet relations assumed a new momentum in 1984, symbolized by the visit of Ivan Arkhipov, first deputy chairman of the USSR Council of Ministers Praesidium, on the last day of that year. He was the highest-ranking Soviet official to visit China in over 20 years, and his discussions with Vice Premier Yao Yilin upgraded the talks to a level just below the top. In the course of the visit, three agreements were signed relating to economic and technological cooperation, scientific-technological exchanges, and the creation of a commission for economic, scientific, and technological cooperation.

Arkhipov was an excellent choice on the part of the Soviets. He had served as general adviser to the Soviet specialists in China in the 1950s and in this capacity had come to know Chen Yun, Bo Yibo, Peng Zhen, and Wan Li, who promptly hailed their "old friend." His visit evoked comments from them and from the media that China would never forget the Soviet specialists who had helped China in its socialist construction.[7]

In July 1985, Vice Premier Yao Yilin visited Moscow, keeping the official contacts at this level. Two economic agreements were signed that called for the doubling of bilateral trade to US$3.5 billion by 1990 and for Soviet assistance in building seven new plants in China and modernizing 17 others built in the 1950s with Soviet aid.[8] Two-way Sino–Soviet trade in 1985 was $1.9 billion. Yet, in comparison with the $19 billion Sino–Japanese trade and the $8 billion Sino–U.S. trade, economic relations with the USSR appear likely to be of much less consequence for the near future at least.

The year 1983 marked the beginning of renewed Sino–Soviet scientific and technological cooperation, with three "investigation teams" exchanged, increased to five teams in 1984, and with an additional number pledged for 1985. In 1984, each side exchanged 70 students, one medical team, and four sports teams. The Friendship Associations of the two countries have resumed contacts, and the first tourists were exchanged in 1984.

These activities are extremely modest in comparison with those under way between China and Japan, Western Europe, and the United States. Is this merely the result of a late start, with Sino–Soviet relations scheduled to "catch up" in the course of time, or are there basic blocks in the path of extensive Sino–Soviet economic and cultural interchanges?

Before exploring this important question, let us turn briefly to the psychological-political mood that prevails among Chinese and Soviet leaders and the more articulate portions of their citizenry with regard to their mutual relations. As noted earlier, the official attitudes as expressed in public statements and press accounts have been optimistic, and Chinese organs frequently demonstrate restraint in dealing with the Soviet Union, especially since the advent of Gorbachev to power. Presumably, this is to make policy changes under the new leadership easier. A period of similar restraint could be noted at the outset of the Brezhnev era. Gorbachev has usually been praised or given neutral treatment, with attention focused on his commitment to domestic reforms and to "innovative new policies."[9] No open criticism of the Soviet system is voiced. Nor is there any public suggestion, as in the past, that the Soviet Union has departed from Marxism-Leninism. On the contrary, various leaders, including Hu Yaobang, have made it clear that the PRC now officially accepts the USSR as a member of the community of socialist nations. On the occasion of the fortieth anniversary of the victory over European Fascism, moreover, one authoritative article gave the Soviet role top priority, with the contribution of the Western allies relegated to a strictly secondary position, even with respect to the Pacific theater.[10] Some of the statements in this article were reminiscent of articles published in the early 1950s. In addition, attention is now being focused upon the assistance given by the Soviet Union to Nationalist China in 1937–1939, a theme long absent from Chinese publications.

Public treatment of the Soviet Union, to be sure, is not uniformly favorable. On some issues, such as the arms race, Chinese organs adopt a "plague on both your houses" approach, doling out criticism in more or less equal measure to the United States and the Soviet Union. The basic thesis is that the two superpowers, in their quest for supremacy and hegemony, are threatening the world with a global holocaust. A subsidiary and derivative theme is that Europe, like the Third World, should assert its independence from superpower domination, achieving in the process a greater unity. Again, these themes are virtually identical to those advanced in the 1960s and represent the persistent strain of xenophobically tinged nationalism that runs so deeply in Chinese politics. It is perhaps not surprising to find Deng Xiaoping telling European guests of his admiration for Charles De Gaulle.

Nor has there been any substantial retreat from criticism of Soviet policies in Indochina and Afghanistan. Much of this criticism is indirect in nature, through quotations from the Coalition Government of Democratic Kampuchea and mujahideen sources, but some of it is direct and forceful. Moreover, at times, as indicated, Chinese commentators raise doubts as to whether Gorbachev, whatever his aspirations and intentions, can carry out dramatic changes in Soviet foreign policy, given the historic proclivities of the Russians and the collective judgments upon which current Soviet policies rest.[11]

To judge merely from Chinese publications and public pronouncements, however, the conclusion might easily be reached that PRC leaders are less favorably disposed toward the United States and the policies of the Reagan administration than toward the USSR under its new leadership. Condemnation of U.S. foreign policy is both direct and sweeping, encompassing policies toward virtually the whole of the Third World (the Middle East, Africa, Central and Latin America) but extending to American policies toward Europe as well (the Strategic Defense Initiative [SDI] and the general matter of arms limitations).[12] There is no hesitation, moreover, in criticizing the domestic policies of the present administration and various actions of the Congress. Doubts are frequently voiced about the future of American society and, most particularly, the American economy.[13] Often, the criticisms are buttressed by lengthy quotations from West Europeans and Americans.

As in the case of the Soviet Union, however, on occasions of official visitation of American or Chinese leaders, a generally optimistic note is struck: "Sino–American relations are advancing, difficulties can be surmounted, and the friendship of the Chinese and American people is firmly rooted."[14] Certainly, the evidence for the first assertion at least is much greater than is the case with Sino–Soviet relations at this point. Whether the measurement be trade, technology transfer, joint ventures, Chinese students and researchers in the United States, or tourism, the recent advances in Sino–American relations are striking and lopsidedly to the advantage of China.

Why, then, the torrent of criticism? The rapid intensification of relations has itself produced specific problems and grievances (on both sides). In addition, the Chinese government has long opposed certain American foreign policies from an ideological and political perspective. Taiwan constitutes a large bone of contention, since it has once again been elevated by Deng and others to a position of high priority because of the worry about the island's political future after Chiang Ching-kuo. There is fear that the process of Taiwanization may make reunification more rather than less difficult. Protectionism and controls over the transfer of sensitive technology by the United States are also sources of grievance.

Beyond these matters, however, there are certain other considerations. The Chinese leaders find it difficult to make a distinction between the pronouncements of the U.S. government and critiques of China, many unfavorable, in the media or by American intellectuals. Some of the reports are strongly resented. The Chinese leaders have also discovered that criticism of the United States carries very limited penalties, in contrast to criticism of the Soviet Union. The U.S. government, through successive administrations, has remained doggedly optimistic about Sino–U.S. relations (officially) and exceedingly careful in any comments about Chinese domestic or foreign policies. Moreover, in the American system, pressure works. Over time, American concessions on a wide range of issues have been forthcoming, although neither in scale nor in scope wholly satisfactory to China. One might also conjecture that the very enthusiasm with which certain segments of the Chinese populace view the United States ("the most advanced society, politically open, affluent, and avant garde") is of concern at a time when China is committed to turning outward and must therefore cope with extensive Western influence; hence, the need to counteract "over-enthusiasm" (spiritual pollution). Finally, if the tilt in policy is clearly toward Japan and the West, this can be camouflaged in some degree by a more circumspect rhetoric.

Not all is based on shrewd political calculations and gamesmanship, however. If nonalignment (and a plague on both your houses) is politically advantageous at present, it is also congruent with some of the deepest cultural-historical features of Chinese (and East Asian) society. In remarkably candid discussions with Theo Sommer and Chancellor Helmut Kohl in the fall of 1984, Deng Xiaoping revealed a side of himself (and of

Chinese leadership) not generally known.[15] Sommer, editor of the respected German newspaper *Die Zeit*, summarized Deng's views by asserting "he does not think much of the superpowers." He then proceeded to quote Deng specifically on both the USSR and the United States. Deng's criticism of the Soviet Union was clearly the more trenchant. While he hoped that relations with the Soviet Union would improve, this would be possible only if it accepted the conditions stipulated by China (the three obstacles), and he doubted that Moscow would agree to such terms. Moreover, Deng made it clear that the Soviet abandonment of China in the late 1950s still rankled deeply, and he concluded with the surprising comment that the Soviet system was neither Marxist nor socialist, thereby separating himself from the present official stance.

But his criticism of the United States was also strong. "It is a weakness of the Americans that their words are not matched by their deeds"—this with reference to Taiwan. And his final observation on these matters was "there is no difference between the superpowers."[16]

On these matters, Deng does not necessarily speak for all key Chinese figures. On the basis of slender evidence, it has been argued that some leaders—among them Chen Yun—remain sympathetic to the Soviet system and in degree are thus more interested in rapprochement with the USSR. Conversely, as previously noted, it is assumed with somewhat greater evidence that a sizable number of intellectuals look to the United States, not merely because of its more advanced technological-scientific foundations but also because of the freedom of research and inquiry allowed.

On-the-scene observations by this writer and various discussions yield the following conclusions. First, the Soviet system, both in its economic and political aspects, remains deeply implanted in China and will not be easily eliminated. At present, however, the thrust of the reforms and experiments is in varying degree away from the Soviet system, whether the field be education, economics, or politics. If this process continues and is reasonably successful (both hypotheses being subject to some uncertainty), China will ultimately possess institutions and policies more compatible with its nature and needs. Today, China's leaders are seeking, among other things, to come to terms with their cultural traditions even as they seek to change those traditions. The resulting edifice will not be Western, but it may permit increasingly meaningful interaction between China on the one hand and Japan and the West on the other.

At the same time, a process of "Asianization" is taking place in East Asia as a whole, a process whereby the interactions between and among the Asian states themselves are intensifying and the centrality of external powers (including the Soviet Union and the United States) are decreasing but by no means rendered insignificant. Current Chinese domestic and foreign policies reflect the partly contradictory thrusts noted above: the drive for rapid modernization, with a corresponding pull toward the advanced industrial world, and the quest for an independent foreign policy that answers only to China's national interests. The links binding these two elements together is a staunch nationalism, itself partly traditional and partly modern in character.

Looking beyond officials, what of the Chinese public and, most particularly, of the articulate public—a small percentage of the total population, yet of considerable importance? Public opinion in China can be molded to a considerable extent by officialdom. If a "hate America" or "love the Soviet Union" campaign were again to be turned on (most unlikely), significant numbers of Chinese would do what was expected of them, and those in opposition would lapse into silence or minimal conformity. At present, however, the signs all indicate that public sentiment, and especially sentiment within the intellectual community, for close relations with the Soviet Union will have to be cultivated. There are exceptions, often noted. Those who received extensive training in the Soviet Union, can use the Russian language, and have Soviet friends may have a nostalgia for the past, a sympathy for the Soviet way, or a hope for enhanced career opportunities through Sino–Soviet rapprochement. Some of these individuals, moreover, are now reaching top positions in the military and civil hierarchy. But scores of discussions with individuals having a Soviet background reveal that opinions regarding their life in the USSR and the Soviet system are, at a minimum, very diverse, with limited desire to emulate Soviet society. (Can similar diversities be found among those now returning from the United States?)

More importantly, the general mood of the Chinese educated classes is running in a direction opposite to that which would support Sino–Soviet rapprochement today. Whether the test be language study (English is overwhelmingly favored, although attention to the Russian language has slightly increased); desire to study abroad (few want to go to the USSR, and the United States is the near-unanimous first choice); or social intercourse (Americans are seen as more informal, relaxed, and friendly), the Soviet Union faces a difficult climb in any popularity contest. One should emphasize that this is certainly not the only factor influencing relations between nations or necessarily the most important one. One does not detect a high level of popularity for the Japanese among Chinese today even though PRC leaders proclaim that Sino–Japanese relations are better than at any time in this century and permit only selective criticism of Japanese policies. Even high officials, however, privately speak more pessimistically about Sino–Soviet relations than in public, at least when talking with Americans. It would also seem revealing that the Soviet encirclement of China and the potentials for Soviet expansionism continue to be stressed in conferences with Chinese scholars and researchers from institutes having governmental ties. This concern is expressed much more forcefully in such settings than in published pronouncements, Gorbachev's Vladivostok speech notwithstanding.

There is a parallel between the private or unofficial remarks of Soviet officials and intellectuals and those of the Chinese to which we have just referred. In 1984, it was still possible for a key Soviet official to assert privately that the central problem of Asia in the twenty-first century would be Chinese expansionism but that a coalition of India, Vietnam, and Indonesia would evolve to meet this challenge.

One can also turn for additional evidence to a series of recent articles carried in the 1985 issue of *Far Eastern Affairs*, a journal of the Institute of the Far East, which is closely connected with the Soviet government. Various distinguished Soviet writers level the following charges against Chinese policies:

China is supporting the build-up of armaments by the United States and accepting Japanese and American efforts to tear China further away from the socialist community, drawing it into the orbit of the world capitalist economy;[17] Chinese officials have echoed the groundless Japanese position on the northern islands and the need for enhanced Japanese military power to counter the so-called Soviet threat; China counts upon the United States to increase its military-industrial potential and expand its influence in Asia;[18] despite internal opposition and an emphasis upon "independence," much of what China does in the world scene does not square with its rhetoric.[19]

Nor are Chinese domestic policies exempt from criticism. Thus, the quest for foreign investors, it is suggested, is to court the subordination of the Chinese economy to foreign control; the "chaotic development" of small-scale industries, it is argued, has seriously aggravated the contradictions between them and large state-run industries; and most importantly, to extend the thesis of the plurality of "national models" of socialism to the general principles of socialist construction, it is asserted, is to run counter both to logic and the principles of scientific analysis.[20]

Given the current efforts of Gorbachev to improve relations with China, these theses may disappear from the scholarly journals of the USSR. Similarly, on command from the Communist Party of China, the concern over the "Soviet threat" may be muted. It seems unlikely, however, that these various concerns will disappear from the minds of officials and scholars on both sides, even if they disappear from the printed page.

Against this complex background, what future scenarios are to be given the greatest credence? A Sino–Soviet alliance or war—to deal first with the extremities—can be dismissed as having far too little possibility to warrant discussion. This paper will choose to focus upon two possible scenarios—one labeled the "maximum accommodation scenario," the other the "minimum accommodation scenario."

MAXIMUM ACCOMMODATION

Maximum accommodation would involve the relatively rapid development of a network of economic and cultural interactions somewhat less in intensity and volume than those between Japan and the United States, but sufficient to create important bonds between Moscow and Beijing and also sufficient to serve as a stimulant to others, particularly the United States, to bid higher for Beijing's affections. To occupy a centrist position between two rivals has both tactical and strategic advantages, as the United States discovered in the mid-1970s when it held that position vis-à-vis Moscow and Beijing. The North Koreans have profited from precisely this stance for many years. Chinese leaders repeatedly assert that they have no intention of playing either a Soviet or American card, but a healthy skepticism is warranted.

Even the maximum accommodation scenario would stop short of Sino–Soviet military cooperation in any active sense, but here too, measures involving risk limitation would be taken, such as discussions between Chinese and Soviet military leaders, a hot line, and prior notification, along with observers invited, to military exercises.

This scenario would require a gradual Soviet accommodation to the advent of China as a regional power. Such an adjustment would include the reduction of close-up Soviet border forces, an acceptance of more extensive Chinese relations with both states on the Korean peninsula, and, above all, an arrangement regarding Indochina involving some degree of Soviet–Vietnamese accommodation to Chinese interests. Over these matters, to be sure, the Soviet Union may not have full or even decisive control. But China's regional interests must be satisfied if Sino–Soviet relations are to reach the highest possible level of cooperation, and it is precisely here that the Soviet Union will find the greatest difficulties in accommodation. Soviet containment policies—vastly more extensive than similar efforts of the United States in the 1950s—will not be abandoned lightly, even if Moscow can find means of adjustments that would not demoralize and antagonize their Asian client states. A "successful" China—one advancing rapidly in economic power, political cohesion and military strength—is not likely to provide the type of assurances of support for or acceptance of Soviet interests in Asia satisfactory to any Soviet leadership. But an "unsuccessful" China, wracked with economic and political woes, would pose a different set of inhibitions to Soviet strategic concessions.

What could China offer the USSR that would make Soviet sacrifices on behalf of a maximum accommodation attractive? Greater ideological accord and the resumption of party-to-party relations would have some value. More important would be a Chinese willingness to refrain from criticizing Soviet Third World policies and support for Moscow's position

vis-à-vis that of the United States in certain key instances. Chinese acceptance of a major Soviet military presence in the Soviet Far East and the
Pacific, viewing it as directed against the United States, not China, would
be a supreme benefit, particularly if the accommodation could extend to
the new Afghanistan, as it was ultimately extended to the new Outer
Mongolia (although Soviet doubts about Beijing's acceptance of the status
quo in Outer Mongolia and Siberia persist). Afghanistan, to be sure, is
an issue that points to Pakistan. Any destabilization of Pakistan would
profoundly concern Beijing, and the Soviet Union will need to keep this
in mind. Chinese assistance in achieving a modus vivendi between the
USSR and Japan—more or less on Soviet terms—would be an added
bonus. Softer Soviet policies toward China and Japan might go hand in
hand if the Soviet leaders were to contemplate a major new direction.

MINIMUM ACCOMMODATION

The minimum accommodation scenario would involve regular increases
in Sino–Soviet trade and some Soviet assistance in plant renovation, but
with these processes lagging far behind China's economic interaction with
the advanced industrial nations and with both nations having their primary
economic interests elsewhere: the Soviet Union with Europe and, increasingly, Japan; China with Japan, other parts of Asia, and the industrial
West. Similarly, cultural relations would advance, in accordance with the
interests of both nations in keeping contact on a wide range of fronts—
science, technology and the social sciences—but such contacts would be
very carefully regulated and circumscribed.

Each side would refrain from the violent polemics of the 1960s and early
1970s, especially in third-party settings, but both would remain critical of
each other on specific issues, and ideological questions would creep into
disputation over concrete issues. The basic theme would be reduction of
tension, not genuine rapprochement. To this end, some agreements on
reduction of border forces and similar measures would be reached. It
might even be possible to get a partial accommodation in Indochina,
depending upon developments. But each side would be cognizant of its
different interests in Asia and unwilling to make basic concessions regarding what it considered to be vital to those interests.

LOOKING AHEAD

The conventional wisdom among outside observers (and, privately,
among Chinese and Soviet observers as well) is that future developments
will accord more with the second rather than the first scenario. In this
case, I am inclined to believe that the conventional wisdom is correct
despite recent Soviet initiatives. One must conjure first with the perceived

vulnerability of both China and the Soviet Union in terms of their respective frontiers and, at the same time, the supreme importance each accords to its existing empire. The situation is fraught with potential for insecurity, hence apprehensions and suspicions. Then there is the overpowering nationalism that exists in both societies. But nationalism in the two societies has quite different psychological underpinnings. In both peoples, xenophobia and racial prejudices remain elements of importance. However, the deeply imbedded insecurity—and feelings of inferiority—manifest in Soviet society stand in contrast to the extensive self-confidence exhibited by the Chinese.

Moreover, on the reaches of Central Asia along the Siberian and Manchurian borders and in such regions as Tibet, an unease prevails. Peoples of diverse cultures are still unassimilated. Russian and Han power is exercised primarily by military means. And no buffer state system exists to cushion the confrontation of two highly nationalistic states. Geopolitics in this instance does not support easy accommodation. The Yellow Peril still looms large in the Russian mind, at the grassroots as well as among elites. And the unfavorable image of past Russian expansion—Czarist and Stalinist—cannot be eradicated from Chinese consciousness. Indeed, it is now a powerfully reinforced image due to the Soviet encirclement of China.

In sum, considerations of security must bulk large in future Sino–Soviet relations, and if the principal threat to the USSR comes from the United States, China's concern can only be with the Soviet Union. The United States poses no threat to China today, and that single fact is of paramount importance in determing the nature of the tilt in Chinese foreign policies.

Economic development, China's second major concern, is best served by a low-risk foreign policy, as I have noted, but that can be achieved through a minimum accommodation scenario. Increased Sino–Soviet economic interaction can be of benefit to both countries, especially as their respective border regions become more developed. It will occur. China's experience with Soviet trade and aid in the 1950s, however, like that of most other countries, was decidedly mixed, notwithstanding the significant support given by the USSR to the initial PRC industrial program. Today, whether it is appropriate or not, Chinese leaders want to be on the cutting edge of technological innovation, and—particularly in fields like energy development and telecommunications—they prefer to turn to Japan and the West. There is every reason to believe that Japan will play the most major role in China's industrial revolution, with the United States counted upon in select high-technology fields. Even where they have had a strong strategic and economic role, as in India, the Soviets will be hard-pressed to keep their overall edge as a nation moves toward ever greater emphasis upon high technology.

Could internal developments in either the Soviet Union or China significantly affect their mutual relations? If Gorbachev and his colleagues can advance a combination of innovation and sophistication in transforming Soviet policies in Asia—and elsewhere—making certain concessions, relaxing the encirclement policies, finding a solution to Afghanistan, and presiding over a Vietnam–China modus vivendi, Sino–Soviet rapprochement could go much further, as has been suggested. The initiative shown in the Vladivostok speech should not be ignored. But rapid progress on all of the above fronts is highly unlikely. Beyond this, even under such circumstances, China would be cautious, not finding it in its interest to become too closely identified with the USSR because of the repercussions this would have on China's relations with other nations.

If the Soviet Union manages to revitalize the Soviet economy and Soviet society under the impetus of substantial reforms, will that be helpful? Far-reaching economic reforms encompassing structural changes in the USSR might enhance Soviet capacities to participate more fully in the dynamic economic revolution now sweeping over Asia and legitimize its current efforts to join GATT and Pacific–Asian regional economic organizations. Such a development might also provide Beijing with useful propaganda about the superiority of the socialist system and, more particularly, about the vital necessity of reform, its own included, Thus, ideological disputation would be further reduced, and greater opportunities for economic interaction might ensue. But a successful Soviet Union would not of itself resolve the security issue for China; indeed, it might cause greater apprehension.

What of Soviet–U.S. relations? Chinese leaders have decided that a reduction in tension between Moscow and Washington is in China's interest, partly because it might increase Soviet flexibility in security arrangements in Asia, as well as put a curb on such developments as space weapons that threaten China's arrangements. Beijing, however, would not want to see Soviet–American rapprochement go too far, since that would evoke in the Chinese mind the possibility of collusion between the superpowers. It should not be forgotten that this was precisely the charge made by PRC spokesmen at certain points in the 1960s, with U.S. and Soviet policies toward India providing evidence at the time.

How might domestic developments in China affect the two scenarios discussed above? A stable China, one in which the economic reforms turned out reasonably successfully and the political succession was managed without undue trauma, would presumably be a more confident China, highly nationalistic and pressing its claims in Asia, but reluctant to jeopardize its ever closer ties with Japan and the West by exhibiting aggressive behavior. At some point, territorial and buffer state issues—Taiwan, among others—might evoke crises, but these would just as logically involve Vietnam as Japan, the ASEAN nations, or the United States. If with stability came a decided growth in military power, the Soviet Union would not be happy.

A "failed" China, on the other hand, might well bring back a higher level of authoritarianism, greater military influence, attempts to reinstitute Stalinist-type socialism, a rising quotient of xenophobia, and a reversal of the "look-outward" policy. However, while such a situation would greatly damage ties with Japan and the West, it would not necessarily cause an improvement in ties with the Soviet Union. In the past, such cycles have produced antipathy to all foreign influence.

It remains only to explore the impact of the two scenarios upon other states, most particularly the United States, Japan, and the two Koreas. It is obvious that the United States would be at a disadvantage by a maximum accommodation scenario, since that would provide greater leverage for both the USSR and the PRC vis-à-vis the United States. Nor would such a scenario be advantageous to other Asian states. It might cause sentiment for non/alignment to increase in Japan, a stiffening of the North Korean position toward the South, and apprehensions both in Vietnam and among the ASEAN states, especially among those states most dubious about China's future intentions.

Minimum accommodation, on the other hand, should not cause great concern. Such a development, indeed, has certain advantages, especially if it enables China to focus upon economic development, keep the military under control, and permit a degree of liberalization, political as well as economic.

It would be a serious mistake, however, to assume that under any scenario applying to Sino–Soviet relations, China's current leaders, or their successors will be less than extremely vigorous in pursuing what they regard as China's national interests. Nationalism is still on the ascendancy in the PRC, having thoroughly penetrated and largely supplanted any ideology, including Marxism-Leninism. For all nations, whether labeled friend or foe, China will represent a difficult and, on occasion, abrasive force—determined to pursue "the Chinese way" and possessed of an extraordinarily high quotient of self-confidence, only occasionally leavened by a recognition of its huge problems yet to be surmounted. If that self-confidence is justified, it is due to the great reservoir of human talent as yet untapped, awaiting the appropriate institutions and policies. Despite the disclaimers of its leaders, the Chinese will assert themselves as regional leaders in the course of events; their size, their pride, and their abilities dictate such a course. Hence, most neighboring states, including the Soviet Union, would prefer neither a chaotic nor a supremely successful China, but one forced to concentrate on internal concerns for the foreseeable future.

DEVELOPMENTS ON THE KOREAN PENINSULA

Since the autumn of 1984, movement in North–South Korean relations has recommenced after a lapse of more than a decade. Do recent developments augur well for a sustained reduction of tension and a growing network of relationships between Pyongyang and Seoul, or are they a charade that is doomed to end in disappointment and bitterness? The signs are mixed. If cautious optimism is warranted, it is primarily because the external and domestic circumstances surrounding the Korea issue seem more propitious as forces for moderation than at any time in the past. Yet agreement remains to be reached on many of the most basic principles that must underlie rapprochement, and the level of polemics remains discouragingly high.

First, a brief recital of the basic facts is necessary. By 1983, developments within Northeast Asia, both as they related to major power relations and interests and as they pertained to trends in the two Koreas, were conducive to a renewed effort to break the impasse. China, with its deepening commitment to economic modernization and a turning outward for science and technology on behalf of this goal, was in the process of widening its relations with Japan and the United States. In addition, hijacking incidents and, more importantly, economic interests had brought China into a growing interaction with the Republic of Korea (ROK). On the other hand, relations between the PRC and the Democratic Peoples' Republic of Korea (DPRK), while proclaimed as fraternal bonds sealed in blood and marked by numerous high-level visits, seemed less stable than in the recent past. Was Pyongyang troubled by what North Korean leaders perceived to be an opportunistic quotient in Chinese foreign policy and uncertain also as to the course of Chinese domestic programs?

In any case, Kim Il-song and his colleagues moved to strengthen their ties with the Soviet Union, a relationship often cool in recent decades. Both economic and strategic considerations played a vital role in this effort to improve relations. The North Korean economy was in trouble, with obsolescence, lowered productivity, and very limited foreign exchange along with a sizable unpaid foreign debt confronting the younger generation of technocrats who were rapidly replacing Kim's old guerrilla faction at the helm. The North's GNP was less than one-fourth that of the South, and this had strategic as well as economic implications. The Stalinist "big push" economic strategy, and the very high degree of autarky accompanying it, had reached a point of rapidly diminishing returns.[21] Pyongyang needed as much economic and military assistance as it could get, and the Soviet Union—deeply worried about what they regarded as a U.S. – Japan – South Korean alliance directed against it and with China on its peripheries—was a logical source of support.

On the other hand, Soviet aid would be limited and no long-term answer to North Korea's economic problems. The Chinese, entertaining a number of high-level DPRK economic and political delegations, sought to persuade them that they should emulate at least certain aspects of the new Chinese program. Perhaps persuasion was not really necessary. In the early 1970s, North Korea had sought to turn outward, as problems in the economy were recognized. Steep price rises due to the oil crisis rendered this effort a failure and bequeathed the debt problem. Nonetheless, North Korea's current leaders have recognized that it would be to their great advantage if they could tap the resources and technology of the advanced industrial world, especially Japan—a most logical source of assistance.[22]

It is probable that Chinese leaders counseled the North that by drawing the United States and South Korea into discussions and participating in tension reduction efforts, the path toward "turning outward" to Japan and Western Europe would be smoothed. Such a course of action would draw upon China's own experience in the 1970s, even though the two situations were far from analogous.

In the summer of 1983, after consultations with U.S. representatives, Beijing engaged in discussions on this matter with Pyongyang, with leaders at the highest level participating.[23] At the time, the Chinese were led to believe that Washington would support tripartite negotiations of the type suggested in the Carter–Park proposal of 1979, a proposal rejected by Pyongyang at that time. On October 8, PRC officials notified the U.S. Embassy in Beijing that North Korea was ready to take part in such talks. The following day, however, the Rangoon bombing occurred, an incident raising still unanswered questions about Pyongyang's decisionmaking process.

Naturally, a great furor arose over the Rangoon incident and North Korea suffered a serious setback internationally, especially after the Burmese government emphatically fixed the responsibility for the bombing on Pyongyang, with irrefutable evidence in the form of two surviving perpetrators. Only in early December did North Korea broach the trilateral concept informally, followed by the formal proposal on January 10, 1984.[24] As initially worded, the DPRK proposal provided in effect for two separate bilateral discussions—one between North Korea and the United States, focused on the issue of troop withdrawal and a peace treaty to replace the armistice; the other between North and South Korea, relating to agreements on a bilateral nonaggression pact, followed by military force reduction and a pact on the nonuse of force between the two governments. The rhetoric accompanying the North Korean proposal appeared to deny South Korea full and equal status in the negotiations.

ROK authorities strongly objected to the proposal, and the United States supported them. In the succeeding weeks, there were hints that North Korea would be prepared to accept South Korea as a full participant and agree to a less rigorously formulated agenda, but neither the South nor the United States showed an interest in testing Pyongyang on these matters. By the summer of 1984, the stalemate seemed unlikely to be broken; only rival polemics were in evidence.

Suddenly, in the autumn, there was a chain of events that formed a striking contrast. In September, serious floods in the South had left several hundred thousand people homeless. North Korea offered basic relief supplies, in all probability expecting the South to reject them; on earlier occasions, each had made similar offers, with the other indignantly denouncing them. On this occasion, however, Seoul announced that it would accept the contributions not because they were needed, but because the process of reducing tensions might be forwarded.

A hitch was overcome. Pyongyang's demand that its supply trucks be allowed to drive to Seoul was rejected, but this time the North backed down, and the transfer of supplies took place at the border and by ship in several South Korean ports. Not to be outdone in the propaganda campaign, the South prepared hundreds of boxes containing transistor radios, wristwatches, clothing and household items as gifts for its Northern compatriots. Barter trade had begun! The hot line between the two capitals was also reopened.

The future remained clouded, however. Kim Il-song continued to insist upon trilateral talks and argued that North–South discussions would only be feasible after the South had regained "all real powers," including total control over its armed forces, repealed anti-communist legislation, and made certain other concessions. Notwithstanding these remarks, another surprising development occurred in November, when the North suddenly announced acceptance of a proposal by the South to hold bilateral discussions on economic relations and Red Cross talks on the divided family problem. The first economic meeting took place on November 15, with the Red Cross meeting following five days later. No preconditions were attached to either meeting, and while no significant agreements were reached, discussions were amiable. From the outset, the South continued to offer very specific proposals relating to trade and other matters, whereas the North sought to broaden the discussion to encompass political-strategic issues.

After the first meetings, a hiatus occurred, with the North using various occurrences as causes for demanding postponements. The second series of meetings, scheduled for December, were canceled because of the incident in which a Soviet defector, Vasily Matuzok, ran across the DMZ: a fire fight followed, killing one South Korean and three North Korean soldiers. A new schedule of meetings for January was later fixed, but once again Pyongyang demanded postponement, this time because of *Team Spirit '85*, the annual joint U.S.-ROK military exercises. The reason for postponement seemed contrived, since these exercises had long been scheduled and no earlier threat of cancellation had been made. Various speculations could be advanced:

North Korean strategy with respect to negotiations was not in place; the Northern leaders wanted to see the results of the South Korean elections of February 1985; discussions with the Soviet Union relating to military aid and other assistance dictated a cautious policy vis-à-vis the South; and there was renewed evidence of independence from China.

Whatever the mix of factors involved in the Northern attitude, the meetings were resumed in May, with the economic talks held on May 17, and the Red Cross talks at the end of the month. A third round of talks was held in June, with working-level Red Cross meetings (three members on each side) taking place on July 15 and 19. The next economic meetings were not scheduled until September 18, with the plenary sessions of the Red Cross meetings on August 27. Since that time, no negotiations have taken place except for those pertaining to the 1988 Olympics up to the end of 1987, although new proposals for bilateral talks have been advanced by the North. These proposals have thus far been unacceptable to the South since they involve an emphasis on political and military issues aimed at rapid reunification on the basis of a formula long proposed by the DPRK. In an effort to make its proposal more attractive, Pyongyang has subsequently expressed a willingness to include economic and humanitarian issues on the agenda.

Any evaluation of the results to date must be complex.[25] On the one hand, the two governments have been drawn into sporadic discussions, with neither side wishing to bear the responsibility for breaking them off permanently. Much has been theater. Some specific agreements were tentatively reached earlier, but these have lapsed for the present at least. Northern proposals to raise discussions to higher levels, both with respect to economic concerns and, more importantly, to reunification issues, have been accepted by the South in principle, with certain modifications, but there has been no agreement or concrete steps to implement the proposals as yet. Here, most of the concessions have been made by Seoul, although the ROK has long advanced proposals for a Chun–Kim summit meeting and has countered Northern proposals relating to steps toward reunification with its own for the drafting of a joint constitution.

No specific agreements on trade or technological exchange have so far been reached, despite various concrete proposals by the South. There is only an agreement to create a North–South joint economic cooperation committee at vice-premier level. On the political front, the South has accepted the North's proposal to hold an interparliamentary meeting, again in principle, but with no agreement on the agenda. The Red Cross working-group meetings once appeared to have narrowed the differences on family visits and related matters. An exchange of separated family members and accompanying folk art troupes was arranged and took place on one occasion, but agreement on further exchanges has not yet been forthcoming.[26] High-level secret talks regarding a Chun–Kim summit have reportedly been held but without result thus far.

In most of these developments, much is tactical maneuvering, with the targets being the domestic and the international audiences. Two separate tracks can be discerned, uneasily coexisting, with no clear sign that they can be successfully meshed. The main thrust of the South's position is toward the creation of economic and cultural relations of a concrete type, with the assumption that the broad political and strategic agreements necessary for genuine progress toward reunification cannot possibly be reached now or in the near future. Understandably, there is no interest in the reunification formula advanced by the North, and a deep suspicion (not unjustified, as will be seen) of Pyongyang's intentions. Thus, the South has signaled that it will press for dual admission to the United Nations despite the improbability that the Soviet bloc (or China) will accept this. And while, for tactical reasons, it advances its own reunification concepts, its primary concerns lie with the establishment of a network of economic and cultural relations.

Using the formula of "one nation, two systems" and demanding full political equality, the North is seeking in every possible way to make the reunification issue the foremost matter on the agenda, with all other considerations weapons to this end. Its interest in economic exchange and the union of divided families is limited by the fear that such developments will perpetuate the political status quo and, of equal importance, expose the North's deficiencies. For the same reason, it has staunchly opposed dual admission to the UN or cross-recognition by the major powers. Yet its reunification plan is totally unrealistic and could never be accepted by any ROK government.

In addition, the rhetoric emanating from the DPRK suggests that Northern leaders have doubts that any agreement with the present government of South Korea is possible or even desirable. Indeed, the call is still explicitly for revolution in the South, albeit a revolution carried out by "the workers and peasants" of the South, with Northern support only indirect.[27] President Chun is variously described as a puppet, traitor, and leader of a military-fascist clique. Typical is a radio comment of July 7, 1985:

On June 24, traitor Chun Du-hwan held a so-called Security Council meeting at Chongwadae. That day, the traitor raved that only when the people are united and maintain superiority in national strength can they prevent a war, thus using the utmost efforts for strengthening the security posture.[28]

On July 10, Pyongyang radio broadcast a statement that

. . . the South Korean military fascist clique should apologize to the people for its criminal acts instead of attempting to conceal the truth of the Kwangju incident and escape the responsibility. It should be deservedly punished.[29]

Thus, while the North Korean government has officially reversed itself by entering into negotiations with a government it once said it would never acknowledge, such language does not augur well for any mutual trust or accommodation. And there are some more ominous statements. On July 9, one of the ranking DPRK politburo members, Pak Song-chol, in a published article, after averring ironclad unity under the leader and party, spoke of the need to "achieve national reunification on one's own and to consummate the Korean revolution to the end."[30] By pursuing "agile tactics and strategies," Pak wrote, "we can advance the revolution and place the enemy (presumably ROK leaders) on the defensive." And he followed with these words:

The Korean revolution still has a long way to go and is full of trials. We should reunify the divided fatherland without fail, establish national sovereignty on the basis of the whole country, and establish a communist paradise on the soil of the fatherland.[31]

In these remarks, there is no mention of "one nation, two systems," but of a continuous revolution with the South clearly an ultimate target. Recent unrest in the South may strengthen the temptation to put an emphasis on destabilization policies, although that course would present its own hazards, among them Pyongyang's relations with the major powers.

Thus, uncertainties continue to abound with respect to the future course of North–South relations. Optimists can argue that the harsh rhetoric of DPRK spokesmen is natural in a situation where the people have long been conditioned to hear only such rhetoric and when explorations of a new North–South relationship are only in their preliminary stages. Further, the evidence supports the thesis that at present, there is no major state—including the Soviet Union—that would benefit from another Korean conflict, and the bulk of the external pressures upon both Koreas is directed toward continuing negotiation until some modus vivendi is found, however long and arduous the route. It is also a fact that conditions in the North are far from favorable for a sustained confrontation with the South, and a new generation of leaders under Kim Jong-il appears to be coming to power who may be more qualified—hence more inclined—to focus their attention on domestic concerns. If this is true, and if the goal of turning outward for science and technology is to be realized, the North risks much in intensifying the cold war with the South, not to mention provoking a hot war.

The pessimists counter with some sober arguments that cannot be wholly discounted. On the military front, it is argued, the North has only 4 to 5 years during which it will still possess military superiority over the South, after which the window of opportunity will close. A military strike from the North would presumably involve the following elements: advantage would be taken of a sizable or major upheaval in the South; Northern involvement would be camouflaged, by the use of ROK uniforms, commando units, and established infiltration routes, all designed to sow maximum confusion in the South and in the world; the aim would be a quick strike followed by a conflict to last at most a matter of weeks or a few months, with no necessity to count on external support.

It remains very difficult to envisage any Northern attack that would not evoke massive U.S.–ROK retaliation, with devastating air and sea strikes against the DPRK, and the use of tactical nuclear weapons not entirely precluded. But despite repeated assurances that the North has "neither the will nor the means" to attack the South, close-up deployments of regular and commando units near the DMZ, the acquisition of new military equipment including American-made helicopters and MiG-23s, and the continued development of underground fortresses near the DMZ as well as tunnels provide a basis for anxiety. Are these merely defensive actions? And is it not significant that the North accuses the South of doing precisely what it has been proven are Northern initiatives, namely, the construction of tunnels, the strengthening of forward units, and terrorist intrusions of various types? Similar charges, it will be remembered, were advanced before the 1950 North Korean attack.

On balance, however, another Korean War seems unlikely—unless the South presents an unprecedented target of opportunity because of internal turmoil. Far more likely is a dual-channel approach by the North, with both negotiations and confrontation pursued, the latter course advanced through propaganda, infiltration, and occasional terrorism—all in the hope of kindling a revolution in the South to which assistance can be given.

If this analysis is basically correct, what are the likely postures of the major states of the area, and what are the implications for regional security? Under present circumstances, the most uncertain element is the USSR. On the one hand, the Soviet Union has had troubled relations with the DPRK at many points in the past, and among Soviet officials there is no great affection for—or trust in—Kim Il-song and the North Korean government. But as has been noted, Soviet concern over a perceived Northeast Asian entente—involving the United States, Japan, and the ROK, with the PRC on the peripheries, directed at containing Soviet power in the Pacific—is real and has deepened in recent years. It is an attractive option to strengthen the DPRK militarily, especially if in the process, certain strategic concessions are obtained from Pyongyang, such as the enhanced use of port facilities and permission for military over-flights. All of this presents the Soviet leadership with a number of delicate problems, to be sure. Does Moscow risk antagonizing China with its gains in Soviet–North Korean relations, jeopardizing the hope for improved Sino–Soviet relations? Does it encourage a degree of North Korean adventurism that it does not want—and might not be able to control? Can it count on the DPRK, or will the North Koreans once again demonstrate their proclivities for a tilt toward China at various points? Certainly,

Moscow cannot expect to establish with Pyongyang the relationship created with Hanoi. Nonetheless, the Soviet Union feels itself the odd man out in Northeast Asia at present and so has less interest in accommodation, especially since this might strengthen the United States or Japan. At a minimum, it wants to be a participant in any agreement pertaining to the Korean peninsula.

China is walking a delicate tight rope on the Korean issue, as suggested earlier. On the one hand, it proclaims support for key North Korean positions such as American troop withdrawal; the "one nation, two system" reunification formula (a formula advanced with respect to Taiwan), and the inequities of the Chun administration. On the other hand, its interests lie strongly in a reduction of North–South tensions and a growing network of North–South relations, rather than in a new war. Its economic relations with the South have steadily grown and may have exceeded those with the North in 1985. Moreover, it has found it important to negotiate with South Korea on a series of problems relating to hijacking and mutiny. Chinese–South Korean contacts via international conferences, sports meets, and in third countries are now commonplace and may be greater than Chinese–North Korean contacts except at the higher official levels. Thus, China is steadily moving toward a two-Korea policy and on balance, its actions in recent years have constituted a positive contribution to a lessening of tension on the Korean peninsula. It is doubtful, however, whether it will be inclined to move from a de facto to a de jure two-Korea position, given the leverage which Pyongyang exercises upon it by using the Soviet card. Indeed, there is considerable concern in Beijing over the most recent warming of Soviet–North Korean relations, and the possibility of an enhanced Soviet military position in this highly strategic area. For the Soviet Union to obtain base rights and other military privileges would strengthen Soviet encirclement of China close to the Manchurian industrial complex.

Japan also follows a two-Korea policy, being careful to tilt decidedly towards South Korea. Indeed, the massive Japanese investment and trade with the ROK, while productive of South Korean grievances, has played an important role in the remarkable economic performance of the South in the last 20 years—a fact that has not escaped Pyongyang's attention. Thus, despite its vehement denunciation of the South's "colonial status," the North has now made a key goal the broadening of economic and cultural relations with Japan. Japan is interested, and will do as much as it can to forward the negotiations between North and South, in an effort to induce the conditions that would permit expansion of Japan–DPRK contacts, but it will not risk its ties with the ROK. And these ties continue to develop, with low-level strategic relations now added to the extensive economic and cultural interactions. In contrast, the economic disabilities of the North provide decided limits to interaction between Tokyo and Pyongyang.

The United States, like China and Japan, has a strong interest in a reduction of tension on the Korean peninsula. It has no intention, however, of removing the 40,000 American troops in the South at present. In addition to memories of 1950, the United States is well aware of the importance of a military presence on the scene to assure Koreans (both North and South) of the American commitment, these troops playing a role similar to that of U.S. forces in Western Europe. In addition, such incidents as the December 1984 DMZ fire fight between North and South Korean soldiers show how easy it might be for an incident to trigger a large-scale conflagration in the absence of any third force. The United States has long signaled its willingness to see cross-recognition take place, although it is prepared to settle for cross-contacts. No restrictions are currently placed on visits by American citizens to North Korea, but there is no encouragement given to U.S. public figures who receive invitations from Pyongyang. In recent times, despite the vituperation heaped upon Washington by Pyongyang organs, North Korea has been soliciting contacts with "Americans with influence," while carefully screening others. The prospects for further positive U.S.–DPRK interaction are dependent upon the course of North–South negotiations and the broader policies of North Korea, but contacts are likely to be limited for the near term at least. In response to Chinese urging, the United States has softened its stance on informal diplomatic contacts in social settings, returning to a position taken prior to the Rangoon bombing. For its part, North Korea has expanded its efforts to contact Americans privately, offering dialogue and reciprocal visits. But advances will be cautious.

Three variables would appear to be of critical importance in assessing future developments on the Korean peninsula. First, the internal political and economic evolution of the two Koreas must be a matter of vital concern. A serious deterioration of conditions in either Korea accompanied by a rising quotient of strife would invite greater external involvement and/or major North–South conflict. Second, the future course of Soviet policy toward the two Koreas and, in a broader context, toward Northeast Asia—together with trends in Sino–Soviet and Soviet–American relations—constitute variables of basic significance, since the Soviet Union is the one major state where attitudes and policies are currently the most flexible and subject to the greatest potential shifts. Finally, the adjustment between the past and present role of the United States in Korea and the Northeast Asian region generally on the one hand and the rising tide of Asianization on the other will represent an intricate, continuous process of commanding importance.

On balance, trends both with respect to Sino–Soviet relations and North–South Korean relations offer hope for some reduction of tension. Yet the distance covered with respect to substantive accomplishments is scant so far, and the road ahead is certain to be very rocky. Retreats as well as advances are likely, and there is no reason to believe that vigilance on the security front can be relaxed. There is now, however, a heightened premium, upon political skills and economic achievements, with reliance upon military power alone less and less promising. Whether political skills will be directed primarily to winning propaganda battles and camouflaging real intentions, or whether they can assist in reaching attitudes and policies conducive to genuine peaceful coexistence remains at present an unanswered question.

NOTES

1. The background of Sino–Soviet relations has been extensively treated. Among the standard sources, see Donald Zagoria, ed., *Soviet Policy in Asia* (New Haven, Conn: Yale University Press, 1982); Herbert J. Ellison, ed., *The Sino-Soviet Conflict* (Seattle, Wash.: University of Washington, 1982); and Richard H. Solomon, ed., *The China Factor* (Englewood Cliffs, N.J.: Prentice-Hall, 1981). For my interpretation, see "In Quest of National Interest—The Foreign Policy of the People's Republic of China" (Berkeley: Graduate Division, University of California, 1983).

2. Chinese criticism has long focused upon the Taiwan Relations Act, the Congressional action which followed the normalization with the subsequent approval of President Carter. But Deng Xiaoping was aware that the United States was not prepared to abandon Taiwan completely and that normalization with the PRC was dependent upon an acceptance of that fact. He may, however, have been misled by certain private statements from a White House source.

3. This position was reiterated by a prominent Soviet official in a discussion with this author.

4. Current Soviet negotiating tactics with the Chinese have been discussed by this author with Chinese knowledgeable about the talks. On May 21, 1985, in his speech at a state banquet given in honor of Prime Minister Rajiv Gandhi, Gorbachev restated the Soviet proposal for a collective approach to Asian security, a theme that has been muted since 1975. Earlier Soviet proposals received very little support from Asian states. Gorbachev, incidentally, took aim at the Chinese attack upon both superpowers, stating that the cause of tension in the world lay in the "attempts by imperialist powers to interfere . . . in the affairs of newly independent countries and to subjugate them to their influence," and not "in the notorious 'rivalry of the superpowers.' " For the text of Gorbachev's speech, see Foreign Broadcast Information Service (FBIS), *Daily Report—Soviet Union*, 22 May 1985, D3–5, and for a brief analysis, see Robert G. Sutter and Richard P. Cronin, "Soviet Leader Gorbachev Calls for Collective Security in Asia—Possible Implications," Congressional Research Service, The Library of Congress, May 28, 1985.

5. For the text of the Beijing statement, see Joint Publications Research Service (JPRS), *China Report—Political, Sociological and Military Affairs*, 1 April 1985, p. 12.

6. Gorbachev's statement is contained in a Xinhua dispatch from Moscow, dated March 11, translated in FBIS, *Daily Report—China*, 12 March 1985, C4.

7. For a Chinese evaluation of the significance of the Arkhipov visit, see Tan Cheng and Yuan Yin, "After Arkhipov's China Visit," *Shijie Zhishi*, No. 3, February 1, 1985, p. 2. According to the authors, "The results of Arkhipov's visit have proved that China and the Soviet Union have made a great stride forward in developing economic, trade, scientific, and technological cooperation." After discussing Arkhipov's meetings with his old friends, the authors note Premier Zhao Ziyang's statement to Arkhipov, "China values highly the traditional friendship between China and the Soviet Union and between the peoples of the two countries. It sincerely hopes that Sino–Soviet relations will improve and will be established on a good-neighborly and friendly basis." The article concludes: "It is gratifying that positive factors in Sino–Soviet relations are increasing. However, there are still negative factors and obstacles hampering the further development of Sino–Soviet relations. Both sides need to make joint efforts to remove obstacles, overcome negative factors, develop positive factors, and normalize their relations through joint efforts."

8. See Richard Nations, "A $14 Billion Deal," *Far Eastern Economic Review* (July 25, 1985): 12–13.

9. For example, see Tang Xiuzhe and Sun Weizi, "Another Change in CPSU Leadership,"

Liaowang, No. 11, March 18, 1985, pp. 6–7. See also Jie Fu, "Gorbachev at the Helm," *Beijing Review* (May 6, 1985): 12–13. In this generally sympathetic account of Gorbachev's first two months, the author refers to Vietnam and Afghanistan at the end of the article in remarkably restrained fashion, calling them the Soviet Union's "more controversial positions," but noting that Gorbachev had signaled no change in USSR policies on either front. For a more equivocal evaluation, see "The Soviet Union Following Gromyko's Transfer to Another Post" in the pro-PRC Hong Kong newspaper, *Wen Wei Po*, July 5, 1985, p. 2.

10. The article is written by Zheng Weizhi, director of the Institute for International Studies and adviser to the Foreign Affairs Committee of the NPC. Zheng is a veteran diplomat, having served as ambassador to a number of countries. The article is entitled, "Historical Tragedy Must Not Be Repeated," and an English version is carried in *Beijing Review*, May 6, 1985, pp. 16–18. Note the following passages: As a result of the war, "Britain and France, two once-powerful capitalist countries, were seriously weakened. Not only did the imperialists get nothing from the war they started; they also hastened their decline and as a result, conditions were prepared for the oppressed peoples to throw off the yoke of imperialism and colonialism. Second, the forces of socialism grew more powerful. The Soviet Union, the world's first socialist country, withstood the severe test of the war. . . . The Soviet people and the Red Army, led by Stalin and fighting shoulder to shoulder with the other anti-fascist countries, defeated Nazi Germany. Their victory was forceful evidence that the socialist system had great vitality. . . . In short, victory over fascism was the victory of the socialist system, the victory of the people of the world." Of equal interest is the emphasis given in this article to the Chinese contribution to victory and the praise accorded the Kuomintang for its acceptance of a united front with the Communist Party. Nationalism and current PRC strategy toward Taiwan are thus united: "China suffered heavy casualties and other losses, and also inflicted greater punishment on the Japanese than any other country. In the course of the war, the Chinese people killed or wounded 1.33 million Japanese soldiers, exceeding the number shot dead or wounded by Britain, the United States and the other countries in the Pacific War combined. . . . By accepting the CPC's proposal for forming a national united front against Japan, the Kuomintang played an important part in the War of Resistance." The article concludes by asserting that China hopes that both the United States and the USSR "can settle down to serious talks and reach a true agreement on stopping the arms race and gradually reducing armaments."

11. See the *Wen Wei Po* article of July 5, 1985, earlier cited. This article concludes with the following comment: "It is really hard to imagine that Gorbachev's assuming power will give rise to a drastic change in the Soviet Union's foreign policy, which is determined by the country's international goals and strength and formulated collectively by the Politburo. Therefore, there will be no major change in the fundamental orientation of its foreign policy. The Soviet Union will continue to scramble for global hegemony with the United States and to use the 'détente' strategy in pursuit of its strategic goals." But then the writer adds, "However, judging from Gorbachev's speeches on foreign relations, one can, after all, find certain changes. . . . Gorbachev has taken the initiative in facilitating contacts with the United States . . . using the strategy of 'détente' . . . he has paid more attention to expanding the Soviet Union's relations with China and Western Europe . . . seeking a new breakthrough in the Soviet Union's relations with Western Europe." Since the USSR wants to concentrate upon economic reform, the author adds, "seeking détente must be the Soviet Union's diplomatic goal at present."

12. For one evaluation, see Jin Junhui, "Reagan's Diplomacy: An Overview," carried in English in *Beijing Review* (June 17, 1985): 21–25. While paying homage to U.S. successes in the contest for influence and power with the USSR and accepting Nixon's definition of Reagan as a "responsible rightist," not a "crazy rightist," the author is clearly not enamored with the policies of the Reagan administration and accuses the United States of a number of negative attitudes and policies: "vilifying the socialist system," "preaching a gospel of market magic and advertising the economic achievements of South Korea and even Taiwan," "intensifying the threat of armed force," stepping up funding for CIA covert activities, pushing "economic hegemonism," and taking "stubborn positions in international organizations and conferences, going against the will and interests of the majority of nations." The article concludes on a somewhat ambiguous note. After asserting that the tilt in America toward a more conservative ideology exists, bolstered by the flourishing U.S. economy and Washington's strengthened position in world affairs, the author asserts: "The moderate policy will persist as a Reagan mainstay, especially since international conditions will impose a growing control upon the hegemonism and national chauvinism of the

United States; yet the conservative trend will also remain very much in evidence, if only as a minor force, throughout the foreseeable future."

13. See Jie Fu, "President Reagan's 'Second American Revolution'," in *Shijie Zhishi*, No. 6, March 16, 1985, pp. 3–4.

14. For example, on the occasion of the fifth session of the Sino–U.S. Joint Economic Commission meetings, Wang Bingqian, Finance Minister, stressed the progress being made in various aspects of economic cooperation, and added that both sides believed that the existing problems would not be difficult to resolve as long as joint efforts were made in accordance with the principles of equality and mutual benefit. FBIS, *Daily Report—China*, June 27, 1985, B1.

15. For an account of this meeting, see the article by Theo Sommer, "The Yellow Emperor's Descendant—Number One in the Middle Kingdom: Deng Xiaoping's View of the World and China's Future," first appearing in *Die Zeit*, October 12, 1984, p. 3, and translated in JPRS, *China Report—Political, Sociological and Military Affairs*, April 9, 1985, pp. 12–15.

16. Ibid., p. 13.

17. D. Petrov, "Japanese–Chinese Relations: Problems and Trends," *Far Eastern Affairs* (1985): 25–34.

18. V. Petukhov and G. Ragulin, "USA—PRC: Ties in the Military Sphere," *Far Eastern Affairs* (1985): 45–53.

19. Ibid., p. 53. See also an intensely critical review of articles written by Su Beihei in the *Xinjiang University Bulletin* (Xinjiang daxue xuebao) on the "Tsarist aggression against the Kazakhs." Su's work obviously touched a raw nerve, raising the issue of the legitimacy of Russian control over Kazakhstan. The review, entitled "Against Distortions of Kazakhstan's History," by R. Suleimen and V. Moiseyev is in *Far Eastern Affairs* (1985): 137–147.

20. S. Manezhev, "Foreign Entrepreneurial Capital in the PRC's Economy," *Far Eastern Affairs* (1985): 35–44; and A. Kruglov, "Small-Scale Industry in China," *Far Eastern Affairs* (1985): 71–79.

21. For several recent accounts of economic developments in North Korea, see Joseph S. Chung, "Economic Planning in North Korea," in a work edited by this author and Jun-yop Kim, *North Korea Today: Strategic and Domestic Issues* (Berkeley: Institute of East Asian Studies, 1983); and Joseph S. Chung, "Economic Planning in North Korea," in a second work edited by this author and Hongkoo Lee, *North Korea in a Regional and Global Context* (Berkeley: Institute of East Asian Studies, University of California, forthcoming); and Suk-Bum Yoon, "Macroeconomic Interaction Between Domestic and Foreign Sectors in the North Korean Economy: A Schematic Interpretation," in *North Korea in a Regional and Global Context* (Berkeley: Institute of East Asian Studies, University of California, 1987).

22. See Hong-Nack Kim, "Japan's Policy Toward North Korea Since 1965," *Korea and World Affairs*, (Winter 1983): 656–676, for background information.

23. For details, see the author's "The Korean Peninsula—Threat and Opportunity," in Robert A. Scalapino and Chen Qimao, eds., *Pacific–Asian Issues: American and Chinese Views* (Berkeley: the Institute of East Asian Studies, University of California, Berkeley, 1986).

24. An English-language translation of the proposal is carried in *Pyongyang Times*, January 14, 1984, p. 1. See also FBIS, *Daily Report—Asia and the Pacific*, January 11, 1984, D1–D11.

25. Detailed accounts of these meetings from various perspectives can be found in issues of JPRS, *Korean Affairs Report*: FBIS, *Daily Report—Asia and the Pacific*; *Korea Newsreview*; *Nodong Sinmun*; and *The Korea Herald*.

26. See *The Korea Herald*, July 17, 1985, pp. 1 and 5.

27. Clandestine Voice of the Revolutionary Party of Reunification (RPR) in Korean, "Workers and Peasants are the Masters of the South Korean Revolution," July 9, 1985, in FBIS, *Daily Report—Asia and the Pacific*, July 16, 1985, D10–12.

28. Pyongyang radio in Korean, "Dialogue and Confrontation Cannot Be Consistent with Each Other," July 7, 1985, D13.

29. Pyongyang Radio, Broadcasting Information No. 320, from the CPRF, in "Dialogue and Confrontation Cannot Be Consistent with Each Other," July 11, 1985, D3.

30. Pak Song-chol, "The Workers Party of Korea Is a Tested Guide Leading the Revolutionary Cause of Chuche on a Single Victorious Road," carried in ibid., July 9, 1985, D1–10 (D5).

31. Ibid., D.8.

TWO

Economic Issues

4

The Roots of Stability: The Economies of Northeast and Southeast Asia

by Lawrence B. Krause

INTRODUCTION

A strong but complex relationship exists between economic progress and societal stability. It is an intricate relationship that requires careful evaluation and is neither monotonic nor unidirectional. Some societies have been known to be quite stable while in a condition of economic stagnation and to become unstable with rapid economic growth; Iran in the 1970s was such a case. On the other hand, other societies were stable when economic growth was quite brisk, but became unstable when progress ceased. Cuba in the 1950s is an illustration. Furthermore, some countries have maintained successful economies until a political disturbance reversed the situation. This was the circumstance in Uruguay, which showed progress until the mid-1960s when it experienced a decline. And while there may be no cases of real political chaos and economic success coexisting, there are instances where political disturbance did lead directly to economic improvement, in a comparatively brief period—for example, the Cultural Revolution in China. What these diverse examples suggest is that a complete structural model must be specified in order to understand properly the relationships involved.

One can begin to come to grips with the relationship when stability is defined in terms of the relative continuity of existing institutions that govern the political and economic life of a society. Evolutionary changes are to be expected and are consistent with societal stability. Instability is associated with institutional discontinuities or revolutions. Thus one can attempt to trace the consequences of economic developments on such fundamental factors as the role of government in the economy, the existence of private property, the form of governance, and the like. The reverse line of causation can also be explored.

This essay will explore the link between economic developments to societal stability in Northeast and Southeast Asia. It will focus primarily on the period since 1973, when the world economy was subjected to several economic shocks. It will also examine certain current economic developments, together with some evolving ones, which pose new challenges to the region in the future. The countries to be examined are Japan, the four newly industrializing countries (NICs) of Asia—Hong Kong, South Korea, Singapore and Taiwan—and the other original ASEAN countries, Indonesia, Malaysia, the Philippines, and Thailand.

THE ECONOMIC RECORD

The most important summary statistic that indicates the economic progress of a country is the growth of its gross domestic product (GDP). The recent experiences of the countries under examination are shown in Table 4.1. In the period before 1973 the countries in the region had good economic performance, but that experience was widely shared among developing countries and some advanced countries. What is particularly significant is that after the 1973–1974 oil crisis, these countries continued to maintain progress, which was not a common development in other parts of the world. Since 1973, the world economy has witnessed a quadrupling of oil prices; a worldwide recession; a normal recovery; another jump in oil prices; another worldwide recession, which was deeper and longer-lasting than the earlier one; an external debt crisis for less developed countries (LDC), and an atypical recovery. With the exception of the Philippines, all the developing countries in the region grew at about 7 percent per year during this unsettled period, and Japan grew at about 4 percent per year. The countries range in per capita income from about US$600 in Indonesia (1982) to about US$10,000 in Japan.

A hypothesis that links economic growth and stability suggests that stability is promoted when the society's reasonable expectations of economic progress are fulfilled, and instability is caused when these expectations are disappointed. A society's expectations are likely to be determined by its own previous experience and the performance of other countries that the population may identify with, such as neighboring countries with similar productive structures and at the same stage of development. This suggests that stability of economic growth promotes societal stability and can in fact contribute to regional stability.

TABLE 4.1. *Compound Percentage Real GDP Growth*

	1967–1973	1973–1978	1978–1983	1984[d]	GNP per capita (US$) 1982
Japan[a]	9.5	3.4	4.1	5.3	10,080
NICs					
Hong Kong[b]	9.0	9.4	10.3	8.0	5,340
Korea, South	12.4	9.8	5.1	7.5	1,910
Singapore	12.5	7.6	8.8	8.5	5,910
Taiwan	11.4	8.4	5.9	10.9	2,479
ASEAN					
Indonesia	8.7	7.2	6.2	4.5	580
Malaysia	9.4[c]	7.0	7.1	6.9	1,860
Philippines[a]	5.9	6.3	3.9	−5.5	820
Thailand	6.9	7.7	5.6	5.9	790

[a] real GNP
[b] average annual growth GDP
[c] 1970–1973
[d] official and other estimates

Figures are rounded.

Sources: International Monetary Fund, *International Financial Statistics Yearbook 1984* and computer tapes. *Far Eastern Economic Review*, February 21, 1985, "Economic Indicators," p. 100. Council for Economic Planning and Development, Republic of China, June 1984, *Taiwan Statistical Data Book, 1984*. World Bank, *World Development Report* (various years).

Table 4.1 portrays a picture of remarkably stable economic growth with three exceptions: Japan pre- and post-1973; Korea during 1973–1978 and 1978–1983; and the Philippines during these same periods. With the exception of these three countries, economic growth has strongly supported societal stability. As for Japan, it is true that the growth rate dropped sharply; however, since it was widely attributed to external events, it was an experience shared by all other advanced countries and, therefore, probably did conform to the expectations of most Japanese. Thus, despite the fall in the growth rate, social stability in Japan was not endangered. Indeed, social stability may have been strengthened, since slower growth led in time to less inflation. In Korea the causation was probably reversed. The economy was showing strains but was still doing reasonably well until the assassination of President Park Chung Hee in 1979. The period of political instability that followed was an important contributing factor to the decline of income in 1980. However, when President Chun Doo Hwan restabilized the political situation, the economy returned to its previous growth path.

The experience of the Philippines is quite different. Compared to others in the region throughout the postwar period, the underperformance of the Philippine economy has probably added to societal instability. The deterioration in economic growth since 1978 has further worsened the situation. The rapidly deteriorating economy in 1984 was probably caused by the worsening political situation that followed the killing of Benigno Aquino in August 1983. However, the economic debacle is also spreading unrest, so the causation runs in both directions. In the Philippines it appears certain that societal stability and economic growth must be restored in tandem. The remarkable election in 1986 that brought Corazon Aquino to power is a step toward restabilization but is not sufficient in itself.

TABLE 4.2. *Inflation: Compound Percentage Change in Consumer Price Indexes*

	1967 to 1973	1973 to 1978	1978 to 1983
Japan	6.8	11.3	4.2
NICs			
Hong Kong	6.7	6.4	12.3
Korea, South	11.3	17.8	15.4
Singapore	3.8	5.9	5.1
Taiwan	5.1	12.5	9.9
ASEAN			
Indonesia	27.5	19.2	14.7
Malaysia	2.7	6.7	5.9
Philippines	9.4	12.2	13.8
Thailand	4.0	9.6	10.1

Figures are rounded.
Sources: Council for Economic Planning and Development, Republic of China, *Taiwan Statistical Data Book 1984*. International Monetary Fund, *International Financial Statistics Yearbook 1984*. United Nations, Department of International Economic and Social Affairs, Statistical Office, *Monthly Bulletin of Statistics* (various issues).

A second important economic variable linked to societal stability is inflation. The inflation experience of the countries in the region is summarized in Table 4.2. Inflation has its impact on societal stability through two mechanisms. Inflation needs to be taken into account in translating money income into real purchasing power, and it thus affects the real standard of living of the people and income distribution among different groups in society. Inflation also affects asset markets (the value of financial assets, real estate, and so on) and thereby the distribution of wealth in the society. Unanticipated inflation can have a very destabilizing impact on society because of its distributional consequences. Even anticipated inflation at a high level may be destabilizing, since different groups in society have different capacities to protect themselves against it. Inflation is often most devastating to the least sophisticated and impoverished members of society.

Table 4.2 indicates a wide variety of inflation experience among the countries in the region since the late 1960s, and it illustrates some interesting and more recent changes. From 1967 to 1973 the region divided into a group of low inflation countries, Malaysia, Singapore, Thailand, and Taiwan; medium inflation countries, Hong Kong and Japan; and high inflation countries, Indonesia, Korea, and the Philippines. The rise in oil prices tended to accelerate inflation in the subsequent period throughout the region, with the exception of Hong Kong and Indonesia. By 1984 price stability had been restored; in the case of Japan and Korea, it was restored to a much lower level than before 1973, which probably added to societal stability. In the Philippines, however, inflation became rampant and contributed significantly to the instability of that country.

A third important characteristic concerns the growth of exports of these countries, as shown in Table 4.3. This is closely related to the balance of payments of the countries shown in Table 4.4. Exports are linked to societal stability because they provide the capacity to purchase resources from abroad, which increase growth and add to the standard of living and quality of life of the people. If foreign resources are absorbed without corresponding exports, then foreign indebtedness is increased (possibly in the form of direct investment) as reflected in the balance of payments. Borrowing from abroad is a natural development if the additional resources made available are invested in assets with the potential to generate foreign exchange earnings. If not, then a repayment burden will be created, which will add to societal instability when the repayment comes due.

TABLE 4.3. *Patterns of Change in Export Growth and Merchandise Exports as a Share of GNP*

	Compound Percentage Export Growth (change in value)		Compound Percentage Change in Volume of Exports		Merchandise Export as a Percent of GNP
	1973 to 1978	1978 to 1983	1973 to 1978	1978 to 1983	1983
Japan	15.4	11.2	9.7	6.6	12.7
NICs					
Hong Kong	17.8	13.8	9.9	3.3	77.9[a]
Korea, South	36.8	25.3	19.7	9.9	32.5
Singapore	20.9	15.0	9.1	10.3	133.8
Taiwan	22.4	16.5	13.9	9.6	50.3
ASEAN					
Indonesia	29.5	29.2	8.1	−2.9	26.0
Malaysia	18.3	14.0	6.5	4.3	51.4
Philippines	14.5	16.9	6.9	6.3	14.4
Thailand	20.9	12.0	13.0	5.2	16.2

[a] GDP (not GNP)

Figures are rounded.

Sources: Far Eastern Economic Review, *Asia 1985 Yearbook.* Census and Statistics Department, Hong Kong, *Hong Kong Annual Digest of Statistics, 1982* and *Hong Kong Monthly Digest of Statistics, July 1984.* IMF computer tapes. IMF, *International Financial Statistics Yearbook 1984* and February 1985 issue. Council for Economic Planning and Development, Republic of China, June 1984, *Taiwan Statistical Data Book 1984.*

The export value figures shown in Table 4.3 are in current prices; they must be adjusted downward to reflect inflation. The estimated growth of export volumes is shown in the second set of columns. This table illustrates that all of the countries in the region, especially the NICs (newly industrialized countries), experienced a rapid growth of their exports. To put these figures in some perspective, they can be compared with the growth of world exports. Between 1973 and 1978, the value of world exports grew 17.8 percent per year. To a great extent this reflected the oil-induced rise of world inflation, as the volume of world exports grew only 4.2 percent per year. Each of the region's NICs, Japan, and all of the ASEAN countries (except the Philippines in value terms) exceeded the world growth of value and volume in this period.

From 1978 to 1983, which was considerably less inflationary but also much less buoyant, the value of world exports grew 6.8 percent per year and the volume only 1.5 percent per year. The decline in the growth of world trade was reflected in the experience of the countries in the region but in an attenuated fashion. Among the NICs, the decline in the growth of export volume was particularly pronounced for Hong Kong, possibly because of its heavy concentration in textiles and clothing, which faced increasingly severe trade barriers. Hong Kong, however, made an adjustment by upgrading its product line in textiles; thus the growth of the value of its exports progressed reasonably well. The other NICs continued to experience rapid export growth, and Singapore actually exceeded its earlier growth rates. Japan's export growth did moderate considerably, but it was still substantially greater than world totals, which indicated that it was gaining a larger share of world markets.

Although the ASEAN performance was more mixed than that of the NICs, it was still remarkably good. Malaysia, the Philippines, and Thailand exceeded world growth of exports even though this was a difficult period for raw material exporters. On the other hand, Indonesia suffered a decline in export volume between 1978 and 1983 because of the reduction in world trade of petroleum. Indeed, most other oil exporters recorded a much sharper decline than Indonesia, although this was compensated for by higher prices.

A comparison of rates of growth of export volumes (Table 4.3) with corresponding growth of GDP (Table 4.1) indicates that in general, export growth was greater and in some cases so much greater as to yield a characterization of export-led growth. This is certainly true for Japan, Korea, and Taiwan, and possibly true for Singapore as well. For the other countries, export-led growth was common from 1973 to 1978, but not from 1978 to 1983 when the world recession was very severe. Although there is no inherent virtue in export-led growth, there may be an indirect link between it and societal stability. Export-led growth requires an outward orientation, which may strengthen a regime by encouraging it to adopt better economic policies. At the same time, however, it may make a country

TABLE 4.4 Balance of Payments, Total Debt and Interest-Service Ratios

	Current Account Balance/Average (US$ millions)		Trade Balance/Average (US$ millions)		Average Total Debt Outstanding and Disbursed[a] (US$ millions)		Total Debt Including Trade Credits (US$ millions)	Average Interest-Service Ratio (US$ millions)	
	1972–74	1982–83	1972–74	1982–83	1972–74	1982–83	1983	1972–74	1982–83
Japan	610.0	13,825.0	4,643.3	24,770.0	—	—	—	—	—
NICs									
Hong Kong	n.a.	n.a.	−3,151.0	−2,290.5	6.6	245.5	—[e]	n.a.	n.a.
Korea, South	−893.7	−2,128.5	−1,026.0	−2,147.0	3,872.3	22,285.2	35,380.0	5.1	6.2
Singapore	−678.0	−1,127.0	−1,537.7	−6,347.5	411.6	1,326.9	—[e]	0.3	0.4
Taiwan	−11.2	3478.2	183.8	4,926.5	n.a.	5,975.5	7,800.0[f]	2.6[c,d]	4.5[c]
ASEAN									
Indonesia	−70.3	−5,831.0	1,176.7	1,428.0	5,270.4	20,193.4	25,380.0	1.7	5.9
Malaysia	−227.7	−3,138.0	335.0	−32.0	756.2	9,367.9	13,840.0	1.3	3.9
Philippines	90.0	−2,984.5	−100.0	−2,565.5	2,000.1	12,830.0	25,600.0[f]	2.0	7.4
Thailand	−62.3	−1,933.5	−328.3	−1,796.0	985.0	9,123.6	11,000.0[f]	1.1	5.9

[a] for Hong Kong, Singapore, Indonesia, and Malaysia, the debt figures refer to public and publicly guaranteed debt (disbursed only). Total debt includes private non-guaranteed debt

[b] the interest service ratio refers to interest payments as a share of exports of goods and services

[c] for Taiwan, the figures refer to the debt-service ratio defined as service payments on external public debt as a percentage of exports of goods and services

[d] data for 1974 only

[e] for Hong Kong and Singapore, the figures cannot be interpreted because of external banking

[f] preliminary estimate

n.a. data not available

Figures are rounded.

Sources: Asian Development Bank, Economics Office, "Estimates of the Total External Debt of the Developing Member Countries of ADB: 1981–1983" by I. P. David, September 1984. Census and Statistics Department, Hong Kong, *Hong Kong Annual Digest of Statistics 1982 Edition* and *Hong Kong Monthly Digest of Statistics*, July 1984. Central Bank of China, *Balance of Payments, Taiwan District, Republic of China*, Annex Tables 1 and 2. International Monetary Fund, computer tapes and *International Financial Statistics Yearbook 1984* and February 1985 issue. The World Bank, *World Debt Tables*, 1982–83, 1983–84 and 1984–85 editions.

more vulnerable to foreign sources of disturbance and to domestic critics who stress excess dependence on foreigners. By the end of the period (1983) merchandise exports constituted a remarkably high share of the GDP of all of the NICs and Malaysia. Exports were at a more moderate level in Japan, Thailand, and the Philippines, but they were still very important to their development.

The balance-of-payments experience of the countries in the region is shown in Table 4.4. Japan is seen as developing ever greater surpluses, as is Taiwan. Neither trend seems sustainable over the long term. Korea, Singapore, Indonesia, the Philippines, and Thailand all had trends towards larger current account deficits. Their sustainability depends on the magnitude, which in the case of Korea and Singapore is quite modest. For the others, it depends on whether domestic investment is being increased appropriately, and on how the deficit is being financed. Malaysia switched from a net surplus country to one in deficit, but the magnitude so far seems manageable.

TABLE 4.5. *Exports of Pacific Basin Countries:*
Total Value and Shares to Major Countries and Country Groups, 1983

	1983 Total Value of Exports (tens of billions of US $)	1983 Export Shares (percent of total)			
		Pacific Basin	ASEAN	Japan	U.S.
Japan	14.70	53.53	10.22	—	29.49
NICs					
Hong Kong	2.20	54.65	10.75	4.40	32.20
Korea, South	2.44	58.42[a]	6.09[a]	15.60[a]	28.80
Singapore	2.18	65.27	23.86	9.20	18.11
Taiwan	2.51	74.30[b]	6.50[c]	9.86	45.11
ASEAN					
Indonesia	2.11	85.38	16.44	45.77	20.18
Malaysia	1.41	70.26[a]	29.99[a]	20.34[a]	11.62[a]
Philippines	0.49	72.71	7.12	19.95	36.35
Thailand	0.64	49.61[a]	15.47[a]	13.69[a]	12.70[a]

[a] data to 1982
[b] excludes Malaysia, New Zealand, and Papua New Guinea
[c] excludes Malaysia

Figures are rounded.

Sources: Council for Economic Planning Development, Republic of China, June 1984, *Taiwan Statistical Data Book 1984*. International Monetary Fund, *Direction of Trade Statistics Yearbook 1984* and computer tapes.

Another important characteristic of the region concerns the trade distribution of the countries by trading partners, which is shown in Table 4.5. This table indicates that the developing countries in the region trade primarily with other countries in the Pacific Basin. At the extremes, Indonesia sells 85 percent of its exports and Thailand about 50 percent of its exports to other Pacific Basin countries. There are two distinct patterns involved. There are the NICs that specialize in manufactured goods and sell between 50–70 percent of their exports within the Pacific Basin. For them, the United States is by far their largest market. The other LDCs are primarily exporters of natural resources and sell between 50–81 percent of their exports within the Pacific Basin. For them, Japan is their largest market. Thus regardless of specialization, the Pacific Basin provides a major market for these countries. To this can be added the rapidly growing intra-LDC trade in the region, which is possibly enhanced by ASEAN. The importance of this pattern to the societal stability in these countries is that it centralizes the sources of foreign disturbance or stimulation and thereby increases the salience of foreign economic relations within the Pacific Basin. If these relations are managed with skill and foresight, then stability of all countries is increased. If they are managed badly, then instability is generated.

INDIVIDUAL COUNTRIES

The links between three economic variables (economic growth, inflation, and international trade and balance of payments), and societal stability have already been examined. At this point, they will be pulled together in the examination of the countries in the region. Needless to say, this is only a brief and preliminary treatment of a complex and difficult subject.

Japan

Japan has been the most successful industrial country in the postwar period in sustaining economic growth. It has also been one of the most societally stable countries, despite its devastating defeat in World War II and the occupation that followed. The two events are very likely linked closely to one another. Recently, however, Japan has been described as a country undergoing relative stagnation, similar to the United States during the Eisenhower years. As noted earlier, the Japanese growth rate did decline sharply after 1973, but this was probably seen as a natural consequence of the oil crisis.

However, the slowdown in Japanese growth cannot be attributed to the two increases in oil prices. If that were the case it would have required a once-and-for-all adjustment in income levels without having any impact on growth, and it would have been partially reversed in recent years. Rather the slowdown in growth is due to fundamental factors, such as the country's unwillingness *and* inability to adjust to competitive imports and to policy mistakes. The most salient fundamental factors are the end of the technology catch-up and the soon-to-be-felt aging of the labor force.

The fact that there is no accommodation to competitive imports means that all adjustment is forced on the export industries, which are the most dynamic in the economy. Finally, the government has misperceived the nature of its fiscal problem and has unnecessarily instituted budgetary restraint, which has caused relative stagnation. However, as long as Japanese society accepts stagnation, stability will not be damaged through internal forces.

Even the rate of growth that has been achieved has been export-led and thus not sustainable. Japanese exports of goods and services as a share of its GNP in fiscal year 1973 was 11.3 percent but in fiscal year 1983 had ballooned to 20.6 percent (both measured in 1975 prices). Whereas small countries can have export-led growth for a number of years, in the case of Japan, the world's second-largest market economy, a near doubling in a decade puts enormous pressure on other countries. Furthermore, that pressure has been greatly magnified because Japan's import share of GNP has not risen, indeed it has fallen marginally. In 1973 the share of imports of goods and services in GDP was 14.2 percent, but this share fell to 13.1 percent by 1983 (again measured in 1975 prices). Thus the Japanese economy is no more open today than it was a dozen years ago. This means it was not in any way relieving the market pressure it was exerting on other countries. There are several mechanisms through which these nonsustainable trends can be arrested and reversed. These include a sharply higher exchange value for the yen and foreign protectionism against Japanese exports.

If the adjustment comes about through a sharply higher value of the yen, some domestic policy adjustment will be required, but societal stability should not be endangered. Some Japanese import-competing production will suffer as well as some marginal exporting activity. However, if the government responds by stimulating the domestic economy, the resources released from the traded goods industries can easily be absorbed in the non-traded areas, such as construction and services. In fact the yen began to rise in 1985 in relation to the American dollar and signaled the start of a long period of advance.

The alternative of greater protectionism, against Japan could be more upsetting, particularly if led by the United States. The policies of the dominant political party in Japan, the Liberal Democratic Party (LDP), have been based on close security, political, and economic ties to the United States. This would be shaken by aggressive US protectionism and political uncertainty would result.

The Newly Industrialized Countries (NICs)

Hong Kong

Hong Kong developed as an entrepôt for trade with the southern part of China. Its peculiar political status as a colony of Great Britain did not seem to matter until 1950. It was then that trade with China was interrupted by the UN embargo which grew out of the Korean War. The only option for Hong Kong was to become a manufacturer of the products it had formerly been transshipping. The question arose as to whether there was anything that the government of the Colony could do to promote manufacturing development. Since there were no obvious policy choices, it was decided to leave Hong Kong's development solely in the hands of private entrepreneurs. Thus Hong Kong became the only place in modern times to accept complete laissez-faire. The only exception from the most narrow conception for government was in the area of housing, where the government did take a more active role to solve a severe shortage.

Hong Kong's only resources are its harbor, its location, and the energies of its people. This combination of resources has proven sufficient to give Hong Kong one of the highest standards of living in the region. Despite the inflow of refugees from the mainland and political uncertainty, the economic progress of Hong Kong has created societal stability.

Hong Kong has the largest service share of GDP of any area in the region. This reflects the skills of its people in trading, insurance, banking, tourism, and the like. Hong Kong has a large manufacturing sector as well, oriented toward international trade. Thus market forces have pushed Hong Kong to make the most of its resources.

The world economic disruptions of the 1970s had more of an indirect than direct impact on Hong Kong. As long as all competitors paid the same price for petroleum, Hong Kong's international competitiveness remained unaffected by the oil crisis. It did require a one-time reduction of income, but only by a modest amount. However, the world recessions have led to greater protectionism in world markets and, as noted earlier, this does affect Hong Kong. Nevertheless, Hong Kong's producers have made several adjustments and have been able to work around trade barriers when they have been created.

Hong Kong is now in transition, in response to the political change to come at the end of the 1990s when China will begin to exercise political sovereignty over the former colony. The future cannot be forecast with certainty; however, in the absence of sharp policy changes not currently indicated, the economy of Hong Kong should remain on its present path, although with difficulty. Manufacturing may begin to decline, and services are likely to become even more dominant as a source of income. However, if Hong Kong remains outwardly oriented and directed by market forces, then income should continue to advance and societal stability will likely be maintained. The slowdown of the U.S. economy in 1985, which spilled over to slower growth in Hong Kong, shows up the downside of outward orientation. World protectionism would be an even more severe threat and would likely end the outward orientation policy altogether.

South Korea

The economy of South Korea began to develop following the end of the Korean War in 1953. An import substitution strategy was adopted, and some growth of manufacturing output was generated. While some basic overhead capital was put into place during this period, the economy was not performing well, which contributed to political disturbances in 1960 and a military coup in May 1961. The government was led by President Park Chung Hee until his assassination in October 1979. During this period, the Korean economy made remarkable economic progress. Korea adopted a Japanese model of development, which meant liberalizing imports as an ingredient in export-led growth. Exports of labor-intensive manufactured goods grew at a phenomenal rate and propelled the growth of the entire economy. Policy was shifted in 1975 to emphasize heavy and chemical industries at the expense of light industry. The shift was very likely premature, but the economy adapted, though with difficulty.

A period of political uncertainty followed the assassination, and the economy actually declined in 1980. After the resignation of President Choi in August 1980, President Chun Doo Hwan came to power, and a new constitution was adopted. A short period of intense political disturbance followed, but political stability was restored and the economy embarked on renewed growth. A new policy of economic liberalization was undertaken and is now being implemented. The Constitution permits a president only one term of seven years, and so a new president is expected to be elected in 1988.

South Korea is a densely populated country of 39 million people with very few natural resources. While the nation was entirely agricultural at the end of the Japanese occupation, the agricultural share is now only 16 percent. Industry makes up 39 percent of output and services 45 percent. The government anticipates the continued erosion of labor-intensive manufactures and is trying to steer the country into higher technology development.

The world disruptions of the 1970s were met by a series of measures in the Republic of Korea. Domestic stimulation was temporarily used to offset the world recession. An overseas construction industry, which catered to the oil countries of the Middle East, was developed to overcome the external cost of higher petroleum prices. The adaptive quality of the economy enabled it to manage reasonably well until political difficulties began in late 1979. These political difficulties, combined with the second oil shock and a sharply lower agricultural harvest, resulted in the decline in income. Korea began to borrow from abroad, and its indebtedness of US $43 billion at the end of 1984 was among the highest of any LDC. Its large export sector, however, permits it to service its debt without much difficulty even though over one-quarter is short-term debt. The Korean economy began to recover before the world recession ended, but it was aided greatly by the world recovery and especially by the renewed growth in the United States, its largest customer.

South Korea faces both economic and political challenges during the second half of the 1980s. Several Korean industries will have to reduce capacity in view of the weakness of world demand. This includes overseas construction, shipping, and possibly shipbuilding as well. Moreover, the country must become less dependent on exports to the United States. The consequence of excessive dependence was seen in 1985, when Korean growth dropped sharply in response to the slowing of US growth.

On the political side, Korea faces its first-ever constitutional change of political leadership in 1988. Under the best of circumstances, uncertainty will rise and the possibility exists for significant unrest until a new leader is firmly in control. This is likely to affect investment and other decisions by business, so a period of more restrained growth is a distinct possibility.

Singapore

Because of its natural harbor, Singapore was developed as an entrepôt and service center for the region. Singapore has made remarkable economic progress and has by far the highest income per capita of the developing countries in the region. This has led to societal stability in Singapore much beyond what was anticipated in 1960 or even 1965, when it was ejected from the Federation of Malaysia.

Although manufacturing has expanded rapidly, it remains primarily a service center. Wages in Singapore have always been above wages in competing countries and therefore, unlike other NICs, it never developed a textile or shoe industry. Rather, Singapore depended on foreign multinational firms to bring in capital and make investment decisions. It developed an electronics industry and other products somewhat higher up on the technology ladder. The government takes a strong hand in promoting economic development but does not distort prices through protection or the like. It has pushed up wages in a deliberate effort to force firms to use labor more efficiently. Singapore is the most outwardly-oriented country in the world, as seen in its remarkably high levels of exports and imports.

In Singapore there has been almost no visible effect of the world economic disturbances of the 1970s, but the 1980s may be different. Rapid growth was maintained in the early 1980s through a boom in commercial construction, but the boom ended dramatically in 1985 when growth ceased completely. Signs of overbuilding are present. Moreover the government's participation in industry seems to have gone sour, as shipbuilding and repair stagnated and a newly completed petrochemical complex faced a near-empty order book. Services are likely to continue expanding, providing Singapore with some flexibility for adjustment. Of course, Lee Kuan Yew will eventually give up his political leadership, but several younger leaders tutored by him are being groomed as replacements.

Taiwan

Taiwan is a rather small island and, with 19 million people, is one of the most densely populated areas in the world. During the Japanese occupation, it was primarily an agricultural producer, although manufacturing was begun. In 1952 an import-replacement strategy was adopted in order to develop manufacturing and employ all of Taiwan's people. The policy did stimulate production, but it reached the end of its effectiveness in 1962. At that time a choice was made to promote exports rather than implement another round of import-replacement. This was due to a variety of factors. The small size of the domestic market prevented reaching economies of scales without exports; exports tended to be labor intensive, and thus could absorb all the excess labor; and Taiwan was short of both capital and skilled labor, which would have been a constraint on secondary import replacement. The export promotion policy was very successful, and Taiwan prospered; it is now one of the richest areas in the region. This has brought societal stability despite political uncertainties.

Agriculture's share of GDP has been reduced to 8 percent. Industry now accounts for 49 percent of GDP, mainly manufacturing. This is a remarkably high value, considering that advanced industrial countries usually have a manufacturing share of GDP between 20 percent and 30 percent. The surprise is the relatively low value for services. At 43 percent, the service share is similar to that in the Philippines, a country at a considerably lower standard of living than Taiwan. It may well be that the artificial separation of Taiwan from the mainland of China contributes to this atypical productive structure.

Taiwan reached full employment in the mid-1960s, and wages began to rise sharply. It was recognized that Taiwan would soon have to rely less on the production and export of labor-intensive goods such as shoes and textiles. At that time Taiwan developed a strategy for upgrading its labor force by greater investment in education. Resources were put into both secondary and higher education, particularly in the sciences and mathematics. Furthermore, many students were sent abroad to further their education, even though a considerable number chose to remain abroad after finishing their schooling. This investment in human capital has given it a comparative advantage in many higher technology industries, as compared to other NICs such as South Korea.

Taiwan was affected by the world economic disruptions of the 1970s but not to a significant degree. Moreover, since it followed a conservative monetary and fiscal policy, Taiwan was soon able to overcome the inflationary effects of the rise in oil prices and improve its international competitiveness. Thus Taiwan adjusted very much like Japan, by increasing its exports and by depending upon export-led growth. This policy stance has also meant that Taiwan has no net external debt but is a lender to the rest of the world. However, like Japan, Taiwan has an unsustainable balance-of-payments surplus, which may lead to external difficulties, with a possible effect on societal stability. Taiwan has also become excessively dependent on exports to the United States, which resulted in slower growth in 1985. The challenge to Taiwan will be to take advantage of a rising Japanese yen to sell more in Japan and replace Japanese goods in third markets.

Association of Southeast Asian Nations (ASEAN)

Indonesia

Indonesia has always been known as a country rich with natural resources, although, given its large population—155 million people—agricultural resources are not plentiful. Rapid economic development did not begin until the political disruptions of the Sukarno period were overcome in mid-1966. In the earlier period, Indonesia followed an import-substitution (IS) strategy similar to LDCs elsewhere. This strategy, however, was not successful, in part because it was run by a wasteful and inefficient administration. Nevertheless, the IS strategy has cast a long shadow, and Indonesia remains less open to international trade than other countries in the region. Indonesia is the only one of the ASEAN countries receiving significant amounts of foreign aid, and as the poorest country in the group, it has the furthest to go to become modernized. Nevertheless, economic advance has been made and shared by all members of society and, therefore, societal stability has been promoted. Pockets of poverty, however, remain and could become a source of instability if mobilized by radical political forces.

Economic development during the last 20 years has sharply reduced the agricultural concentration of the economy and agriculture now only accounts for one-quarter of the GDP. Industry has made rapid advance led by minerals, especially petroleum. Despite some growth, manufacturing is only 13 percent of GDP, the smallest in the region. With the density population of Java, Indonesia is thought to have the potential to develop a comparative advantage in labor-intensive manufactures. Some evidence of this possibility exists in its recent advancement in textiles and clothing.

Given its oil resources, the disruptions of the 1970s began as a positive development for Indonesia. As occurred in other oil-exporting countries, however, the windfall led to overindulgence and abuses. When it became clear in the late 1970s that the national oil company was recklessly expanding its domain, was financially overextended, and had unrealistic plans, the Suharto administration changed its leadership and cut it down to size. In addition, Indonesia's currency was devalued to restore the balance of payments and the international competitiveness of the rest of the economy. When the second oil crisis came, Indonesia used the resources to reduce its dependence on petroleum. Thus Indonesia remains an oil exporter, but it is not only an "oil country." Although Indonesia has a foreign debt of about $20 billion, this does not constitute a serious repayment problem because it arose from foreign assistance and is, therefore, owed to foreign governments and international institutions, primarily on a long-term basis.

Thus Indonesia's success since 1973 can be attributed to the fact that unlike LDCs without oil, its terms of trade improved, and it managed its resources better than other LDCs with oil. As long as economic progress continues and is widely distributed, societal stability will be enhanced. However, the economic future is clouded by the sustained weakness in oil prices. Petroleum is Indonesia's largest export and a reduction in its price and lower export volume has slowed economic progress. Furthermore, political uncertainty will increase when President Suharto nears the end of his term in office.

Malaysia

Malaysia is incredibly well endowed with natural resources, resources that have been the basis for creating one of the highest standards of living in the region. Malaysia is the world's leading producer of natural rubber and palm oil; it is near the top in tin and is a net exporter of oil and gas. In fact, there is probably no important natural resource needed for modern industry that is not found in Malaysia. With these natural resources, the reservation wage to industry in Malaysia has been too high to permit the development of traditional labor-intensive manufactures. Nevertheless, Malaysia's manufactures have made progress and have been given a boost as wages in Singapore climbed considerably above local levels. Indeed several multinational firms in electronics have shifted their operations to Malaysia because of wages and labor availability. The economic progress has been essential to help overcome the racial cleavages that exist in Malaysian society. Indeed it is hard to believe that societal stability could be maintained without economic progress.

The economic disruptions of the 1970s came rather late to Malaysia. The rise in oil prices themselves marginally helped the country. The worldwide recession caused exports to decline in 1975 which led to a pause in growth, but the world recovery quickly spread to Malaysia the following year. Remarkably, Malaysia's term of trade hardly changed until the second rise of oil prices, which sharply boosted its export prices relative to import prices. The deep worldwide recession that followed the second rise in oil prices, however, did impede Malaysia's growth. The stagnation of world trade also resulted in lower levels of economic growth. Furthermore, the slide in world commodity prices completely wiped out the country's terms of trade gain. Nevertheless, the decline in the growth rate would have been even steeper if the government had not been prepared to take some action. In 1981 and 1982, the government adopted a stimulative fiscal policy to offset the stagnation in exports that seems to have been reasonably effective in sustaining growth. Prior to this period, Malaysia had practically no foreign debt; however, as part of the fiscal stimulation policy, the government began to borrow abroad. Fortunately, the amounts were well within the country's ability to service and reached about $5.6 billion in 1983. While Malaysia also owed about $8 billion in trade credits, this has not increased in recent years. Malaysia was able to raise funds in Europe below the London LIBOR interest rate, which testifies to the high regard in which Malaysia is held by international lenders.

One can conclude from reviewing the experience of Malaysia that it avoided the economic distress that afflicted many other countries because of a variety of factors. These include a great variety of natural resources; a commitment to growth, on which its social stability depends; the government's diligence at maintaining social stability, and the fact that the government is prepared to take action when required. Of course some of the government's program has been ill-advised (such as promoting the Malaysian car), but it seems to be stepping back from excessive folly. Still, Malaysia is not immune to the problems of other countries and it shared in the worldwide slowdown of growth in 1985.

The Philippines

The economy of the Philippines, while reasonably successful when judged by the average of all LDCs, has consistently underperformed when measured against other developing countries in East and Southeast Asia. The society has long suffered from widespread corruption at many levels of government. During the years under Ferdinand Marcos, the economy was subjected to intense cronyism, whereby friends of the "first family" were helped in pushing aside other entrepreneurs—including the other distinguished families of the country. Furthermore, the country has never had a real land reform, which has perpetuated an unequal distribution of income and wealth.

Another reason why the Philippine economy has done relatively poorly has been the particular economic policies that the government has followed. Philippine policy somewhat resembles that of Latin American countries. The Philippines instituted an ambitious import-substitution (IS) strategy that did manage to promote manufacturing but worsened income distribution in the process. The manufacturing share of GDP is higher in the Philippines than in other ASEAN countries. The IS strategy, combined with other policies, caused several crises, and it became evident that Philippine industry was inefficient and was misdirecting its scarce capital resources. There was a halfhearted move toward an outward orientation, but Philippine industry remains highly protected and relatively inefficient. Another resemblance to Latin America is seen in the build-up of debts to foreign banks. The Philippine external debt was estimated at $26.5 billion in 1986, of which over half is short term and, therefore, constitutes a repayment problem for the country. These economic problems have been an important cause of societal unrest.

An oil-importing country, the Philippines were hurt by the economic disruptions of the 1970s. The first oil crisis worsened the terms of trade, but some of the negative consequences were offset by increases in the volume of Philippine exports, particularly of such nontraditional agricultural products as bananas, canned pineapple, and some manufactures. The second oil crisis was more severe in that the deep worldwide recession limited new export successes and worsened terms of trade. Also, the mismanagement of the economy became more apparent. Despite the recovery in the world economy in 1984, the Philippines suffered a sharp decline in GDP because of the deteriorating domestic political situation, and the economy declined further in 1985.

The coming to power of the Aquino government in 1986 may have marked the end of the deterioration, but even under the best of circumstances, several years will be required to put the economy right. First, it will take time for the population to create realistic expectations and build a consensus behind a recovery program. Second, many required policies will take several years to implement. For example, the plan to privatize government-owned enterprises will require five years. Finally, the recovery of raw material prices in world markets, which is necessary to relieve the Philippine foreign exchange shortage, did not occur in 1986 and may not in 1987. Thus, the economic basis for political stability may be slow in coming, and this will test the skills of political leaders.

Thailand

A remarkable characteristic of Thailand's economy is how little politics and political change affect its economic development. The government is served by a group of able technocrats who appear to be untouched by political maneuvering. There is a certain amount of corruption, but probably no more than is necessary to make the system work reasonably smoothly. The Thais have tried several economic development strategies, including import substitution, but have never carried them to extremes. The policy has been quite pragmatic, which has led it to become more outward oriented in recent years. Indeed, the hallmark of the Thai economy, and possibly Thai society, is that it is adaptable. As a result, the economy has performed very well. Economic success and societal stability may be determined simultaneously without causation in either direction being dominant.

Thailand is reasonably well endowed with natural resources, although less so than some of its neighbors. Its agriculture is rather broadly diversified in food and industrial crops. Until recently, the Thais practiced extensive agriculture, as new lands could be brought into production when needed. Now they have reached the end of those possibilities and more intensive cultivation has begun. Thai agriculture is remarkably responsive to world market signals and shifts from products whose prices are weak and where demand is falling to others whose prospects are more encouraging. However, the weakening of commodity prices in 1984 and 1985 was so widespread that it affected all of Thailand's crops, and growth suffered. Thailand has been deficient in domestic energy resources; however, natural gas has been found and is now being produced in increasing quantities. Industrial production has made some progress in recent years but remains a lower share of GDP than in other countries in the region.

Thailand was hurt by the world economic disruptions of the 1970s. As with other oil importers, terms of trade deteriorated, and since Thailand was heavily involved in international trade, exports were curtailed by the world recession. Nevertheless, the Thais overcame most of the disruption with only a moderate decline in the country's growth rate. Some foreign borrowing has been necessary to finance the deficit in its balance of payments, but of reasonable amounts. Thus the Thais have continued to make progress by being pragmatic and adaptable. The slowdown of the U.S. economy in 1985 was another such challenge and did have a negative impact on its growth.

FUTURE CHALLENGES

Numerous developments could conceivably upset the economic progress being made by the countries in the region. If economic progress ceases or is reversed, then societal stability will be put under severe stress in most of the countries. The danger that appears to warrant the greatest concern is that of a possible breakdown of the international trade regime. However, since the consequences of such an eventuality are more certain than those raised by other issues and are extremely negative for the region they need not be further analyzed here. Rather, two other developments will be examined because their effects are less certain, and therefore require greater attention and consideration. These developments are rapid changes in technology and the emergence of the People's Republic of China.

Technological Change

Remarkable developments are occurring in four technological areas: microelectronics (including robotics), biotechnology, optics technology, and materials technology. In combination they constitute a significant change, a process that Professor Walt Rostow has dubbed the "Fourth Industrial Revolution." Microelectronics will not only make more things possible; through robots it will be labor saving. It is unclear, however, what type of labor will be displaced from existing production. It could be skilled labor, in which case Japan would be most affected, or unskilled labor, in which case Korea, Taiwan, and ultimately the Philippines and Indonesia would be most affected. Furthermore, it is unclear where the new production will take place. With respect to the other three technologies, the issue is essentially one of producing new products or increasing the productivity of existing processes rather than new process technology. However, these developments could have important impacts on reducing the demand for natural resources, which will affect countries such as Malaysia and Thailand.

Since it is impossible to predict the product implications of the new technologies, their impact on the economies cannot be traced; however, it is obvious that the countries that will be hurt will be the ones whose economies are least able to adjust. If labor markets clear and entrepreneurs live by their own wits, then an economy can do well even with a considerable disturbance. The countries that will benefit most by the new technologies are the ones where there is a close link between pure scientists (whether in universities or government laboratories), risk-taking entrepreneurs, business enterprises with research and development capacity, and a capital market that can allocate resources into the hands of creative people. The countries with such links will be the primary producers of the products generated by the new technologies.

The Emergence of China

Another challenge will arise if China can maintain its current economic reforms—that is, domestic liberalization combined with an outward-oriented external strategy—and if the returns are successful. A consistent policy in China maintained for an extended period of time would be a unique event, but at this time such an event seems likely. If only that part of China with easy transport with the rest of the world is considered (the coastal provinces and those on Yangtze River), this is still a country of over 300 million people.

China could have an impact on the Pacific Basin during the next 25 years similar to that of Japan since World War II. This implies a combination of market opportunities for some goods and services and stiff competition for others. The characteristics that will turn the challenge into a great opportunity for a country, rather than a serious disruption, are no different than those noted above. However, foreign policy considerations are also critical. This will obviously pose a particular challenge for Taiwan and an opportunity for Hong Kong (assuming local autonomy) and Singapore. The other countries will have to come to grips with China as a major economic player in the world; some will adjust better to this development than others. If the challenge becomes too severe, political unrest could occur.

The important point is that economic decisions being made throughout the Pacific Basin will have to take China into account, something that many firms may already be doing. China even has the potential to rescue Japan from its creeping stagnation. What will be required for this to happen is a mechanism for Japan to transfer large amounts of capital to China. This, in turn, will permit Japan to continue running a current account surplus. No finance channel of this dimension now exists.

CONCLUSIONS

The message to be drawn from this essay is that the countries of East Asia and Southeast Asia have managed to enjoy a remarkable amount of economic success during the difficult economic environment since 1973. This is seen in numerous economic indicators and reviewed in the tables. Overall, the picture is one of economic progress, and for the developing countries it is a picture of substantial advance along the path of modernization.

Economic success has likely contributed to societal stability. Stability and change have gone hand in hand. Thus it is dynamic stability that has been attained, that is, the stability of a bicycle rider rather than of a person at rest. Stability has been increased despite rapid change because the societies are prepared for change by being very adaptable.

No doubt the causation also runs in the opposite direction, since societal and political stability have furthered economic progress. This was seen most clearly when political stability was undermined in Korea in 1979–1980 and in the Philippines in 1983–1984.

In the future there will be challenges that will disturb the economies in the region. Aside from the possibility of the breakdown of the international trade regime, which would be an unmitigated disaster for all countries in the region, the other challenges are likely to be met and overcome as long as the countries remain adaptable. Adaptability is the very characteristic that helped them achieve dynamic stability in the past. Thus preparation for meeting future challenges should be addressed through the education and training of the labor force, the removal of protective devices and other government props for private enterprise, the reduction of oligopolies in markets, and increased government responsiveness to economic developments. These are the kinds of policies that improve the workings of the labor market, the product market, and the allocation of capital. Although the countries in the Pacific region have progressed quite far in this regard by world standards, there is more that can and should be done.

5

Future Prospects for Economic Cooperation in Asia and the Pacific Region

by Ryokichi Hirono

INTRODUCTION

Not a single month has past since 1980 without a meeting being held somewhere in the world on the past, present, and future of the economic growth and structural changes of the Asian and Pacific countries and, in particular, economic cooperation among western Pacific countries.

In 1985 alone, several regional meetings were held. In the middle of July, at the two-day post-ASEAN Foreign Ministerial Conference in Kuala Lumpur, the ASEAN foreign ministers met with their counterparts in the five dialogue countries, i.e., Australia, Canada, Japan, New Zealand, and the United States, and discussed broad-range issues of common interest, including further regional pursuits in human resources development. The last week of April, at the Fourth Annual Meeting of the Pacific Economic Cooperation Conference in Seoul, high-level politicians, government officials, business leaders, and academics met to discuss additional possibilities for regional and subregional cooperation in energy, primary commodities, industrial development, trade in manufactures, technology transfer, and financial flows, including direct foreign investment. At its annual session in March, the United Nations Economic and Social Commission for Asia and the Pacific (ESCAP) discussed, among other things, further possibilities for economic and technical cooperation among developing countries (ECDC/TCDC) of the ESCAP region. In February, the heads of state from Bangladesh, Bhutan, India, Maldives, Nepal, Pakistan, and Sri Lanka met in Dacca, Bangladesh, to establish the South Asian Association for Regional Cooperation (SAARC) in an attempt to intensify their cooperation in economic and cultural areas at the subregional level.

In addition, a number of meetings are being held in the respective countries in the Asia and Pacific region, to enhance understanding of basic issues, and to promote national efforts for economic cooperation among themselves at regional and subregional levels. These meetings deal not only with such traditional areas of economic cooperation as international trade, investment, technology transfer, and aid between developing and industrial countries, but also with similar aspects of ECDC/TCDC. They also are increasingly concerned with possible international cooperation on such urgent issues for developing countries as human resources development, including skills formation, supervisory training, and development of middle-level management.

Sector-specific subjects have become major focuses at these meetings, such as agriculture, fishery and forestry, mining, metal fabrication, plant maintenance and renovation, health and nutrition, computers and communications, power generation and distribution, railway and airline transport, banking and insurance, port development and warehousing, advertising and public relations, tourism, and public enterprise management. Possible methods for expanding and improving existing schemes of regional cooperation in trade, investment, and financial and technical assistance in the respective sectors are being discussed, at both the working level and the policymaking level.

This paper will discuss economic cooperation in the Asia and Pacific region in terms of (1) trends and overview; (2) major issues; and (3) future prospects.

TRENDS AND OVERVIEW

During the last two decades and a half, the world has witnessed a remarkable record of economic performance by both the newly industrialized countries (NICs) and the middle-income developing countries (MICs), as well as some industrial market-economy countries (IMEs) in the region, as indicated in Table 5.1. The region's share in the world's gross national product (GNP), export and import trade, and financial flows, including direct investment overseas, have increased substantially. Intra-regional trade and investment flows, both within the larger Asian and Pacific region and within the subregional groupings such as ASEAN (Brunei, Indonesia, Malaysia, the Philippines, Singapore, and Thailand) have also expanded enormously, particularly during the last decade (see tables 5.2 through 5.5).

Though supported and accelerated in varying degrees by government

TABLE 5.1 Basic Economic Data for Asian and Pacific Countries, 1965 and 1984.
Population and Gross Domestic Product and Distribution of GDP by Sector

	Population (million) Mid.-1984	GNP per capita ($) 1984	GDP ($ million) (annual average) 1965	GDP ($ million) (annual average) 1984	GDP growth rates (%) 65–73	GDP growth rates (%) 73–84	Agriculture 1965	Agriculture 1984	Industry 1965	Industry 1984	Manufacturing 1965	Manufacturing 1984	Services 1965	Services 1984
Low-income Countries														
Bangladesh	98.1	130	4,380	12,320	(.)	5.0	53	48	11	12	—	—	36	39
Burma	36.1	180	1,600	6,130	2.9	6.0	35	48	13	13	9	9	52	39
China	1,029.2	310	65,590	281,250	7.8	6.6	39	36	38	44	—	15	23	20
India	749.2	260	46,260	162,280	3.9	4.1	47	35	22	27	15	15	31	38
Nepal	16.1	160	730	2,290	1.7	3.1	65	56	11	12	3	4	23	32
Pakistan	92.4	380	5,450	27,730	5.4	5.6	40	24	20	29	14	20	40	47
Sri Lanka	15.9	360	1,770	5,430	4.2	5.2	28	28	21	26	17	14	51	46
Middle-income Countries (Lower middle)														
Indonesia	158.9	540	3,630	80,590	8.1	6.8	59	26	12	40	8	—	29	34
Papua New Guinea	3.4	710	340	2,360	6.7	1.0	42	34	18	9	—	—	41	58
Philippines	53.4	660	6,010	32,840	5.4	4.8	26	25	28	34	20	25	46	41
Thailand	50.0	860	4,050	41,960	7.8	6.8	35	20	23	28	14	—	42	52
Middle-income Countries (Upper middle)														
Hong Kong	5.4	6,330	2,150	30,620	7.9	9.1	2	1	40	22	24	—	58	78
Korea, Republic of	40.1	2,110	3,000	83,220	10.0	7.2	38	14	25	40	18	18	37	47
Malaysia	15.3	1,980	3,000	29,280	6.7	7.3	30	21	24	35	10	19	45	44
Singapore	2.5	7,260	970	18,220	13.0	8.2	3	1	24	39	15	25	73	60
Industrial Countries														
Australia	15.5	11,740	23,260	182,170	5.6	2.4	10	—	41	—	28	—	50	—
Japan	120.0	10,630	90,970	1,225,006	9.8	4.3	9	3	43	41	32	30	48	56
New Zealand	3.2	7,730	5,580	23,340	3.7	1.4	—	9	—	32	—	23	—	60
All Asian and Pacific Countries	2,504.7		268,740	2,247,036										

Source: IBRD, World Development Report, 1986.

TABLE 5.2. *Merchandise Exports of Asian and Pacific Countries (APCs)*
by Major Trading Partners, 1970 and 1985
(in percentage)

To: From:	APCs[b]		Developing APCs		Japan		Australia		North America		Western Europe		Eastern Europe	
	1970	1985	1970	1985	1970	1985	1970	1985	1970	1985	1970	1985	1970	1985
APCs[b]	36.7	39.0	22.0	25.9	11.1	9.8	2.5	2.6	26.2	32.3	18.5	16.1	3.3	2.0
Developing APCs	42.8	66.3	—	—	20.5	29.9	2.0	2.9	19.9	30.0	22.1	20.8	4.7	2.4
Afghanistan[b]	23.4	30.9	23.2	30.2	0.2	0.4	—	0.3	2.7	1.7	29.8	39.6	39.7	24.6
Bangladesh[b]	—	31.8	—	22.9	—	7.2	—	1.4	—	0.3	—	19.9	—	7.1
Brunei	99.5	88.0	83.7	9.3	0.5	78.2	11.7	—	—	7.0	0.4	0.1	—	—
Burma[a]	63.1	61.1	55.3	53.2	7.6	7.1	0.2	0.7	0.3	4.8	24.0	19.7	3.7	5.9
Fiji	29.2	43.8	9.2	22.7	4.2	3.0	8.8	13.5	27.3	7.1	32.2	30.0	—	—
Hong Kong	25.5	44.8	14.9	38.3	7.1	4.2	2.8	2.0	38.4	34.0	25.5	14.8	0.1	0.4
India[a]	26.1	25.5	10.1	14.0	13.9	10.0	1.7	1.3	15.3	25.6	19.7	22.5	19.4	14.9
Indonesia[a]	68.6	65.7	24.2	16.1	40.8	47.3	3.6	1.3	13.0	25.5	14.9	5.3	2.4	0.7
Iran[a]	50.4	25.3	11.5	8.1	37.7	17.2	0.5	—	3.7	6.7	36.7	54.9	—	4.2
Lao, People's Democratic Rep[a]	71.1	58.1	70.9	51.6	0.2	6.5	—	—	24.2	16.1	3.0	12.9	—	—
Malaysia	53.0	64.9	32.0	38.5	18.3	24.6	2.2	1.7	14.9	13.6	20.9	15.4	5.4	1.5
Pakistan	22.1	33.0	13.0	20.6	5.9	11.3	2.7	1.0	13.1	11.1	25.9	26.9	10.6	6.2
Philippines	48.6	40.7	8.0	19.7	40.2	19.0	0.5	1.7	41.9	37.8	8.6	17.0	—	0.8
Republic of Korea	37.7	30.1	9.1	13.7	28.2	15.0	0.4	1.2	49.5	42.5	8.6	14.2	—	—
Samoa[a]	53.3	44.2	44.4	11.5	—	3.9	—	7.8	6.7	28.9	40.0	19.2	—	—
Singapore	54.5	55.7	43.1	41.9	7.6	9.4	3.4	3.3	12.3	23.4	17.5	11.8	4.3	1.3
Sri Lanka	16.3	11.8	7.6	7.7	3.3	3.1	3.6	0.8	9.8	15.3	33.3	12.6	7.5	2.3
Thailand[a]	59.6	44.2	33.5	29.4	25.5	13.0	0.5	1.6	13.6	18.9	19.9	22.6	0.3	1.3
Papua New Guinea[a]	—	50.5	—	11.2	—	29.5	—	8.8	—	3.5	—	44.0	—	1.0
Vietnam[a]	—	75.4	—	55.7	—	18.3	—	1.4	—	0.6	—	8.5	—	3.6
Australia	49.3	55.6	17.7	23.0	26.2	27.8	—	—	15.6	11.9	21.8	14.9	2.4	3.5
Japan	29.5	30.8	25.9	27.1	—	—	3.1	3.1	34.1	43.3	13.0	14.3	2.5	1.9
New Zealand	24.6	47.7	5.9	17.2	9.9	14.5	8.7	16.0	20.6	18.1	44.9	21.4	2.0	1.9

[a] 1985 figures not available. Computations made by reference to 1984 figures, and for Afghanistan and Brunei by reference to 1980 figures.
[b] Percentages computed by reference to total exports of Asia and Pacific Countries (APCs).

Source: ESCAP (i) Development in Trade and Trade Policies: Issues and Problems (E/ESCAP/TRADE.24/10/Add.1) September 20, 1982, and
(ii) Quarterly Bulletin of Statistics for Asia and the Pacific (Vol. XVI No. 3) of September 1986.

TABLE 5.3. Merchandise Imports of Asian and Pacific Countries (APCs) by Major Trading Partners, 1970 and 1985
(in percentage)

From: / To:	APCs 1970	APCs 1985	Developing APCs 1970	Developing APCs 1985	Japan 1970	Japan 1985	Australia 1970	Australia 1985	North America 1970	North America 1985	Western Europe 1970	Western Europe 1985	Eastern Europe 1970	Eastern Europe 1985
APCs	31.5	43.9	14.3	26.9	10.9	12.2	5.4	4.1	27.8	20.0	19.9	16.4	4.5	1.6
Developing APCs[a]	39.8	61.2	—	—	22.1	36.8	3.1	5.4	21.1	18.0	24.1	22.7	3.7	2.5
Afghanistan[a]	33.3	53.0	15.8	35.5	17.4	17.5	0.1	0.0	4.3	2.0	17.5	14.6	35.1	24.8
Bangladesh	—	39.4	—	25.0	—	13.0	—	1.3	—	13.2	—	16.2	—	3.6
Brunei[a]	85.6	73.8	57.6	57.8	13.7	15.3	14.3	0.6	0.0	12.1	10.1	13.1	0.0	0.0
Burma[a]	51.2	64.7	22.4	28.3	26.2	35.7	2.6	0.8	8.1	3.5	27.9	28.8	6.8	1.0
Fiji	64.6	80.1	13.8	14.3	15.2	15.0	23.7	33.8	5.6	4.7	22.4	11.6	0.2	0.2
Hong Kong	40.8	72.0	14.4	47.2	23.8	23.0	2.4	1.4	13.9	10.2	21.8	13.8	0.7	0.4
India[a]	9.7	29.4	2.7	21.1	4.6	7.3	2.3	0.9	36.5	12.4	19.7	26.4	14.0	8.1
Indonesia[a]	49.7	45.8	17.5	18.7	29.4	23.8	2.8	2.7	17.8	20.9	21.6	17.8	2.3	0.7
Iran[a]	16.6	24.9	4.1	8.4	11.3	12.1	1.1	2.7	21.0	2.2	50.4	54.8	4.8	10.1
Lao, People's Democratic Rep[a]	59.9	68.3	45.1	56.7	14.2	11.7	0.6	—	24.1	—	14.3	10.0	0.8	—
Malaysia	53.5	57.7	29.5	29.9	17.5	23.0	5.7	4.1	9.7	16.6	25.0	17.4	2.2	0.4
Pakistan	17.2	33.2	4.5	16.7	10.9	12.6	1.6	3.9	32.6	15.4	32.4	23.8	0.0	1.6
Papua New Guinea	—	87.0	—	18.1	—	14.9	—	48.6	—	5.8	—	5.1	—	—
Philippines	43.9	47.5	7.9	29.6	30.6	14.0	4.7	3.4	31.1	25.9	17.7	10.2	0.0	0.4
Republic of Korea	52.1	41.1	10.3	12.8	41.0	24.3	0.7	3.6	30.7	25.0	10.8	12.9	0.0	—
Samoa[a]	70.2	86.5	11.2	45.2	10.5	9.0	16.4	9.0	15.7	6.0	11.9	6.0	0.8	—
Singapore	52.8	59.8	28.4	39.6	19.4	17.1	4.5	2.6	11.4	15.7	17.6	13.5	1.4	0.3
Sri Lanka	36.2	52.3	22.1	32.7	8.4	15.4	4.8	3.1	8.6	9.5	27.4	18.5	5.9	1.3
Thailand[a]	49.3	56.3	8.3	27.1	37.4	26.9	3.2	1.9	15.6	9.5	26.3	15.3	1.4	1.1
Vietnam	—	64.4	—	41.7	—	22.0	—	0.4	—	4.4	—	15.1	—	3.9
Australia	22.2	38.7	7.1	11.5	12.7	23.1	—	—	29.4	24.7	39.5	26.8	0.6	0.3
Japan	25.6	37.1	16.7	30.7	—	—	8.0	5.7	34.4	25.5	10.2	9.5	6.5	1.3
New Zealand	36.3	49.1	6.7	10.7	9.8	20.9	20.9	17.5	17.5	18.7	38.0	24.7	0.4	0.2

a 1985 figures not available. Computations made by reference to 1984 figures, and for Afghanistan and Brunei by reference to 1980 figures.

Source: ESCAP (i) Development in Trade and Trade Policies: Issues and Problems (E/ESCAP/TRADE.24/10/Add.1) September 20, 1982, and
(ii) Quarterly Bulletin of Statistics for Asia and the Pacific (Vol. XVI No. 3) of September 1986.

TABLE 5.4. *Direct Investment Flows Among Asian and Pacific Countries, 1976*
(In millions $US)

From: / To:	Japan	US	Canada	Hong Kong	Taiwan	Korea	Singapore	ANICs	Thailand	Malaysia	Philippines	Indonesia	ASEAN	Asia Total	Australia	New Zealand	Total
Japan	0.	1018.6	39.2	12.7	5.8	0.	0.	18.5	0.	0.	0.	0.	0.	18.5	0.	0.	1479.7
US	1178.0	0.	5907.0	0.	0.	0.	0.	0.	0.	0.	0.	0.	0.	1178.0	0.	0.	30770.0
Canada	273.4	31564.6	0.	36.2	0.	0.	0.	36.2	0.	0.	0.	0.	0.	309.6	39.4	0.	39781.9
Hong Kong	75.4	196.0	0.	0.	2.7	0.	13.1	15.8	10.6	0.	2.4	0.	26.1	104.2	19.0	0.	397.5
Taiwan	246.6	491.8	0.	7.8	0.	0.	0.	8.0	0.	0.	0.	0.	0.	246.6	0.	0.	1546.8
Korea	429.3	106.5	79.0	7.8	0.2	0.	0.	8.0	0.	0.	0.	0.	0.	437.3	0.	0.	676.5
Singapore	213.8	502.1	0.	0.	0.	0.	0.	0.	0.	0.	0.	0.	0.	213.8	0.	0.	1522.7
ANICs	965.1	1296.4	79.0	7.8	2.9	0.	13.1	23.8	10.6	0.	2.4	0.	26.1	1001.9	19.0	0.	4143.5
Thailand	74.6	30.5	0.	11.0	22.8	0.	1.9	35.7	0.	0.	0.9	0.	7.6	116.0	1.1	0.	195.1
Malaysia	255.0	107.6	3.6	121.2	0.	0.	197.1	318.3	0.	4.8	0.	0.	197.1	573.3	20.4	0.	953.8
Philippines	134.4	175.2	11.9	4.3	31.8	11.2	0.	47.3	0.	0.	0.	0.	0.	181.7	24.3	0.	521.0
Indonesia	2044.1	1000.3	78.8	546.1	0.	0.	162.0	708.1	0.	0.	0.	0.	162.0	2752.2	185.0	0.	5192.5
ASEAN	2721.9	1815.7	94.3	682.6	54.6	11.2	361.0	1109.4	0.	4.8	0.9	0.	366.7	3837.0	230.8	0.	8385.1
Asia Total	3473.2	3628.6	212.5	703.1	63.3	11.2	374.1	1151.7	10.6	4.8	3.3	0.	392.8	4643.6	249.8	0.	12485.6
Australia	256.4	1076.6	89.1	0.	0.	0.	0.	0.	0.	0.	0.	0.	0.	256.4	0.	0.	2615.0
New Zealand	20.6	78.4	8.2	0.	0.	0.	0.	0.	0.	0.	0.	0.	0.	20.6	124.3	0.	373.9
Total	5201.6	36348.2	6216.8	739.3	63.3	11.2	374.1	1187.9	10.6	4.8	3.3	0.	392.8	6408.2	413.5	0.	86026.4

Notes:
1. Figures are outstanding or cumulated approval amount of direct investment (DI) based on those governments' reports.
2. Singapore is included in both A(sian) NICs and in ASEAN.
3. For countries which report only in home currency terms, cumulated approval was converted into U.S. dollars at year-average exchange rates in 1976.
4. Latin American Statistics are not listed as statistics were short at the time of making the matrix.
5. Since some countries only cover manufacturing, or a limited time period for making cumulated figures and statistical definition varies, the matrix serves for only rough observation.
6. Figures for Malaysia are for 1977.

TABLE 5.5. Direct Investment Flows Among Asian and Pacific Countries, 1980
(In millions $US)

From: / To:	Japan	US	Canada	Hong Kong	Taiwan	Korea	Singapore	ANICs	Thailand	Malaysia	Philippines	Indonesia	ASEAN	Asia Total	Australia	New Zealand	Total
Japan	0.	1611.6	76.8	73.1	18.9	0.	0.	92.0	0.	0.	0.	0.	0.	92.0	0.	0.	2552.3
US	4225.0	0.	10074.0	0.	0.	0.	0.	0.	0.	0.	0.	0.	0.	4225.0	0.	0.	68351.0
Canada	431.6	1206.7	0.	69.3	0.	0.	0.	69.3	0.	0.	0.	0.	0.	500.9	83.2	0.	51811.5
Hong Kong	120.9	218.2	0.	0.	5.6	0.	16.0	21.6	13.4	0.	16.8	0.	46.2	172.7	20.2	0.	537.2
Taiwan	457.7	776.3	0.	0.	0.	0.	0.	0.	0.	0.	0.	0.	0.	457.7	0.	0.	2718.4
Korea	612.3	231.8	79.0	12.5	0.6	0.	0.	13.1	0.	0.	0.	0.	0.	625.4	0.6	0.	1141.6
Singapore	517.5	957.8	0.	0.	0.	0.	0.	0.	0.	0.	0.	0.	0.	517.5	0.	0.	3275.5
ANICs	1708.4	2184.1	79.0	12.5	6.2	0.	16.0	34.7	13.4	0.	16.8	0.	46.2	1773.3	20.8	0.	7672.7
Thailand	76.6	28.3	0.	17.2	31.5	0.	3.2	51.9	0.	7.8	0.9	0.	11.9	137.2	2.2	0.	229.0
Malaysia	225.9	79.7	7.8	119.0	0.	0.	277.1	396.1	0.	0.	0.	0.	277.1	622.0	27.2	0.	1100.3
Philippines	299.1	752.1	56.0	84.2	4.2	6.0	12.7	107.1	0.	0.	0.	0.	12.7	406.2	34.5	0.	1519.0
Indonesia	3372.4	575.2	83.0	1062.3	128.6	84.8	145.1	1420.8	0.	60.4	292.6	0.	498.1	5146.2	208.6	0.	9446.2
ASEAN	4491.5	2393.1	146.8	1282.7	164.3	90.8	438.1	1975.9	0.	68.2	293.5	0.	799.8	6829.1	272.5	0.	15570.0
Asia Total	5682.4	5231.0	302.6	1368.3	189.4	90.8	454.1	2102.6	13.4	68.2	310.3	0.	846.0	8176.9	293.3	0.	22519.5
Australia	2101.4	5094.1	236.7	0.	0.	0.	0.	0.	0.	0.	0.	0.	0.	2101.4	0.	0.	16342.6
New Zealand	4.7	236.1	25.3	0.	0.	0.	0.	0.	0.	0.	0.	0.	0.	4.7	360.7	0.	1325.7
Total	12445.1	15767.9	10638.6	1437.6	189.4	90.8	454.1	2171.9	13.4	68.2	310.3	0.	846.0	15008.9	737.2	0.	160350.3
Chile[a]	49.8	5098.5	767.2	14.1	1.2	2.8	0.	18.1	0.	0.	0.	0.	0.	67.9	12.0	0.	6991.0

Notes: Notes (1)–(5) in the previous table apply here, too.
1. Inflow investment in home currency terms are converted into U.S. dollars at the year-average exchange rates. Adding these figures to 1976-end amount, cumulated approval or cumulated investment in 1980 were made.
2. Figures for Malaysia are for 1979.
3. Data for 1975–1982 period provided by Arturo Wenzel of the Chilean Embassy in Tokyo.

policies for higher growth and structural changes in most cases, the complex network of trade, investment, and other economic cooperation among western Pacific countries thus has been built up significantly, essentially through the interplay of market forces.

Partly because of this phenomenal economic performance, which distinguishes the region from the rest of the world, increasing attention has been given among some western Pacific countries to some possibilities for institutionally-enhanced economic cooperation in the region to sustain the momentum of economic growth and structural changes in their respective countries. Without question it was, however, the three-year world recession, which began in the fall of 1980, and the subsequent stagnation of the global demand for primary commodities that substantially reduced the growth rates of GNP, volume of exports and imports, and foreign investment inflows in practically all the Asian and Pacific countries. And that has been instrumental to the heightened interest and concern among countries in the region in some form of loosely organized, institutionalized regional economic cooperation.

INTRA-ASEAN ECONOMIC COOPERATION

Since 1980, there have been renewed national efforts among the ASEAN countries for enhanced subregional economic cooperation. While strategic factors have remained the most important in binding ASEAN nations together since the organization's founding in 1967, as evidenced by the adoption of the Zone of Peace, Freedom and Neutrality (ZOPFAN) and the ASEAN proposal for political solution to Cambodian issues, progress in intra-ASEAN economic cooperation has been quite slow, even after the 1976 Bali Declaration that reaffirmed the need for enhancing such cooperation. Major instruments of intra-ASEAN economic cooperation have been expanded—e.g., the preferential trading arrangement (PTA), ASEAN swap arrangement (ASA), a food security reserve (FSR), joint ASEAN industrial projects (AIP), ASEAN industrial complementation programs (AIC), ASEAN industrial joint ventures (AIJV), and the ASEAN customs code (ACC).

So far, the preferential trading arrangement to reduce tariffs among ASEAN states has been the most successful instrument of intra-ASEAN economic cooperation. While the effects of this arrangement, as evidenced by the slower than expected expansion of intra-ASEAN trade, have been less dramatic than had been hoped for, the number of traded items covered by scheduled tariff reductions increased substantially during the first few years after its inception in 1977. Since 1983, automatic tariff cuts of 20 to 25 percent have been extended to all items whose import values would amount to US$10 million or less per annum, while tariff cuts up to 50 percent have been offered for all other items.

ASEAN industrial projects, on the contrary, so far have been among the least encouraging of all the schemes for intra-ASEAN economic cooperation. An AIP is supposed to be jointly owned and managed by the ASEAN governments, with its host country providing one-half of its equity capital and the other member states providing the rest. To take advantage of economy of scale, the products of an AIP are to be marketed free of tariffs in all ASEAN countries. However, so far, only two urea plants—one each for Indonesia and Malaysia—have been set up under the AIP scheme. Thailand has yet to choose a site for a rocksalt soda plant, and the Philippines have not chosen a project—possibilities include an ammonium sulphate fertilizer plant, a copper fabrication plant and a pulp and paper plant. Confronted by some practical difficulties, posed by other member states, Singapore abandoned its AIP proposal to set up a small diesel engine plant, and established it outside the AIP scheme.

Lack of progress is also seen in terms of ASEAN industrial complementation (AIC) programs. Under this plan, different member states are assigned production of different products; to optimize economy of scale, all member states are requested to refrain from either expanding their existing production facilities for two years or establishing new facilities within four years, for those products assigned to other states. Industrial joint ventures (AIJVs) have also been slow in coming in all ASEAN countries. Member states have agreed under the program to provide tariff preferences to any products of ASEAN firms whose majority shares are owned by nationals from two or more member states. There is a possibility that the ASEAN Finance Corporation (AFC), established in 1981 to co-finance promising investment projects in member countries, may become instrumental to the establishment of AIJVs in the future.

Economic Cooperation among Pacific Island Countries

Efforts have long been made to expand and improve economic cooperation among the island developing countries of the South Pacific that have in common small population size, geographic isolation, and poor land resource endowments. The results of such cooperative efforts, as made by the South Pacific Bureau for Economic Cooperation (SPEC)—the secretariat set up by the South Pacific Forum (SPF) in 1973—have been noteworthy in some respects.

However, these efforts have not had encouraging results in the traditional areas of trade, investment, and air/marine transportation. While the South Pacific Regional Trade and Economic Cooperation Agreement (SPARTECA), effective since 1981, provides for tariff concessions by Australia and New Zealand for exports of 10 Pacific countries, it has not been substantial in terms of its impact on trade and development in the island developing countries. The Pacific Forum Line, a regional shipping line in which most of the SPF countries participate, has been run with a mounting deficit. On the other hand, greater progress has been observed in technical cooperation efforts, such as tertiary education—e.g., the establishment of the University of the South Pacific in Fiji and technical and professional training in various occupations.

Economic Cooperation among South Asian Countries

Since approximately 1980, the countries of South Asia have intensified, although without much apparent success, their respective efforts for enhanced economic cooperation on the subregional level. So far, their only achievement has been the signing by foreign ministers of the New Delhi Declaration, which established the South Asian Association for Regional Cooperation (SAARC) and an integrated program of action under the group's auspices. SAARC's major emphasis appears to be on strengthening national development capabilities rather than initiating concrete schemes for economic cooperation among its member states. It is encouraging to note, however, that several working committees have been set up to investigate the potential for cooperation among member states in the fields of agriculture, rural development, telecommunications, health, science, technology, arts, culture, and sports.

In addition, the work of the Committee on Studies for Cooperation in Development in South Asia (CSCD), whose academic member institutions come from all the member countries of SAARC except Iran, seems to be facilitating the efforts of SAARC member states toward enhanced economic cooperation.

OTHER REGIONAL COOPERATIVE ARRANGEMENTS

In addition to these broad, all-inclusive programs for subregional cooperation among the ASEAN, Pacific Island and South Asian countries, a number of functional cooperative schemes have been operative for some time in the Asia and Pacific region, both at the regional and subregional levels. They were installed mainly by the United Nations Economic Commission for Asia and the Far East (ECAFE) and its successor, ESCAP, as well as other United Nations specialized agencies, such as UNESCO and FAO, in order to assist member countries in this region to improve their performance in specific economic and social spheres through mutual financial and technical cooperation.

There is the Asian Clearing Union (ACU), founded in 1973 mainly by South and West Asian countries under the auspices of ECAFE, to promote trade expansion. The amount of funds channeled through ACU, denominated in Asian Monetary Units (AMU), in 1981 reached the equivalent of only US$228 million, less than one percent of member states' total external trade. The Bangkok Agreement on Trade Expansion was initiated in 1976 by Bangladesh, India, the Lao People's Democratic Republic, the Republic of Korea, Sri Lanka, the Philippines, and Thailand, although the last two have not ratified the Agreement. It has fostered product-by-product negotiation of trade concessions among its partners. But the consequences of such efforts have not been significant, as evidenced by its small intra-Agreement trade as a percent of the total trade of its member countries.

Other examples include the Asia-Pacific Telecommunity, participated in by 21 countries of the region; and the Asian Highway project and Trans-Asian Railway Network, both of which include a large number of Asian countries as participants. There are also a few regional organizations with membership limited to commodity-producing countries, such as the Association of Natural Rubber Producing Countries (ANRPC), the Southeast Asian Lumber Producers' Association (SEALPA), the Asian and Pacific Coconut Community (APCC), the Regional Mineral Resources Development Centre (RMRDC), and the Southeast Asian Tin Research and Development Centre (SEATRADC). Efforts are also made by ESCAP, together with other international organizations, to assist producer countries to form associations for jute, tropical timber, and silk. There are two standing committees for the coordination of joint prospecting for mineral resources in offshore areas, one active in the East Asian subregion (CCOP) and another in the South Pacific (CCOP/SOPAC). Two major projects have been set up in the Pacific region to promote and coordinate national efforts to minimize the damage caused by typhoons (Typhoon Committee) and tropical cyclones (Panel on Tropical Cyclones).

There are two principal regional institutions in Asia and the Pacific, each acting as a clearinghouse of information on technology development and transfer. One is the Regional Network for Agricultural Machinery (RNAM) at Los Banos in the Philippines; the other is the Regional Centre for Technology Transfer (RCTT) at Bangalore, India. In 1980, a region-wide Asian and Pacific Development Centre (APDC) was also set up in Kuala Lumpur, Malaysia, a result of amalgamating and integrating the four regional research and training institutions to promote policy-oriented research and training in a broad spectrum of development issues.

In the field of international finance and insurance, the Asian Development Bank, located in Manila, has been supplementing the development loans and technical assistance provided by the World Bank and the International Development Association (IDA) in this region. The Bangkok-based Asian Reinsurance Corporation (ARC), which began underwriting in 1980, has provided a good example of how ECDC/TCDC is perennially confronted with inadequate foreign exchange earnings and reserves in this region.

In addition to these instruments of multilateral economic cooperation at the regional and subregional levels, a large number of bilateral cooperative schemes have been initiated between developing Asian and Pacific countries and IMEs, in and outside the region as well as among the former themselves. They range from financial to technical cooperation, with the latter increasingly significant and diversified to meet the changing and higher requirements of developmental tasks. With a few centrally planned economies in the region, such as Democratic Kampuchea, the Democratic People's Republic of Korea, the Lao People's Democratic Republic, the People's Republic of China, the People's Republic of Mongolia, and the Socialist Republic of Vietnam, financial and technical cooperation among some of them, particularly in the Indochina Peninsula, and between these countries and like-minded countries outside the region has been increasing.

MAJOR ISSUES

In spite of the clear-cut rationale for promoting regional and subregional cooperation among interested countries, critical issues abound in such cooperative agreements, arrangements, and institutions. The need for collective self-reliance, resilience, and solidarity vis-à-vis the rest of the world and, in particular, the economic and military superpowers is quite obvious to a smaller number of countries participating in subregional groupings that are often in geographical proximity and sometimes share common identities of culture, language, and lifestyle.

The logic behind regional and subregional cooperation is clear to countries participating in such cooperative schemes. Costs are minimized while the benefits of national and international economic activities in specific functional areas of production, research and development, information processing, marketing, and/or in specific sectors including agriculture, industry, and finance, are to be maximized. But yet, many regional and subregional cooperative efforts and institutions have failed, faltered, or are just lingering on.

In discussing the major issues facing both subregional groupings such as ASEAN, SPF, SAARC and various regional/subregional cooperative schemes in specific functions and sectors in the Asian and Pacific region, it is important to note again that varying gains—at times substantial— have accrued to the countries participating in these regional/subregional cooperative arrangements. It should also be noted that even in generally successful subregional groupings some cooperative schemes have failed while others have succeeded.

The major issues facing both subregional groupings and regional/subregional cooperative schemes can be classified into two types: (1) those internal and (2) those external to such institutions and arrangements. Both internal and external issues are intertwined and reinforce each other, while basic underlying factors constraining such cooperative efforts are at work in common to both of these issues. Some of the more important factors constraining regional undertakings are the lack of political commitment among member countries; the diversity and/or conflicts of national interests; the fear among smaller member countries of large-country domination and exploitation; the diversity of historical and economic linkages with outside powers; the lack of cultural, linguistic, and historical ties among themselves, and the inadequate provision of financial resources.

Major Internal Issues

Constrained by the above-mentioned factors, most regional and/or subregional arrangements, while agreeing basically on broad objectives, direction, and scope of work, often suffer from differences regarding the strategies to be adopted in pursuit of objectives, as well as from differences and, at times, conflict in assignment of priorities for the different tasks.

It is well known that differences have emerged among the ASEAN countries in their strategies toward intra-ASEAN economic cooperation, particularly with respect to AIPs. Outsiders believe that Singapore's decision to participate only nominally in urea fertilizer projects for Aceh and Bintulu under AIP aegis is a reflection of its irritation with the difficulties posed by some other ASEAN governments in regard to its own proposal for setting up a small diesel engine project under the AIP schemes. While to some extent this may be so, the decision also stems as much from their firm, long-held belief in the free enterprise system and free market approach and from a lack of practical interest in the product in the country due to the near absence of domestic demand for it.

The AIP scheme necessarily involves governments providing equity and loan capital, running corporate management and day-to-day project implementation, and providing the special legal and administrative environments conducive to successful project execution. With both Malaysia and Thailand joining Singapore in moves toward further privatization of their public enterprises and statutory bodies and further deregulation and promotion of private-sector business activities, AIP schemes may have a long way to go before completion. There is some likelihood that one ASEAN government after another may, in the future, decide not to participate in such government-owned joint industrial projects. Much of the earlier intentions of the ASEAN governments to promote their respective industrialization programs through the AIP scheme had essentially already been achieved more efficiently in the marketplace. It may be high time that the ASEAN governments adopt AIP projects more selectively so that only those, for reasons of optimum efficiency and risk minimization, necessarily require joint ASEAN government efforts in finance and markets may be taken up for future consideration. Otherwise, the AIP scheme will lose its raison-d'être against the background of rapidly growing industrial capital, technology, and entrepreneurship in the ASEAN private sector.

Another important internal issue facing regional and subregional cooperative efforts in Asia and the Pacific is the difficulty of agreeing to a common policy stance—whether for agriculture, manufacturing, or international trade—among their respective member countries. This stems essentially from the inability of the governments of these countries to adjust and coordinate the dissimilar interests of the different productive sectors and segments of the population in their own countries. Logically speaking, it should be easier to thrash out or contain such internal differences, and at regional forums to come up with a more flexible and cooperative policy stance, in those countries whose governments are more authoritarian; this is likely to be the case in many developing countries as compared with IMEs. Even there, governments often give up their attempts to resolve such internal differences and tend to present a rather rigid policy stance, one not amenable to negotiation and compromise.

A third issue is the oft-criticized institutional weakness of the secretariats—which are often poorly financed, manned, and organized—and the effect on any regional and subregional cooperative arrangements. This weakness is partly a reflection of the lack of political commitment by the member countries participating in such cooperative activities and partly of the lack of intellectual leadership at the top of such bodies. After the initial fanfare announcing the birth of new regional cooperative arrangements, the political leadership often loses interest in sustaining such arrangements. The placement of mediocre bureaucrats, often retired from national civil services, at the top of such regional/subregional bodies, precipitates the waning of the initial hopes, aspirations, and interests shown by member countries in such cooperative arrangements. Such leadership tends to bring together professional men and women of mediocre capabilities, with organizational morale slipping away, beginning the slow process of institutional death. Also, when faced with the necessity of cutting national budgets, most countries assign lowest priorities to regional and subregional arrangements, because they have no constituencies to speak for them and hence no political support.

Major External Issues

One of the most serious external issues facing regional and subregional groupings in the Asia and Pacific region is the pressure, whether military or economic, exerted by external powers on such groupings. To respond means establishing common external policy stances vis-à-vis these powers in economic and political relations.

When it is difficult for member countries to agree even on the basic internal policy measures affecting their respective national economic management, it is all the more difficult to formulate common external policies that take into account all the needs and requirements of the member countries. No nation, however willing to compromise in the interest of attaining the common objectives of regional/subregional groupings, is ready to surrender sovereign rights over its domestic affairs and foreign relations. The complex network of bilateral economic, political, cultural, and historical ties between each member country and the external powers makes agreement on a common external policy stance nearly impossible.

When finally agreed upon, in the name of collective resilience and solidarity, any common external policies of a regional/subregional grouping tend to take into account all the needs and requirements of its weakest member countries. Thus, policies will be neither creative nor entirely positive, unless the economically stronger members are willing to shoulder heavier burdens. The tendency, therefore, is for regional and subregional groupings to discriminate against outside countries in favor of its members in the areas of trade, investment, and other areas of economic cooperation. The divisive effects of such groupings thus tend to be as important, if not more important, than the creative effects. This is the reason why regional and subregional groupings often have been described as promoting trade and economic cooperation internally but protectionist externally.

Another major external issue confronting many regional and subregional cooperative arrangements is the difficulty of enlarging their membership to include other interested countries. ASEAN, in spite of its charter provision that the organization is open to any interested countries, since its founding in 1967 has accepted only Brunei as its partner, although a few other countries, such as Sri Lanka, have informally sounded out the possibility of joining ASEAN. Chances for successful application seem scarce, because a consensus among the existing ASEAN members is required for any new admissions. Conversely, there are quite a number of regional and subregional arrangements that, in practice, are open to any countries interested in joining. However, not many countries are interested in joining, since these arrangements appear neither attractive nor beneficial to them.

The third major external issue lies in the absence of effective communications and working relationships between such groupings and national institutions engaged in similar efforts for regional cooperation. In spite of a rapid improvement in telecommunications and information technology and despite repeated warnings by member governments against duplication, it is amazing to learn of the substantial amount of duplication of work between them that often results not only in the waste of precious money, time, and manpower but also in the loss of credibility with such regional bodies. Inter-organizational cooperation has often suffered, not because of simple ignorance by either party but because of the personalities of the organizations involved. Similar problems have persisted between regional bodies, also.

FUTURE PROSPECTS

In spite of all these shortcomings and the issues involved both internally and externally, there has been a phenomenal growth of cooperative arrangements in Asia and the Pacific at the regional and subregional levels during the last three decades. Between the end of the 1950s and 1982, the number of these arrangements—governmental and nongovernmental and encompassing more than two countries—increased from 10 to 322 in the region, including those national bodies providing ECDC/TCDC. And the number seems to be still growing, albeit at a much slower pace, as a result of intensified efforts for expanded regional cooperative projects among the developing countries.

As shown in the case of APDC, however, efforts for rationalization and reorganization of regional institutions are being intensified to minimize duplication of work and to increase the efficiency of regional cooperation. The future trend is toward gradual phaseout of the small, fragmented regional and subregional projects that have outlived their utility and whose impact have been negligible. Nations and IMEs, in particular, today are much more cautious in adding any new cooperative arrangements to those already existing in this region. The importance of having adequate subregional infrastructures—including transportation and communications links—and sharing cultural values, both the cause and effect of such cooperation, is understood much better now. People and nations are also much more realistic about the cost and benefit of any regional cooperative arrangements and entertain less illusions about them.

Also, efforts have been intensified in recent years to promote Pacific economic cooperation among countries in and around the Pacific. After the first three meetings in Canberra, Bangkok, and Bali, the fourth annual meeting of the Pacific Economic Cooperation Conference (PECC), held in Seoul, called for the ASEAN national committees to provide positive support for Pacific economic cooperation, as shown by Australia, Canada, Japan, New Zealand, ROK, and the United States. An energy forum has been created by PECC to better enhance understanding of energy issues and, if possible, to bring about better coordination of national energy policies among the participating regional countries.

With respect to the formation of the Pacific (Economic) Community, there are, as it stands today, too many unknowns and uncertainties among the potential member countries in terms of major objectives, scope of cooperation, and membership. The small island countries of the Pacific and ASEAN countries fear the possible adverse impact such enlarged cooperative schemes might have on their own subregional groupings, such as SPF and ASEAN. They are quite sensitive to a possible Chinese role in a PEC and even suspicious of a possible extension of a PEC to include a regional defense or security arrangement against the USSR and its allies.

It is all the more unlikely, therefore, that a head organization of the type found in other parts of the world, such as the Organization of African Unity (OAU), the Organization of American States (OAS), the European Community (EC), and the Council of Mutual Economic Assistance (CMEA), will be installed for the Pacific region in the foreseeable future. There seems to be a long way to go before the Pacific countries may become interested enough to form such an institution at the regional level.

The future of economic cooperation in the Asian and Pacific region thus appears to be pointing toward strengthening the all-inclusive subregional groups such as ASEAN, SPF, and SAARC, through better planning and implementation of cooperative projects and schemes among some or all of the respective member countries. It also points toward the reorganization and streamlining of a large number of functional cooperative arrangements at the regional and subregional levels. Even here, participating countries will have to be more broadminded and willing to commit themselves to the principle of changing the international division of labor geared to dynamic comparative advantages and to make their cooperative arrangements open to all those countries willing to share the costs.

In every Pacific country a stronger commitment to the principle of mutually shared benefits under freer trading and investment regimes will increase the possibility that international trade, investment, and aid flows will expand in the Asian and Pacific region. This will lead to further steady economic growth, structural changes, and continuing improvement in the quality of life for all the countries both inside and outside the region.

THREE

Political Issues

6

Domestic Developments Affecting Stability and Regional Relationships in Northeast Asia

by William H. Gleysteen, Jr.

INTRODUCTION

Northeast Asia still faces the potential danger of military conflict (in Korea, Taiwan, and on the Sino–Soviet border). Political institutions in much of the region have yet to demonstrate durability or long-term effectiveness, and few other parts of the world are as vulnerable to economic developments elsewhere. Nevertheless, domestic conditions within the region have been stable for some time and may well continue to evolve in patterns which reduce local tensions and ease foreign relationships. The contrast with the situation of twenty or even ten years ago is striking.

China is obviously the biggest element of change. Preoccupied with economic modernization, the People's Republic of China (PRC) has abandoned policies of economic autarky, ideological coercion, and orchestrated turmoil in favor of a pragmatic approach that has relaxed the country internally and lowered the risk of confrontation abroad. Japan's economic strength and political stability have combined to make it by far the steadiest country in the region. Disappointing some by its reluctance to change certain economic and security policies, it has reassured others—including its neighbors—by avoiding abrupt moves that might alter the area's strategic equilibrium. Stability on the Korean Peninsula remains tentative, largely because of the North/South military confrontation but also because of political and other domestic issues that will test the Republic of Korea (ROK) and Democratic People's Republic of Korea (DPRK) over the next few years. Similar tentativeness hangs over Taiwan, which has, however, demonstrated a strong capacity for survival. Generally, developments in Northeast Asia seem more in harmony with geopolitical realities than during any other period since World War II, a condition both reflecting and contributing to domestic stability in the area.

DOMESTIC STRENGTHS AND WEAKNESSES IN THE REGION

At the risk of oversimplification, the countries of the region—with the partial exception of the DPRK—share certain qualities which contribute heavily to their current stability. Most important are their national strategies for rapid economic development, coherent governing structures, large administrative bureaucracies and a tendency toward pragmatic, as opposed to ideological, behavior. All the countries of the region also have governments that generally subordinate individual interests to the group. In democratic Japan, the function is performed through time-consuming procedures to reach consensus; in the other states, which are to varying degrees authoritarian, strong leaders and technocrats decide issues more arbitrarily, but they too are responsive to popular desires for progress, efficiency, and a reasonable degree of social and economic equity.

Each of these societies, except North Korea, is in a practical phase of its development, leaving ideology at its lowest ebb in the twentieth century. China is diluting its socialist ideology through practical adoption of incentives and market forces. In South Korea and Taiwan, the anti-Communist ideology of the war years is wearing away, even though fear and concern remain strong. Throughout, the trend is toward flexibility, defusing of conflict, and greater acceptance of coexistence with external antagonists.

The sense of threat, from within as well as from outside the region, is also diminishing. Rhetoric aside, South Korea is considerably less fearful of a North Korean attack than a decade ago. China's willingness to deemphasize its military expenditures suggests convincingly that it foresees no major threat for at least the next few years, not even from the Soviet Union. Japan, while frequently angered by Soviet behavior and always bothered by Soviet military expansion in East Asia, does not feel under imminent danger from any quarter. Even Taiwan, with all its anxieties about its future, does not suffer an overwhelming sense of threat, seeing its problems largely in political and economic, rather than military, terms. North Korea may be an exception, given what it would probably be tempted to do if it enjoyed the dominance South Korea has achieved. Although these relaxing trends in Northeast Asia may, in the long run, make it harder for leaders to justify arbitrary political behavior to their citizens and mobilize popular support for expanding military capability, they have not increased instability or reduced powerful incentives to excel.

These qualities of domestic strength that underlie Northeast Asia's current stability are nevertheless offset by substantial strains and vulnerabilities. The very fact that rapid economic development is the centerpiece of stability makes the region exceptionally vulnerable to outside economic trends. Japan, South Korea, Taiwan, and, to a lesser extent, China are heavily dependent on foreign markets, technology, energy, food, and raw materials. A serious wave of global recession or protectionism could have devastating consequences, not only on the economic well-being of these countries but also on the lubricant that has kept their political machinery functioning. The problem could be compounded by economic rivalry within the area.

Stability in all countries of the region, except Japan, is weakened by political strains never very far below the surface. One aspect of this weakness is the lack of reliable mechanisms for leadership succession. China, for example, could be semi-paralyzed by policy disputes and leadership rivalries at a time of political succession, while the ROK faces its next presidential election without ever having had a peaceful transition. Another aspect is the lack of sufficiently effective ways to compensate for the breakdown of traditional authority or to accommodate the complex demands of rapidly urbanizing populations. Military and security services play a disproportionate role in much of the region, reminiscent of considerably less-developed parts of the world. Often they have been important in the modernizing process; normally they are tolerated in their political role by other elements of the population; and occasionally they are even welcomed as a last resort against chaos. However, armies have generally had an inhibiting effect on the growth of institutions that might ease political tension.

Without doubt, these political weaknesses are the most worrisome threat to stability in Northeast Asia. Growing sophistication and the growing stakes that the people of these countries have in stability may constrain some of the more extreme possibilities, but most of the region still suffers from the political dilemma of stability enforced during long periods of strongman rule, but frequently followed by tumultuous release of pent-up opposition during the inevitable interregnums.

Domestic stability in all the countries of the area is dependent on a certain equilibrium in security relationships, and these could be upset by changes within or outside the region, such as an (unlikely) large-scale build-up of Japanese military forces or a diminished American military presence.

Finally, there is the problem of nationalism, effectively disciplined or subordinated to other factors in most of Northeast Asia during the last four decades. At present, this emotion appears the least of the threats to the area's stability. The potential for trouble is growing, however, from developments within the region as well as from outside it. With such effective competitors at work, inter-area rivalries could develop rather naturally or even be encouraged by leaders who do not wish to be flanked on the issue of national self-esteem. This issue is especially crucial among younger generations, who are impressed by their national accomplishments, less respectful of their Western tutors, less inclined to be bullied, and sometimes simply bored with the mundaneness of economic development. Although xenophobic extremes seem unlikely, chauvinism could develop rather easily if not firmly controlled.

China

If only because of its recent and spectacular record of domestic turmoil, China seems the logical point to begin a review of the region's prospects for stability. Although the thrust of events since the cultural revolution has been encouraging, China still has great potential for instability, not surprising given the problems with which it must cope. No other government has even had to administer a society of one billion people and to do so with such an unfavorable ratio of people to resources. Faced with massive problems of control and diversity of conditions, Chinese governments have long had difficulty finding the right balance between central and local control. Perhaps more serious is the effect within China today of the prolonged leadership struggle that, for the most part, has bitterly frustrated but not destroyed former or potential opposition elements. The process has left the population distrustful and cynical about authority, including the state ideology of communism.

Despite these circumstances, China is managing itself quite impressively as it introduces incentives and market forces to invigorate its socialist economy, reduces arbitrary political pressures on its people, and turns to the West for help with its modernization plan. The odds are better than even that it will continue to do so for the next few years at least. Reform and change are being implemented carefully in striking contrast to the impulsive style of Mao Zedong. Deng Xiaoping has been essentially successful so far in a series of key organizational steps. He has selected and progressively turned responsibilities over to new party and government leadership, having, however, to draw the process out as he deals cautiously with conservative leaders in the party and army. Many of them share his dismal view of Maoist radicalism but fear that his pace of change is too rapid and may carry China out of the socialist realm. Apart from ideology, they also resist changes that affect their perquisites and status.

Equally delicate and certainly more cumbersome, the current leadership has not only set out to rectify the Communist Party at all levels but also to deflect it from administrative responsibilities into a policy and oversight role. In parallel, the army has been gradually pushed out of its political role and reduced in its budget priority. Resistance is great, and progress is slow. Throughout, but especially in the government and army apparatus, the accent is on youth, education, and professional competence. Ideology has been relegated to the role of morality and as a (not very effective) hedge against abuse of the liberalization process.

An uneasy consensus, which is periodically challenged, has allowed changes in China's structure of authority—emphasizing the priority of government bureaucracy over the party and army, as well as reducing the scope of direct controls. The adjustment would have been more difficult if the Cultural Revolution had not thoroughly discredited many potential opponents of reform or if proponents of greater reform were not restrained by fear of future retribution. Ideology has faded considerably as a force. The Government's ability to keep people in line has not been fundamentally challenged, however, not only because the leaders have deflected political dissatisfaction with the prospect of economic progress but also because the state's coercive structure remains in place.

Although some people missed the full import of his message when Deng told visitors, even before his troubles in 1975, that China's modernization program would require a long period of domestic stability and international peace, his persistence toward these goals for over a decade has convinced most doubters. In any event, changes in leaders, policies, and style have given China its longest period of consistent direction and domestic stability since the founding of the PRC. External policies strengthen the trend. The search for foreign markets, technology, investment, aid, or student training entangles China with the outside world to a degree that constrains its foreign policy and reinforces the need for domestic stability. China's central strategy reduces the prospect of external trouble that could undermine domestic programs. The PRC has sustained its U.S. connection in a form that is likely to prove durable—less effusive than before but reinforced by a modest military relationship that benefits China immediately, as well as potentially in case of conflict with the Soviet Union. At the same time, China has adopted a less hostile posture toward the USSR, demonstrating determination not to provoke external threats when military modernization has been given a low priority, as well as a desire to position itself better in triangular relations with Washington and Moscow.

China's regional relationships, which also reflect the need for domestic stability, have helped to reduce tensions and open new possibilities. Improved relations with Japan, so critical to regional stability, go back to the Mao–Zhou era, but a similar sophistication has begun to characterize China's approach to the far more troublesome areas of Taiwan, Hong Kong, and South Korea.

So long as they are successful, China's current policies have the decisive advantage of being overwhelmingly more popular than those of any previous phase of socialist development in China. Although the departures from doctrine are demonstrably uncomfortable for many older Marxist leaders, sometimes including Deng, the new measures are being implemented as the most rational way to modernize China in a hurry. In present circumstances, where pragmatism so clearly outweighs ideology, rivals to the current leadership have only limited opportunities to attack. China's present stability is, nevertheless, far from solid; in fact, quite vulnerable.

The greatest threat is the complexity of administering so many people during a period of difficult change, with a ruling structure that has yet to pass the test of survivability and with a bureaucracy that is far too big, inadequately educated, and too self assuming. In fact, the quality of the administrative structure remains the Achilles' heel of the leadership. Current reforms may help ease the problem, but only if China can quickly devise new mechanisms of a more self regulatory nature to replace bureaucratic fiat and the mass of old controls. For both practical and ideological reasons, China cannot sacrifice the principle of equity to complete deregulation and all-out competition. Ways will have to be found, for example, to subsidize poorer areas without returning to the kind of egalitarianism that would negate the incentive for better-endowed areas, such as Shanghai, to pull even further ahead. The scope for individual initiative will have to be expanded, without allowing the wide variations of income and conspicuous consumption that would create very serious tensions in a society that has not yet forgotten all its propaganda lessons. Corruption will have to be contained to prevent it from destroying one of the most basic gains of the revolution. In a related way, the pace of foreign exposure will have to be modulated if the excesses of an increasingly hedonistic population are not to play into the hands of conservative leaders who deeply fear the "spiritual pollution" they periodically decry. For the next decade at least, these problems will probably be more vexing for the authorities than pressures for greater pluralism and democratic institutions.

No one has the capacity to determine China's prospects for coping with these problems. Setbacks are almost inevitable given the complexity of the effort to introduce a freer, less centralized, and more market-oriented economy. Some have already occurred, particularly the overheating of the economy, problems with price reform, and abuse of new liberty by local authorities. If these multiply, they would open the leadership to much more serious attack than it suffers today. But stability would be most seriously challenged if the reforms were to run out of control, for example, through spiraling inflation, leading to reversals and uncertainty that would play into the hands of leadership rivals. The challenge would be compounded if it were to occur during the delicate period of the next leadership succession without the deterrent prestige of Deng to fend off critics. Foreign policies, especially the Taiwan issue, could run into difficulties, complicating matters even further. Such a worst-case scenario would be conducive to political maneuver and perhaps to demagogic manipulation of popular frustration. If so, another costly period of confusion could occur at the expense of the Chinese people and China's neighbors. At a minimum, China's modernization campaign would lose its élan and coherence; but even if the nation's mood turned sour, a return to the Cultural Revolution seems highly unlikely and even a return to socialist orthodoxy would probably be short-lived. For Northeast Asian stability, however, the damage would be a major tear.

Taiwan

Domestic instability in Taiwan could have an effect quite disproportionate to the island's size, because events of recent history have tied it so closely to the United States. Although Taiwan's vulnerabilities are numerous and serious, its prospects for relatively stable survival are better than fair—an impressive prognosis, since the Republic of China's identity is under challenge by Chinese on both sides of the Taiwan Straits and complicated by lack of diplomatic recognition in most of the world. But it is not surprising in the light of Taiwan's strengths, including the capacity of its people to function vigorously without a very clear blueprint of the future.

Whereas the existence of the Taiwan Straits, maintenance of a credible defensive capability, and U.S. support have protected Taiwan's security, the island's domestic stability has depended critically on its economic performance and careful handling of delicate issues. Most likely, the economy will be able to go on playing this stabilizing function. Taiwan could, of course, be badly hurt by adverse developments abroad, because exports constitute such a huge percentage of its GNP. It will, moreover, face more competition from the PRC and other less-developed countries in labor-intensive exports and from Korea, Hong Kong, and others in higher technology industries. But there is no apparent reason why Taiwan will not be able to cope effectively.

Politically, however, Taiwan must undergo a series of adjustments, difficult at any time but especially so in the context of political succession to Chiang Ching-kuo. The first set of adjustments involve the balance of power between the relatively small "mainland" element which still controls the governing structure, and the far larger indigenous "Taiwanese" element of the population. To be sure, a considerable adjustment has already occurred, and much more has been promised. The Kuomintang no longer dominates virtually all aspects of society. As in the army and security services, while leadership control is still monopolized by mainlanders, the overwhelming majority of Kuomintang members and officers are now Taiwanese. Almost all elected officials, including the vice president, are Taiwanese, as are the majority of effective members of legislative organs. Taiwanese constitute the business class and dominate most aspects of the economy. More important over the long run, sharp lines between the two communities are blurring as a result of inter-marriage, education, and common experience.

While these developments have softened the bitter antagonism of the 1950s, they have not obscured the fact that the mainlanders retain ultimate control of almost every facet of the ruling structure. Taiwanese resent this, and it is an obvious threat to stability. Pressures for political liberalization intensify the difficulty. Due to communal concerns, but even more by the desires of an increasingly affluent and sophisticated society, there is much pressure for more representative government, freer expression, less political surveillance, and freedom to organize formal political opposition. Although government authorities have been able to control this pressure, partly through a program of slow—but recently accelerated—liberalization, it clearly complicates the already delicate issue of political succession.

Chiang Ching-kuo has been an exceptional leader, widely feared before coming into power, yet so widely respected today that his demise is anticipated with genuine anxiety by Taiwanese as well as mainlanders. The most stable variety of succession would be arrangements that signified a further shift of power toward the Taiwanese, stopping short, however, of moves alarming to the mainlander element on the island or provoking the considerable anxiety of the PRC that the Taiwanese might lead Taiwan toward juridical independence of China. Even though diehard elements could conceivably try to block an adequate adjustment, a degree of accommodation is likely, probably through arrangements where symbolic changes are greater than real ones and where power is shared by a group in which Taiwanese will be well represented. The pattern of Chiang's senior appointments seems to point this way, although he may be overestimating the willingness of the Taiwanese to content themselves with symbols.

Measured by Taiwan's great capacity for evolutionary change over the last three decades, these further changes should be manageable. Extremists on both sides could endanger the process, especially if it were to coincide with a difficult phase of the political liberalization program. Assuming, however, that the economy continues to perform reasonably well, radical tendencies on the Taiwanese side should be moderated by the large stake the people have in the island's accomplishments, while conservative and reactionary tendencies among the controlling elite should be constrained by the Taiwanese majority in the ranks of the party, government, police, security services, and armed forces. All groups, moreover, seem quite aware that a major domestic upheaval would jeopardize their stand in relation to the PRC.

The second set of adjustments would involve Taiwan's identity and relation to the mainland. The common, and not incorrect, approach to this issue is to estimate the likelihood of a serious effort to modify Taiwan's international legal status, ranging from the radical concept of declaring independence from China to the idea of formally giving up Taiwan's empty claims to exercise sovereignty over the mainland but retaining its identity as part of China. If the so-called "independence" option were to boil up as a major issue in Taiwan, it would have a most unsettling effect. Mainlanders on the island would see it as revolutionary, threatening to emasculate the ruling structure, while the PRC would presumably mount an all-out campaign to prevent the loss of a Chinese province. Fortunately, Taiwan seems unlikely to attempt such an effort in the foreseeable future. Quite possibly, a majority of the population would put independence high on their wish list but realistically, more and more of them seem to appreciate that they will have to live indefinitely with their Chinese identity, largely because of opposition to independence among mainlanders on Taiwan as well as from the United States and PRC.

Less radical changes in Taiwan's status, which also do not seem very likely, would not necessarily pose a major threat to stability in that some arrangements might be consistent with the probable evolution of domestic politics and would offer less of a target for PRC objections. In any event, this question of international identity is likely to remain a function of domestic developments, not a determinant of them.

As a practical matter, Taiwan's internal conditions may be more profoundly affected by another less dramatic and frequently overlooked aspect of the identity problem, namely how the government and people of Taiwan relate over a substantial period to the reality of China, particularly if the PRC refrains from serious threats to Taiwan and continues its own domestic reform programs. Quite possibly, the impact of a "reforming mainland China" in Taiwan will not undermine the government's firm opposition to formal negotiations with the PRC, but it may very well feed sentiment favoring a more relaxed approach to China in trade, travel, sports, and other unofficial contacts. PRC reversion to a threatening posture would negate this effect, as would a reversion to hard-line policies within China. Short of these developments, however, the government in Taiwan may eventually come under considerable pressure to adopt a live-and-let-live policy of coexistence with the PRC.

Japan

Only brief discussion is warranted in the case of Japan, whose solid domestic stability makes the search for vulnerabilities an exercise in manipulating improbable scenarios. Of all the contemporary societies in Northeast Asia, Japan seems to have been the most successful in adopting a domestic structure suitable to its political, economic, social, and cultural needs. Its elaborate process of developing consensus strikes some outsiders as slow and cumbersome, but the system has been remarkably effective in protecting the country from error as it has shifted step by step from its reclusive post-occupation role to its present major power status. Similarly, conservative dominance of the political structure, while not free from abuse and corruption, has not obstructed democratic practice or constructive evolution of policy. Significantly, Japanese opposition parties have had to shift toward Liberal Democratic Party positions, suggesting the government has effective mechanisms for staying in tune with major trends of public opinion. As a result, Japan, unlike other countries of the region, has not been faced with potentially chaotic political succession. Granting that Japanese voters may not be endeared forever to rule monopolized by the LDP, they are not likely to abandon lightly either the policies or structures that have served them so well.

Parallel to and to some extent influenced by the stable centrist pattern of domestic politics, Japan has in many ways become the pivot country for regional cooperation. Even its continuing substantial inhibitions against regional military relationships are diminishing. The passage of time, new generations entering the political arena, and a virtually perfect safety record have permitted Japanese governments to be less hyper-cautious about constitutional restraints, while the ideological character of opposition has faded. Although a palpable sense of threat from abroad has not existed, security concerns and foreign relations have been very much involved in this process. Japan's friendly relationship with China and the build-up of Soviet military forces in East Asia have been most important. Relatively comfortable acceptance, so far, by other Asians of Japan's expanded defense capability has also been helpful. The result is a complex, evolving equilibrium of domestic and foreign factors that allows scope for a considerable Japanese regional role.

The greatest vulnerabilities in this stable structure are foreign rather than domestic, first and foremost because of Japan's dependence on the outside world for resources and markets. A massive wave of protectionism in the United States and Europe, leading to retaliation and trade wars, could lower Japan's standard of living, take the luster off conservative leadership, undercut many of Japan's basic policies, and perhaps stimulate unhelpful nationalistic behavior. Growth of the latter would rapidly antagonize other powers and reactivate powerful fears of Japan, now largely latent. The foreign and domestic consequences could be profound. Souring of Japan's relationship with China—whether caused by events in Japan or China—would reintroduce domestic strains in Japan, perhaps affecting the U.S. base structure. Either a more threatening or a more accommodating Soviet policy toward Japan could complicate events within Japan, although only marginally. Generally, no external development over the next few years seems likely to undermine Japan's domestic stability or foreign policy orientations—with the possible and worrisome exception of major friction with the United States over trade matters.

South Korea

For many, South Korea remains a kind of dangerous vortex in Northeast Asia because of the war that left the peninsula divided, continuing tensions, the security entanglement of four outside powers, and a record for dramatic events as well as considerable turmoil. These are inescapable realities, yet South Korea has managed to pick itself up from wartime rubble to develop into one of the area's most impressive societies. Despite periodic turbulence, its government and other structures function effectively to ensure national defense, economic development, and equitable distribution. They do so, moreover, in a society that has high standards of education as well as great social and economic mobility. The country's reputation for drive and economic momentum has now spread through much of the world. Fading ideology and growing self-confidence have led the ROK to seek more peaceful forms of coexistence with the DPRK and a cooperative relationship with China and the Soviet Union, unimaginable 15 years ago, all with a distinctly beneficial effect on regional stability.

Although the ROK is not the precarious entity pictured by its detractors, its society is vulnerable. The most obvious danger is military attack from North Korea, a danger that requires costly defense expenditures, constant vigilance, and a degree of dependence on the United States that creates problems of its own. Since North Korea has been effectively deterred and restrained, however, South Korea's problems are more likely to be of non-military origin. The most serious is dependence on exports for the performance that underlies Korea's economic success and, equally important, permits Korean politics to survive potentially destructive vibrations. This vulnerability will diminish over time if the Korean domestic economy grows, but like Taiwan, South Korea has an extraordinary stake in essential continuity of the present international trading system. Koreans have every reason to worry excessively about global recession and American protectionism.

The ROK's most dramatic vulnerability is its political system, which remains too authoritarian and too restrictive for many of its citizens and has yet to permit a peaceful succession of political power. The problem is sometimes exaggerated. The almost constant political turmoil among Korean students is not necessarily indicative of basic political health or the national mood. The Korean bureaucracy has acquired the sophistication and stature to compensate for much of the disruption at times of trouble. And recent Korean governments, for all their problems of establishing legitimacy, have done well in meeting the prime demands of the majority of people for security and welfare. Outsiders also view the shortcomings of Korea's political system too abstractly. The authoritarian and centralizing tendencies, which characterize both government and opposition political behavior, have a long, almost unbroken tradition that is to some degree a response to the quarrelsome, combative quality of Korean political culture. In short, Koreans—in both North and South Korea—have a relatively high tolerance for regimentation and roughness.

Nevertheless, the South Korean political system will have to be relaxed if it is to accommodate the demands of a rapidly growing middle class and the complexity of a modern society dependent on external relationships. While the odds are that it will, progress may be uneven, increasing the risk of trouble and the cost of change. The most critical element of change will be the empirical evolution of a nonviolent process of leadership succession that accommodates a reasonably broad spectrum of political views. The overwhelming majority of Koreans, including law-and-order-minded Army officers, agrees emphatically on this point. Koreans know they cannot afford the risks of another succession by military coup or a less violent succession that abuses constitutional requirements and popular views. They see the need for restraint on both sides to head off the kind of confrontation that might precipitate such moves, and this sentiment appears to be serving as a constraint today. But the test has yet to come in a society where political compromise is rare and the army, police, and security forces are checked mostly by the restraint of their leaders and only vaguely by the diffuse reactions of the populace. Prospects for an untroubled presidential election in 1988 are, unfortunately, poor.[1]

A fourth and hopefully diminishing vulnerability involves a complex of psychological and cultural factors. Fear of North Korean military attack and political subversion has been promoted among South Koreans for over three decades, reflecting both genuine belief and convenient rationalization for political shortcomings. Although this sense of threat has been deeply embedded in the Korean psyche, softening reactions to authoritarian rule, it has not played a particularly positive role in South Korea's modern development, which has occurred *despite* the threat. In any event, worry about an external threat is diminishing. Deterrence appears to most Koreans to have worked, and few of them feel any imminent threat. With generations passing, memories of the Korean War are inevitably fading. While many South Koreans look on the current round of North/South contacts rather cynically, they clearly favor the interchange and hope it will reduce tensions. South Korea's sense of competition with the North, which has increased with pride over recent accomplishments, may now play a more significant motivating role than fear of war. Ideology has never been of much importance in South Korea, except that anti-Communism has reinforced practical reasons for vigilance against the North. Erosion of this role would seem more than offset by gains in flexibility in dealing with North Korea, China, and the Soviet Union. The excessive zeal with which Koreans often approach challenges is a potential liability, largely as a compounder of troubles from other sources. This national trait, which is also reflected in the nation's drive, may cause setbacks but is unlikely to do serious damage unless it were fed into an emotional issue.

South Korea's rapid development has generated a degree of self-confidence that has drawn it into major challenges, such as hosting the 1988 Olympics and initiating greatly eased relations with Japan, and that has permitted Seoul to take bold initiatives toward Pyongyang. These are major benefits. An even greater potential gain is that self-confidence may offset the liabilities inherent in South Korea's dependence on the United States for security and prosperity. Without self-confidence, this dependence, which tugs hard at Korean pride and leads to unfavorable comparisons with the North, could engender growth of more and more vicious anti-Americanism and Korean chauvinism. A self-confident ROK should be able to cope successfully with its dependency syndrome while still keeping its self-esteem short of hubris.

North Korea

North Korea's domestic situation is elusive in the absence of reliable information or, frequently, any information. On the basis of inferred knowledge, the society should have fractured long ago under the weight of a huge military burden, a personality cult that should embarrass even loyalists, a lackluster economy, and numerous policy failures, most prominently the murderous attack on the South Korean presidential party in Rangoon. The DPRK has, nevertheless, survived without signs of any massive discontent. Many factors may be responsible, including a charismatic leader who has developed great nationalistic appeal as a result of his handling of the unification issue as well as relations with China and the Soviet Union. North Korea's economy, although dragging, has performed well enough to give North Koreans a fairly high standard of living, vastly better than in the early postwar years. Opposition is undoubtedly kept down to size by a ruthless administration that monopolizes all sources of information and compartmentalizes society. Pumped up by propaganda, fear of the South has probably dampened efforts to challenge the system. And Korean tolerance for regimentation must be a major factor holding the strange society together.

There are, nevertheless, at least three clear signs of strain, difficulty, and possible change. First, the North Korean economy is not growing fast enough to sustain military outlays and a sense of progress among the people. The contrast with the South is increasingly painful, and the leadership seems to recognize the need for foreign business connections, especially the infusion of modern technology. Second, both China and the Soviet Union have been unwilling to assist North Korea's capacity for military adventure. Despite Sino–Soviet rivalry, they have limited their rewards to the North. Soviet supply of MiG-23 fighter aircraft, a move delayed long after equivalent aircraft were introduced in the U.S./ROK inventory, is unlikely to alter this stance, although the Soviets may gain some leverage from it. China has applied obvious pressure both to deter the DPRK from adventure and to push it toward more moderate policies. Third, a difficult leadership succession is in process in Pyongyang. Beijing and Moscow have had great trouble accepting Kim's dynastic succession and worry that it may not hold. No voice of objection is ever heard from within North Korea, but it can reasonably be assumed that there is discontent that may well manifest itself after Kim Il-song departs.

Fragmentary signs occasionally lead to the inference that these and other questions, particularly policy toward the South, are the source of serious debate within the governing elite, conceivably with factions that compete for Kim's support. There is no way of detecting whether the army and technocrats are divided in any significant way or what the ultimate direction will be, but at least some grudging tactical adjustments toward more practical policies seem to be taking place, in a pattern suggesting lack of unanimity if not struggle among the power elite. North Korean interest in contacts with the South is the most obvious facet of this change, which may eventually develop momentum. Some movement in this direction while Kim is still alive might stabilize the situation after his demise. In any event, it is hard to see how DPRK policies could persist indefinitely without significant adjustments in the changing context around North Korea.

South Korean developments, which over the longer run may prove beneficial in bringing about change in the North, have, in the short run, increased the North's sense of rivalry and anxiety. These could intensify to the point of paranoia about the South, blocking change and even encouraging desperate measures. To some extent the matter will be beyond Seoul's influence, but it would help if the ROK were to resist the temptation to build its armed forces beyond "equivalence" with the DPRK and were to avoid highlighting the North's inferior status. Such restraint would, unfortunately, run against the grain for many.

CONCLUSIONS

Viewed historically, domestic stability and developing regional relationships in Northeast Asia have improved to a point unimaginable 15 to 20 years ago. At that time military conflict seemed far more likely, both in Korea and along the Sino–Soviet border; China was in turmoil; economic prowess in South Korea and Taiwan had not yet manifested its capacity to change the complexion of those societies; and Japan's steady course was far less certain than today. Viewed in a global perspective, Northeast Asia has been responsible for a disproportionate share of the economic transformation that has finally demonstrated the importance of East Asia to Americans and Europeans. Many factors underlie this extraordinary development, among them the skills of the Northeast Asian people, the military and economic role of the United States, and crucial changes in the region's balance of power. Although the pattern may get more complicated or be disrupted for periods, Northeast Asia's strength and stability will almost surely continue to grow.

The speed with which it has emerged as a major factor on the world scene is not matched by the strength of its defenses against adversity or the solidity of its political institutions. No other region of the world is as dependent on the continuity of the world trading system. The American market, which has been critically important to the export-driven growth of Japan, South Korea, and Taiwan, has already demonstrated that, while not saturated, it will no longer absorb imports at the rate of previous years. The diversification of trade to other areas has been difficult, compounded by the entry of new competitors, including China. A prolonged, severe global recession could jeopardize much of the progress achieved.

Of less immediate concern, Northeast Asia's stability is based on global and regional factors in the balance of power that are not immutable. The triangular relationship involving the United States, the Soviet Union, and China is unlikely to change radically, but even modest changes could have adverse effects in a place such as Korea or Taiwan. Japan's growth toward major power status faces obstacles, especially from neighbors, including China, who are comfortable with current balances but still deeply suspicious of Japan's power and intentions. A surge of nationalistic feelings in the area could inflame the problem.

Most serious, however, is the threat to the region from domestic political systems that have depended heavily on economic development to offset political failings as well as frequent resort to the coercive powers of the state. With the exception of Japan, no nation in the area has either reliable mechanisms for leadership succession or ways of balancing the ambivalent desires of their peoples for security and freedom. As the area continues to develop, pressures for more pluralistic, less authoritarian regimes will intensify, while governments may be slow to recognize the reality. The area, thus, seems likely to go through periodic turbulence which could be dangerous, although hopefully not disastrous.

NOTE

1. With the advantage of hindsight, some readers might validly argue that this assessment, originally written in the summer of 1985, understated the potential for student-led popular unrest as manifested during the summer of 1987. Similarly, they might reasonably take a more sanguine view of the prospects for a successful leadership transition as a result of reversed positions and constitutional changes that have occurred in the wake of the popular unrest.

7

Korea: A Tricycle in Transition

by Hongkoo Lee

Forty years after the end of World War II, Korea remains one of the few cases in which the legacies of the war and the changes in peace are juxtaposed in a highly uncertain manner. If the end of the Yalta era and the consequent transition from a postwar adjustment to an emergence of a new international order was a worldwide phenomenon, then Korea could not escape from such an historical trend. There are indeed certain indications in both North and South Korea that seem to reflect the fact that the two systems are currently in a stage of critical experiment for restructuring and reorientation. At the same time, however, Korea remains a divided nation, 40 years after the peninsula was artificially partitioned by the United States and Soviet Union. Korea thus represents one of the uglier scars of the Yalta era, and the prospects for unification continue to be discouraging. In the meantime, the tensions resulting from the cold and hot wars of the past four decades are perpetuated on a semi-permanent basis by over one million soldiers lined up on both sides of the demilitarized zone (DMZ), making Korea a most dangerous area, where the possibility of a major military conflict seems quite high. In short, while Korea as a divided nation remains tense, important changes are going on both in and around it.

In this brief essay, the current situation in Korea will be examined with an accent on change rather than continuity. From such a perspective, Korea can be described as a tricycle in transition; the first wheel representing the domestic changes; the second, the international environment; and the third, the relationship between the two Koreas.

THE FIRST WHEEL: DOMESTIC PROBLEMS

During the past four decades, historical circumstances forced Korea to experiment simultaneously with two sets of modernization drives in the peninsula. In the North, a special blend of communism has almost totally transformed both the physical and social organization of that half of Korea; in the meantime, in the South a modernization drive based on an open-market, or mixed-economy, model has made this half of Korea one of the prime examples of so-called newly industrializing countries. It is not necessary here to evaluate the relative success or failure of those two experiments. What should be noted, however, is that those experiments, which have succeeded in making gigantic transformations in both Koreas, seem to have reached the point where major structural changes and policy reorientations are needed to sustain the modernization drive. The two Koreas, each in its own way, seem to be facing the limits of growth and the necessity to rechart the future course of development. These limitations and situational requirements are not the property of any one dimension, such as the economy, but are comprehensive in range, organically related to all aspects of society. Thus the discussion on the present need for restructuring and reorientation in both Koreas has to proceed in a synthetic manner, examining not only the parts but also the whole of the transition process.

Given the extreme scarcity of reliable information about North Korea, it is somewhat hazardous to attempt a diagnosis of the situation there, but one can begin with an observation that North Korea is perhaps the most successful case of a totalitarian experiment in modern history. The term "totalitarian" is not used here in any pejorative sense; instead, it is employed to describe an all-out effort by a political system to achieve rapid modernization through total control and planning of nearly all aspects of society through the absolute authority of one leader, one party, and one ideology. The achievement of the North in rebuilding and modernizing its system following the total destruction of the country during the Korean War has been a considerable one. Either as a socialist experiment or as a totalitarian venture, the North Korean system has demonstrated in the last three decades no mean degree of efficiency and corresponding success in material production as well as social control. What is it then which seems to force North Korea to seriously consider a reorientation of its basic policies, or at least its foreign policy?

There appear to be three basic reasons which, separately or collectively, contribute to the necessity for change. First, a heavy reliance on regimented hard labor and an emphasis on autarky could no longer be considered the most effective policies for sustained growth and modernization. To reconstruct the war-torn country and to increase the production of agricultural and other basic commodities, regimented hard work under central planning and direction was quite effective. However, as the system began to require more sophisticated technologies and management, regimented labor alone could not produce the required growth, and overly centralized planning and control may have been a hindrance to development. Isolation from the international economic system further aggravated matters, because it grossly limited the inflow of capital and technology that could help to remedy the problems brought about by too much regimentation and central planning. In the last number of years, the North Korean leaders have become, it seems, acutely aware of the weakness of their orthodox strategy for sustained growth. Perhaps the modernization drive in China has made a strong impression on their minds.

Second, there seems to be a limit to the ability to keep the system and the people in a semi-permanent atmosphere of emergency. The Korean War ended with the ceasefire in the summer of 1953, but ever since then North Korea has effectively maintained the wartime total mobilization of the population, justifying this by the need to defend the country from aggression by South Korea and the United States, to prepare for liberation of the South, and ultimately to achieve national unification. Given the changing international environment—for example, the cordiality between the United States and China, the relaxation of tensions between the United States and the Soviet Union, and the new developments in North–South relations—it might become increasingly difficult to sustain the same degree of enthusiasm and responsiveness from the people for such regimentation. The point may have been reached in the tolerances of the public and the system where a readjustment is required to maintain vitality.

Third, the politics of succession in socialist countries often provide momentum for significant changes in policy and style, and North Korea is no exception. The dynastic succession of power in North Korea is almost complete, and it serves no useful purpose to wonder how this could happen in a socialist state or to ridicule it as a feudal practice lacking common sense. It is happening, and it does make sense if it is seen in terms of the preservation of an effectively functioning totalitarian system. The new leadership could be more sensitive than the old one to the need to reorient the system in order to remedy the current problems, and it may see this as a useful way to legitimize and strengthen its power.

For the reasons cited above, North Korea can be considered to be in the process of transition. The extent and direction of change will, however, be partly dependent on developments in South Korea and the international environment. If South Korea and its allies proceed on the assumption that the North is, in fact, in a period of transition, this might have the effect of further encouraging or accelerating the changes there.

During the past four decades, South Korea has pursued modernization on two fronts. First, it tried to promote rapid economic growth by adopting an open-market mixed economy, closely tied to the international economic system. Second, it attempted to nurture a democratic political system on the Western model. On the first front, South Korea is often cited as a success story, and there are more than enough facts and statistics to justify this. On the second front, however, judgment could be mixed. The Korean effort to institutionalize democracy could not be called an absolute failure nor characterized as a success. It is the clear discrepancy between the performances on the two fronts that provides the reason for uncertainty about the future development of South Korea. Success in capitalism may be a necessary condition, but certainly not a sufficient one to ensure success in a democracy.

It is not appropriate to engage here in a detailed discussion of the problems inherent in the institution and operation of democracy in South Korea. It can merely be noted that while the economy and society have gone through tremendous qualitative and quantitative changes in the last 40 years, political modalities and practices have changed very little. In this may lie one obvious cause of the problem: society has become much more pluralistic and complex, but the political system has stayed more or less monolithic and simplistic. Such an inadequacy is partly due to historical reasons, partly to circumstances. The disruption of the body politic during the colonial era deprived Koreans of an opportunity to develop modern political institutions and practices through normal process. Forty years of national division and confrontation have necessitated the maintenance of an extraordinarily large military establishment, which has resulted in an inordinate amount of military influence over the political process. These reasons notwithstanding, it might be the judgments, or misjudgments, of the national leadership that have further aggravated political difficulties during this time.

The judgments or misjudgments might have stemmed from a lack of commitment to the norm of popular political participation and from a less than adequate understanding of popular support as crucial to legitimacy. With such shaky commitment and understanding, the successive national leaderships might have entertained an illusion that marked success in vital fields—national security, economic development, social welfare, and international prestige—could substitute or compensate for a failure to accommodate political participation. This is a trap into which successful bureaucratic authoritarianism can easily fall, and, unfortunately, successive leaders in South Korea have paid scant attention to it. When things go well, the danger of falling into such a trap seems minimal; but when signs of possible crisis appear, it becomes quite urgent to see that there is no substitute for popular political participation and that it is therefore important to try to find ways to accommodate it. South Korea today may be in such a period of transition. But what are the signs of possible crisis?

It would certainly be an exaggeration to say that the Korean economy is about to face a serious crisis. In spite of some difficulties, South Korea was expected to have a growth rate close to 7 percent in 1985, lower than originally forecast but still respectable by international standards. (In fact, the growth rate was 12.5 percent in 1986.) What makes Koreans in general unsure about the future of the economy is the pervasive feeling that the good days could easily come to an abrupt end. The job of diagnosing the state of the economy should be left to the economists. However, there are at least five factors that together seem to work against any excessive optimism and produce doubts in the minds of the people:

1. The sheer size of foreign debt, $43 billion at the end of 1984, makes interest payments an increasingly heavy burden.
2. The outlook for Korean exports is clouded by the growing protectionist tendencies in international markets, particularly in the United States, which is, for all practical purposes, the locomotive for the Korean economy.
3. The industrial structure is showing its limitations, while the prospect of acquiring technologies, particularly high technologies, is uncertain.
4. The financial structure of business and industries as well as the national structure, which contains a large underground economy, show unmistakable signs of weakness and malfunction.
5. Labor problems seem to be surfacing after a long period of being artificially submerged.

The last factor is especially troublesome because it has not only direct political ramifications but also mutually incompatible tendencies. Put more simply, low wages and unemployment are the causes of popular unrest, but the price of labor-intensive Korean products is higher than those from countries with even lower wages, thus hurting Korean exports in competitive markets. The prospects of an effective policy to increase wages and employment seem, therefore, less than bright.

Despite the problems and limitations cited above, the economy will perform fairly well, given its excellent past track record. But a crisis, to repeat the point made above, is sometimes a product of psychological factors peculiar to a given country and a given situation. Koreans have enjoyed an annual growth rate of around 10 percent for nearly two decades, and they are used to it. Growth rates of 5 percent or 6 percent are acceptable, but one lower than 4 percent could precipitate a psychological crisis, if not a structural one as well. A series of protectionist measures and legislation by the executive and legislative branches of the U.S. government have had a shock effect, shaking the confidence of Koreans in the future of their economy and in the strength of the United States–Korea alliance. Accordingly, the leadership could not take the symptoms of crisis lightly and will most probably try to devise measures to bring major changes in the structure and operation of the Korean economy.

The worrisome economic difficulties have to be seen in conjunction with the unsatisfactory development of means to resolve social and political conflicts. During rapid modernization, it is not unusual for pluralistic and centrifugal forces to produce conflicting claims and opposing interests, and the Korean situation has to be understood in this light. What makes it especially unsafe, however, is an extremely slow, if not retarded, development of mechanisms for conflict resolution. History, notably the disruption of national political life during the 35 years of colonial rule, has deprived Korea of most traditional means of resolving conflicts, particularly in social and economic settings, and the modernization process of the last few decades has failed to create new methods to fill the vacuum. The current unrest among students, workers, and other so-called dissidents is in part the result of this failure.

Perhaps most important is the lack of a functioning elite. Everyone in Korea agrees there is a need for dialogue, negotiation, and compromise. But who will conduct them and how? First of all, it is very difficult to identify the elite who represent or have influence in certain sectors. Second, there are almost no functioning channels for communication, negotiation and compromise. In short, there is no infrastructure by which to resolve the social, economic, and political conflicts in South Korea today. It is, for example, impossible to identify elites representing the university communities and labor movements, largely because successive national leaders have not recognized the importance of nurturing them and bringing them together into a functioning body. Instead, a bureaucratic elite with authoritarian tastes has dominated and monopolized national affairs. If social unrest grows, the government will increasingly face the need to resort to extra-governmental mechanisms to resolve conflicts. A crucial question is whether such mechanisms will be available.

What makes the task of promoting both economic growth and political stability extremely difficult is that the contemporary political scene in Korea, including voting patterns in national elections, is embedded with anti-government sentiment and behavior. Most political commentators in and outside Korea expressed surprise at the strong showing of the opposition parties in the parliamentary election held in February 1985. In fact, the ratio of votes split between the government party and the opposition parties in 1985 was about the same as that in the 1978 election. It seems a constant in Korean electoral politics that a sizable majority of people are inclined to vote against the incumbent government party, not necessarily to support a particular opposition party or candidate, but often to express their displeasure and dissatisfaction with the government. Given this tradition of opposition in the Korean political culture, there seems to be a built-in tendency among the incumbents to circumvent the fair democratic election process sometimes openly, at other times more delicately. As the promised peaceful transfer of power in 1988 gets nearer, the political burden of finding a successful resolution of this dilemma is undoubtedly becoming heavier. All in all, it can be concluded that South Korea is also in a period of transition, to prevent an economic and political crisis and to enter into a new phase of national development.

THE SECOND WHEEL: THE INTERNATIONAL ENVIRONMENT

If domestic developments constitute the first and front wheel of the Korean tricycle, the international environment of the Korean peninsula is the second wheel, with the North–South relationship as the third. If nothing else, the geopolitical situation alone has throughout history intertwined the fate of Korea with the fortunes of the surrounding powers and the period since the end of World War II has been no exception. Some major developments or new tendencies which seem to have direct relevance to the Korean situation are therefore discussed below.

Since the inauguration of President Reagan, the American commitment to honor its security treaty with South Korea has been reaffirmed and reinforced. The Korean policy of the United States has in fact been fairly steady and the policies of the Reagan administration do not represent any significant change from the past. But the short-lived controversy about the proposed withdrawal of U.S. ground forces from Korea during the early days of the Carter administration and the uneasy period in U.S.–Korean relations that followed have made the present state of the relationship look better than ever. President Reagan's policy of building up the military readiness of the United States to check and balance the Soviet Union has also had positive effects, psychologically and strategically, further fortifying the U.S. commitment to the security and stability of South Korea. It might be reasonable to assume that the effectiveness of deterrence against North Korea has improved accordingly.

What has surprised Koreans, perhaps both in the South and North, is the rapid progress of a cooperative relationship between the United States and China. It is not appropriate here to try to explain the reasons for such a rapid improvement in Sino–American relations. What is of most interest is the degree to which the United States and China seem to share common views about the need to maintain peace or to avoid war in the Korean peninsula. This is certainly the most constructive development since 1945 in the international environment of Korea, in terms of the possibilities it opens up for concrete moves to resolve the difficulties and tensions that result from the division of the peninsula. South Korea has welcomed this development of common ground between the United States and China and has tried to gear its foreign and unification policies accordingly to utilize the new opportunities that are presented. North Korea, too, could not ignore the development, and various North Korean moves clearly indicate that Pyongyang is also trying to reexamine positions in the light of the change.

In the meantime, it is Japan, more than any other power, that has made remarkable progress in upgrading its image and position in relation to the Korean peninsula in recent years. As the defeated power in the Pacific War, Japan was relegated to a secondary role when it came to participating in international discussions of the Korean question. The United States and the Soviet Union originally partitioned Korea. China, through the intervention in the Korean War, secured a legitimate claim to a position on the Korean question. Now, Prime Minister Nakasone, by skillfully engineering a number of diplomatic moves to improve Japanese–Korean relations, including the exchange of state visits by the heads of the two governments, seems to have succeeded in elevating the status of Japan to that of a primary actor in the Korean question. Such a role fits the traditional Japanese position in the region and may also be in harmony with an increase in nationalistic sentiment in Japan. Koreans are, of course, quite aware of this and are in the process of sorting out the various implications of the increased Japanese role.

It can safely be said that China, Japan and the United States seem to share a common interest in maintaining peace in the Pacific region in general and the Korean peninsula in particular. What of the remaining power in the region, the Soviet Union? There is nothing to suggest that the Soviet Union is against the maintenance of peace either in the Pacific or in Korea. It might be fair, however, to ask what the political dividends are for the Soviet Union in sustaining the status quo, or the current state of international relations, in Asia. While Soviet military power has increased rapidly in recent years, its political influence has not; hence, the Soviet Union may be dissatisfied with its position in the region. If such is the case, how might Moscow move to remedy the situation? In searching for a plausible answer to this question, the steady improvement in Soviet–North Korean relations in recent years should be taken into consideration. It is important to emphasize that the recent improvements in these relations are most clearly indicated in the area of military cooperation. The transfer of MiG-23 fighter aircraft, the visits of Soviet naval contingents to North Korean ports as far south as Wonsan, and the reported overflights of Soviet aircraft across North Korea from the East Sea to the Yellow Sea are cases in point. It might be too early to draw definite conclusions about these Soviet actions, but South Korea is, of course, gravely concerned about them and is trying to assess their implications for various scenarios. It could be the Soviet Union more than any other power that holds the key to the future developments in the international environment of Korea, and, in fact, to developments within the peninsula as well. A dialogue between the United States and the Soviet Union, including summit talks, could open a new possibility for the Korean question.

THE THIRD WHEEL: NORTH-SOUTH RELATIONS

The most significant development in the relationship between the two Koreas in recent months is the resumption of direct talks after a long break. Since there are to be a series of dialogues—the Red Cross talks, economic talks, and preliminary talks between parliamentarians—it seems wise to withhold any comment or prediction on future prospects until they are further advanced. At the moment it seems there is a good chance for them to continue. A number of reasons support such an assessment.

North Korea does seem prepared to pursue a two-front strategy in conducting its foreign and unification policies. As noted earlier, the leadership seems to be aware of the limits of its totalitarian and autarkic development policies and of the necessity to open up its economy and establish some links with the international economic system. At the same time, it has had to accept the fact that China has developed cordial relations with the United States and Japan and is indirectly encouraging North Korea to do the same. If good relations with the United States could be established, this would have the significant effect of undercutting South Korea and promoting the withdrawal of the United States forces from the South. Thus, North Korea has decided to launch a peace offensive aimed primarily at the United States and Japan and only secondarily at South Korea. The North has made its proposal for tripartite talks with the primary objective of establishing relations with the United States and bringing about a troop withdrawal; the resumed talks with South Korea are a tactical move to support the primary objective. Such is the North Korean move on one front.

If the North Korean move on the peace front represents a change of its strategy, its stance on the war front only signifies the continuity of the commitment to national unification by any means. This continuity is partly based on the Vietnam syndrome. The dream of replicating the outcome of the Vietnam War in the Korean peninsula is something that the leadership of North Korea cannot give up. Preparation for a contingency in which a combination of disintegration in the South and a military push from the North could lead to unification seems to have top priority, hence, the continued military build-up and forward deployment of offensive forces. The crucial point to note is that North Korea has not only decided on a two-front strategy but has acquired the military and political capability to execute it. This new development poses a severe test for the South Korean government, which must respond to both the hard and soft policies of the North simultaneously and successfully.

It is South Korea that has, since 1982, repeatedly proposed direct North–South talks at any level, any place, and any time; it is therefore quite natural for the South to welcome the North Korean move to resume the dialogue, irrespective of the suspected motives behind it. There are other practical reasons for the South to enter into direct talks with a positive attitude. First, such talks might enhance the prestige and legitimacy of the South Korean government at home and abroad. Second, the direct contacts might provide occasions to strengthen the national consensus within South Korea on some of the basic issues confronting the country. Third, a series of successful and continuing talks will be very conducive in producing the stable atmosphere necessary for the 1988 Olympics. These and other reasons seem to induce South Korea to maintain a positive and active position toward North–South talks.

The leadership in South Korea is held by basically pragmatic people who put greater emphasis on survival and success than on any ideological commitment. Given the requirements of a situation that demands some major changes on all three wheels, the chances are that the leadership will try in one way or another to bring about those changes. In the process, with good luck, it might be able to develop a new mode for the politics of accommodation that would enable the tricycle to continue to run, not perfectly but with reasonable steadiness and speed. In the meantime, there is no a priori reason to believe that the emerging leadership in North Korea completely lacks a pragmatic perspective and enthusiasm for change. Perhaps a period of transition in Korea will be witnessed in the coming months and years. Such a transition would not immediately result in Korean unification; however, it would certainly enhance the development toward a national community, or even a commonwealth, which would conserve the tradition and identity of the Korean people and promote the welfare of the people in both parts of the peninsula.

8

The Philippines:
Years Out of Crisis

by Jesus P. Estanislao

The euphoria from the February 1986 revolution has at last simmered down. Except in a few isolated quarters, the sense of expectation that further major upheavals are imminent is gone. Many sectors of Philippine society have started to settle down and dig in for the longer haul. The time for self-congratulation and waiting is ended; the more difficult time for facing up to the facts and decisively grappling with them has begun.

The Aquino government that was installed by the failed election and the successful revolution of February 1986 was confronted with very harsh facts. Political foundations and institutions, after years of unbridled abuse and manipulation, suffered from flawed legitimacy and questioned credibility. The economy was so drained after two decades of kleptocracy and crony capitalism that growth had stopped, development had been reversed, and bankruptcy had become widespread. The underbrush of ideological tendencies that had sprouted during the Marcos era and had been repressed by authoritarian rule came into full bloom once they could bask unobstructedly under the sunshine of freedom.

It came as no surprise that during the first year after the revolution the Philippines appeared to be perched atop a very loose foundation. Any strong wind or false move seemed capable of toppling it down the precipice again. The Marcos loyalists had a new plan to bring the dictator back each time the previous one failed: they always had a new date to which to look forward. A small core of Enrile loyalists within the military have openly advertised themselves as not above plotting a coup and trying to effect it. The communist insurgents and the leaders of various minority factions claiming to have a legitimate grievance against the fledgling government are vociferous and adamant, and once redress could not conform to their impossible demands—which ranged from giving them partial reins of government to total surrender of the government—they returned to the path of violent struggle.

A YEAR OF TRANSITION

A "miracle" helped topple the Marcos dictatorship and install the Aquino government. Perhaps no less than a miracle helped keep it in power, for the forces arrayed against it were formidable and from the standards of ordinary reckoning, impossible to master. After all, President Aquino had branded herself an ordinary "housewife," and Mr. Marcos, during the height of the presidential campaign, condescendingly and chauvinistically taunted her to "get back to the bedroom." Instead, she simply went to work on whatever problems public duty had thrust upon her.

The democratic marginalists, whose vaunted familiarity with constitutional law may have blinded them from seeing through the improprieties that Marcos had inflicted upon the country's fundamental law, were aghast at the declaration of a revolutionary government and the proclamation of a "Freedom Constitution." As though the February 1986 revolution had never occurred, they insisted that President Aquino should serve under the Marcos-imposed 1973 constitution and strike up a modus vivendi with the Marcos rubber stamp parliament, the Batasang Pambansa, which had blatantly disregarded the people's will and connived with Marcos in officially declaring him the winner of a fraudulent presidential election. Unable to deter President Aquino from cutting the country loose from the untenable moorings of Marcos's "democratic" authoritarianism, these marginalists proceeded to state that the foundation for the authority of government had been radically altered, democratic continuity had been breached, and the constitutional basis for Aquino's presidency had been cast adrift in the open sea. Her government was declared unstable.

Because the February revolution made President Aquino a de facto absolute ruler in whose hands all powers of government were concentrated, she tried to move as quickly as possible to rebuild democracy in the Philippines based upon a traditional separation of powers, much as she had promised during the campaign. She appointed a new slate of justices to the Supreme Court, which she vowed would be independent, and the quality of her appointments, which included the more independent justices from the Marcos Supreme Court as well as new faces regarded as luminaries by the legal profession, gave immediate guarantee that her vow was meant to be fulfilled. She abolished the Marcos parliament and appointed an independent commission to draft a new constitution; and deeply impressed by the need to have a new and firm basis for democratic government, she gave the commission a deadline that was too exacting to produce a document outstanding in every respect.

While the commissioners were rushing their draft constitution, critics were debating the propriety of appointing them instead of democratically electing delegates to a constitutional convention. It was imperative to submit the draft constitution to the people for ratification as quickly as possible, but the critics—wrapped up in their purist concerns—would hear nothing of an appointed commission. They did not even wish to clean up the previous padding of the Marcos's electoral lists by a general re-registration of all voters—a process that itself had to take time. Time was also needed to explain the provisions of the draft constitution to the people.

In the end, despite the pressure for a rapid transformation, nine months passed from the time appointments to the Constitutional Commission were made to the final ratification of the proposed draft constitution. Criticisms were given full airing. The campaign leading up to the plebiscite was fully open, and the election itself was unparalleled in the virtual absence of fraud and in the active participation of the electorate. The plebiscite results have now resulted in elections for a new Congress in May 1987 and for all elective local government positions in August 1987. Thus, within 18 months after coming to power, the Aquino government is set to fill the constitutional void left by Marcos and is putting in place a fully functioning democracy.

If action to fill the void in the political arena has been quick and decisive, the program to deal with the economic crisis has been fraught with ambivalence. The overhang from the foreign debt crisis took more than a year to settle, and much of what needed to be done in the economic field was overshadowed by the need to renegotiate successfully the servicing and repayment terms with foreign creditor commercial banks.

Nevertheless, the most pressing domestic economic concerns vied for immediate attention. Unemployment was at 12.8 percent in April of 1986 and remained at a high 11.8 percent in October of the same year, as the economy wallowed in the mire of depression.[1] A high percentage of installed industrial capacity was left idle, and many businesses, particularly large-scale industries, were bankrupt. It was estimated that in the second half of 1986, capacity utilization rates in many industries may have been under 50 percent.[2] The National Treasury was in an equally precarious situation as deficits were piling up. Indeed, the Aquino government was expected to do too much with too little.

A broad consensus quickly formed around the need to get away from the monopolies, the heavy-handed intervention by government, and the autocratic dictation by the presidential palace on economic and financial affairs that were the hallmarks of Marcos's crony capitalism. A more market-oriented framework for economic policy found immediate and ready acceptance. A frantic search for the hidden and not so hidden wealth of Marcos and his cronies was launched by an independent commission armed with extensive powers to retrieve what they could find.

However, while it was easy to come to a quick agreement on the broadest economic priorities and policy framework, the Aquino government appeared to be divided when deciding on more specific approaches. Intense debates, over the posture to take in handling foreign debt and the tempo of import liberalization, took up much of the cabinet's time. There was almost interminable discussion about the need for a growth facility, the temporary use of SGS (Société Generale Surveillance) services to help customs administration, and the use of external auditors in addition to the Commission on Audit for the rehabilitation of the major government financial institutions.

Indeed, the apparently conflicting positions of the country's economic managers gave the impression of drift. Since the fractiousness of the cabinet on major economic issues dominated the newspaper headlines, the perception soon became widespread that a definitive economic program was still being sorted out, and that until this was done, prudence dictated a wait-and-see attitude.

The widespread hesitancy of the business community was aggravated by the restiveness of labor. Strikes appeared to have multiplied, partly encouraged by the well-meant but much misunderstood remarks of the minister of labor, who was perceived to harbor leftist leanings. There were 571 strikes in 1986 versus 371 in 1985. About 3.6 million work-days were consequently lost in 1986 due to strikes, as compared to 2.5 million work-days lost in 1985.[3] Thus, despite the formulation of the broad outlines of an economic program within the first four months of the government's assumption of power, and the subsequent specification of all sectoral programs three months afterwards, the business community had to be cajoled into action and eventually scolded for its lethargy.

With such lack of enthusiasm, even the endorsement by the International Monetary Fund (IMF) of the country's economic and financial program and the announced support by the World Bank for an economic recovery package did little to rouse the business community to a higher level of investment. Net investments by registered corporations and partnerships from March 1986 to January 1987 declined by 12.36 percent on a year-to-year basis.[4] Despite the agreement on the scaling and timing of import liberalization and on the rehabilitation of the Development Bank of the Philippines and the Philippine National Bank, it was nonetheless difficult to shake off the perception that the government had yet to put its economic act together.

The business community could not be easily convinced even by the macroeconomic indicators that at last started to point in the right direction. Real GNP during the second semester of 1986 managed to post enough positive growth so as to offset the continued decline of 2.2 percent during the first semester. Although the net result for the entire year for real GNP growth was just a shade above zero growth at 0.13 percent, the downtrend at least had been reversed.[5] Select industries managed to notch up respectable growth rates in sales volume during the few remaining months of 1986, and an increasing number of companies were already reporting acceptable profit levels. Consumer industries achieved robust growth rates of 20–25 percent in their sales for the fourth quarter of 1986 as against the fourth quarter of 1985.[6] Presumably, these were more the exceptions than the general rule. However, the market facts were positive in that interest rates had fallen back to more normal levels. After zooming to over 40 percent in 1984, nominal loan rates plunged to an average of 16.78 percent over the period March 1986 to February 1987.[7] Prime lending rates are now down to as low as 8–9 percent. Foreign exchange rates started firming up, even in the open market for U.S. dollars, and have for some time now remained around P 20.51 = $1.00.[8] Inflation, as measured by the Consumer Price Index taken on an annual basis, has chalked up a mere 0.05 percent over the period March 1986 to February 1987.[9] While these market facts may have been unable to raise business enthusiasm, they must have helped to turn the tide in business operations.

The reluctance on the part of the business community to be impressed in the face of these market facts was warranted. There was little for which the economic managers in the Aquino government can claim credit in bringing about the improvements noted. The fall in oil prices and the rise of commodity prices in world markets gave a boost to the Philippine economy: they helped to stem the fall of Philippine real GDP and to pull the inflation rate further downward. In July of 1986, international crude oil prices hit their lowest levels in over a decade. Saudi Arabian light was selling at $8 a barrel. Kuwaiti crude at $5.50, and North Sea Brent crude between $9.60 and $9.80.[10] Coconut prices (very important for the Philippines, where 18 million of its people live in coconut-growing regions) rose by a whopping 262 percent from May 1986 to January 1987.[11] The weakness of the U.S. dollar in international financial markets made it easier for the Philippine peso to maintain its exchange rate against the falling dollar. The relative absence of demand for funds in domestic financial markets and the easing of inflationary pressures mandated that interest rates should fall.

Thus, if the economic problems of the Philippines remained daunting, the external and internal environment took some of the pressure off during the first year of transition from the revolution to the restoration of democracy. The economic policy debates, the hesitancy of the business community, the limited real accomplishment by the cabinet notwithstanding, a basis for future rapid growth of the economy had been laid.

Restoring the foundations of a democracy government and laying the basis for economic development may seem insufficient when viewed against the urgent and critical problems the Aquino government inherited. They pale beside the apparently graver issues posed by the insurgents and secessionists. They look like feeble accomplishments when contrasted with the incapacity of articulate segments of Philippine society to cope with the changes that have occurred. To the extremists on the right, even to talk with the communists is to be pink; to their counterweight on the left, even to talk with the World Bank and the IMF is to be a lackey of imperialism, neocolonialism, and multinationalism; and to the more narrow-minded loyalist forces wedded to the past, to do things differently from Marcos is to be incompetent and unfit to govern.

THE RESIDUE FROM THE YEARS OF CRISIS

The common sense of the majority of Filipinos was expressed during the February 1987 plebiscite. Most Filipinos voted for their security under a democracy. As they said "yes" in record numbers to the constitution, they implicitly said "no" to the extremists of both the right and the left. And with a dramatic finality, they chose to relegate Marcos definitively to the past.

The wisdom of the common people can be the beginning of the decisive phase for getting the country out of its long and humiliating crisis. The broad principles that must underlie society have already been articulated and approved by the majority. Administrative talent and legislative genius must now be brought to bear upon the need to operationalize them in all key segments of Philippine life.

The road ahead, however, is far from clear; it is likely to be arduous precisely because the crisis that is now being put behind the Philippines has sharpened the politico-cultural traits militating against progress. In the afterglow of the revolution that succeeded because of a people's resolve to put society above self and their willingness to contribute to the common welfare, the compulsion to engage in what seems to be a national pastime— to trade rumor and idle political talk—soon reached habitual proportions. Coffee shops are full, talk shows have spread from breakfast to midnight, and light banter takes up much of the day. In this environment, little serious work gets done, and far too much attention is riveted on those who can create enough of a stir to land in the sensationalist headlines of Manila's many newspapers. The politicians continue their posturing to add spit and polish to their image, to get photographed for the front pages, or to appear on television. Style is often made to predominate over substance, and individuals are given far too much importance instead of the institutions they are supposed to be rebuilding.

President Aquino works in direct contrast to the traditional politicians. She sets a tone far different from the one to which they are accustomed, and she plays by rules at variance with the ones they have been using. It has thus been easy to call her by different names depending on which side of the fence one sits. She is either eulogized as a refreshing change or is seriously underestimated; but obviously, the common people like her as she is and as she has performed thus far. However, it is a measure of the expectations of Filipinos with regard to the behavior of politicians that many have failed either to appreciate the phenomenon that she is different or to understand the reasons why she stands apart from the norm.

The difficulty of standing apart from the others is gleaned from the dilemma of those who now occupy positions of government. In a country where everyone feels it important to talk directly to persons perceived to have an influence upon official decisionmaking, a good portion of a top government official's schedule is taken up by having to talk to people. A time for reflection and quiet study is a priceless luxury, and any insistence upon indulging in it during office hours means that many phone calls will not be returned, most demands for a personal appointment in the office will have to be denied, and a great majority of the meetings one gets invited to will have to be attended by one's representatives. Very soon word spreads of one's inaccessibility, and complaints of one's lack of contact with the people get readily broadcast—a polite euphemism for arrogance.

To avoid the deadly charge of arrogance, many people in government do little else except to see those who insist on "only a few minutes" of their time, and much of their real work can get done only after office hours. The widespread insistence on personal access not only lengthens the day of those who work in government; unless they take care, it also tends to center decisions around individuals, thereby weakening the mechanisms of institutional decisionmaking. The informal, interpersonal contacts often substitute for the formal procedures that institutions must follow. The many requests for "preferential attention" from those at the top of a government office can create havoc and destroy the orderly processing of papers at lower levels. The signal goes out that priority is to be given to those "who see the boss," and if this becomes the general rule, it can rapidly degenerate into the operative principle that action gets taken only upon instruction of the higher-ups. It is not surprising that those appointed to head a government office are so warmly congratulated, with the appointment widely regarded as a grant of a personal fiefdom, as though a whole bureaucracy were now at one's beck and call.

The depiction is an exaggeration, and few in government operate in precisely this fashion. Most are wiser and less arrogant than they are made out to be. Nonetheless, the pressures are intense, and without a strong character and the commitment to dedicated service, an individual soon becomes enamored of power and the temptation to believe in one's own importance becomes difficult to resist. It would be a pity if no strenuous effort were exerted to resist this temptation in Philippine politics, particularly so soon after the successful people's revolution and all that it stood for.

The February 1986 revolution has come to mean different things to different people. The romantic view, which many Filipinos are proud to entertain, is that the people forgot about their individual selves and showed themselves ready to take on whatever burdens the collective national enterprise might impose. Quite a few literally braved M-16s, tanks, and helicopter gunships.

A few facts since then have tended to dispel such a romantic view: cabinet ministers insisting on their individual point of view; government officials showing a total lack of teamwork; and ordinary employees throwing all discipline to the wind and angling for their personal advantage even to the exclusion of institutional welfare. These are jarring manifestations of the fact that Filipinos have not learned to shed their extreme individualism.

Excessive individualism is often disguised because of the Filipino's innate tendency to be nice and appear pleasant. Frequently, the stress on form prevents many Filipinos from getting into the substance of issues; these are left unresolved for another day. The delay this causes in government administration and even in corporate decisionmaking has often led to monumental inefficiency. Everyone is kept waiting until the other shoe is caused to fall, simply because confronting an official with the request for a definitive decision is an unwelcome form of behavior. People are supposed to wait.

Those who prefer not to wait and instead insist upon their position and demands are looked down upon as contentious characters, whose pushiness must be met with quiet opposition. They are given the silent treatment, and their papers either get lost or remain unacted upon. In the end, they often fail to get what they want; moreover, they leave a bitter taste in the mouths of their colleagues.

Teamwork and the art of dialogue have to be learned and practiced if a more efficient administration and better-considered policies arising out of the collective wisdom of people working together are to ensue. The recent past has not been propitious on this score, and many opportunities were missed as a consequence.

If economic opportunities were allowed to slip away, it was partly because of far too much stress on the macroeconomy, an emphasis on controls, checks, and balances. The first year of the Aquino administration can hardly be faulted when it comes to broad policy statements and control of financial balances. But the microeconomic aspects were minimized as though they could take care of themselves.

The appropriate broad policy themes were all clearly articulated. But the Filipino people, who had been used to too much dictation from above, kept on waiting for guidelines on how general policy was to be translated into specific working programs so that they could then proceed to make their concrete business plans. As many waited, uneasiness grew not only among those in government but also among the more perceptive observers of the business scene. Government economic managers could not understand why their former colleagues in the private sector did not move much faster and more aggressively when the macroeconomic environment was being quickly improved. Many in the private sector felt uncomfortable with the fact that so much money was left idle in the banking system at a time of low utilization of industrial capacity and very high unemployment. They could not understand why government did not take a lead in putting all the elements together to resuscitate the economy. They could not appreciate that the private sector was now meant to be the primary engine of economic growth, as government retreated from the high interventionist posture of the Marcos years.

Private business was still involved in the numerous meetings to which businessmen had become accustomed under Marcos. Consultation meetings were scheduled beyond anyone's capacity to handle them. Each industry wanted its own special rules. Each sector wanted its specific working relationship with government. Indeed, big business and government were once again acting as though the economy were a series of *specialized* compartments, whose content could be regulated in a particular manner both for the mutual advantage of each industry and for the economy as a whole. In rhetoric, they were all for the market economy; but in practice, many often preferred to forget that the market economy means *generalized* rules applicable to everyone.

Understandably, big business was still battling for preferential attention to each industrial group. Tariff protection became a war cry that had to be raised, with only limited and spaced liberalization grudgingly allowed as a necessary concession to the World Bank and the IMF. It was as though the economy were a zero-sum game, where one's loss must equal someone else's gain. The interrelationships within the economy were completely missed, and few saw the dynamic interdependence between lower tariffs, lower costs of imported materials and supplies, lower prices of manufactured goods, presumably better quality of such products due to the threat of competing imports of finished goods, and higher prospects of a turnaround for export sale in outside markets.

Big business preferred to spend much of its time in dialogue with government. This lack of interest in seeking to understand the entire systemic flow of goods and funds within the economy plunged big business into contradictions and disappointments. The discipline of the market was for someone else; domestic business did not need to compare the price and quality of its products with those of competing imports, to which Filipino consumers might have access under a more liberalized regime. Government assistance was taboo for everyone else but itself, little realizing that this had been the operating principle behind crony capitalism, which it had roundly condemned.

In a market economy, dialogues with government do not produce results; only decisive action to become competitive can generate jobs and income, earn profits, and secure higher rates of growth. Despite the many meetings with government officials, businessmen came away with the feeling that they had been through that wringer too many times in the past and that these meetings have remained what they have always been: little more than frustrating exercises in futility and an opportunity to exchange the usual pleasantries.

Pleasantries and a high level of visible activism do not lead to concrete results. A clear framework is imperative so that all actions can be made to fit logically together in pursuit of clear goals. Many Filipinos are still too "pragmatic" and "atheoretical," distrustful of conceptual frameworks. But hopefully, a happy combination can be struck so that there can be as many specifics as are necessary and as much strategic consistency and vision as are desirable.

This combination could have saved the Philippines the long and bitter acrimony between Juan Ponce Enrile and many of President Aquino's advisers. There should never have been any doubt about the ideological commitment of most people in government: in consonance with popular common sense, which is strongly pro-democratic and anti-communist, the members of the Aquino Cabinet, including those suspected of leftist leanings, had a core of unquestioned beliefs in the ideals of freedom under a democracy. And there should never have been any argument about the need for trying the path of peaceful negotiation with the communist insurgents as the Philippine military was being rebuilt into a fighting force, rather than allowing the issue to become a political tool. Unhappily, the necessary conceptual framework was not clearly articulated, and the strategic initiatives and operational activities were not fully discussed. As a result, the appearance of disunity and dissension was made much greater, quickly assuming crisis proportions.

An unnecessary crisis can arise from the colonial remnants whose attitude borders on paranoia against the United States. To the Filipino ultras who give patriots a bad image, the Americans are perceived as plotting at every turn of Philippine events. The illusion has been broadcast that the Philippines occupies such a strategic and all-important position in the American and multinational corporate schemes that under every bed there is a CIA man, and behind every policy prescription there is a heavy American hand. Since this view is often held with blind conviction, no room is left for enlightened discourse and reasoned argument.

Argument is needed against the narrow nationalistic romanticism that puts self-interest, in the guise of national interest, above all things and disregards the real facts of a dynamic, more interdependent modern world.

142   *Jesus P. Estanislao*

The extreme nationalists notwithstanding, no nation is now so large or important as to singlehandedly influence the course of current and future developments. For all of the love Filipinos have for the Philippines, and precisely because of such love, they have to wake up to the reality that the Philippines is just one more nation in the international community. It must accept and live by the facts of international trade, investments, and finance. These facts are impervious to empty rhetoric; they are moved and influenced only by decisive actions that take advantage of the rules that govern all aspects of international relations. Interminable discussions about the fairness of those rules have some use; but concrete results are achieved by quiet and persistent actions that bespeak of serious homework accomplished in economic competitiveness, administrative effectiveness, and politico-social stability.

GETTING OUT OF CRISIS

Now that the initial hype has quieted down and the usual confusion that attends the aftermath of a successful revolution has been partly cleared, the time for serious homework has come. Both President Aquino and the Filipino people could sincerely claim that the first year after the revolution was taken up by the all-consuming task of reestablishing democracy. The almost universal consensus is that this was an essential task for securing political stability, the *conditio sine qua non* for eventual economic progress. Having accomplished it, both the president and her people are turning their eyes to the next bottom-line results: more jobs, more purchasing power, and socioeconomic reforms that can help secure peace and win the fight against the Marxist hard core.

These results can be achieved only if Filipinos can show that they have as much talent for organization as for staging a successful nonviolent revolution. It would be a pity if the lessons they lived and learned from the 1983 assassination of Senator Aquino to the installation of Corazon Aquino as president were soon to be forgotten. They had learned how to spell out specifics in implementing a comprehensive program that involved strategies that had to be pursued by phases. They had lived by a spirit of unity, which allowed many initiatives to flourish and which enabled the self-sacrifice and generosity of hundreds of thousands to flow towards a common purpose.

The experience with success is there. Can the leadership now inspire the people to use it for a goal no less noble than the one they have already achieved? If they were so committed to bringing democracy back, they must now be challenged to make it work. Democracy must now translate into greater efficiency, the provision of all the people's basic needs, and the further enhancement of each individual's personal dignity.

The odds are great and the task is difficult. The Philippines will have to pass multiple tests if it is to overcome the odds successfully and accomplish the urgent task at hand. Continuing commitment has already been demonstrated by thousands of young men and women, more than a few of whom are highly educated, who have decided to stay in the hills and fight for a Marxist solution to Philippine problems. Their idealism is not suspect, and their capacity for dedication to the communist cause is boundless. They must find their match. And they will find it only in the thousands of no less educated men and women who are now in the mainstream of Philippine society, who must be motivated to find their self-fulfillment in their contribution to the strengthening of the institutions so essential to making democracy and development in the Philippines a dual success. The gradual de-emphasis on personalities and the rapid introduction of efficient systems and procedures may well be tasks that reap no headlines; they may look ordinary and unglamorous; but the extent to which Philippine institutions can be made to function effectively, professionally, and independently of passing personalities will determine the pace by which Philippine society as a whole is strengthened.

The test of visionary pragmatism has been passed by the young entrepreneurs of medium-sized enterprises, who within weeks after the successful revolution decided to shed their wait-and-see attitude and adopt a more risk-taking stance by acquiring idle plants and restarting industrial activity. These are the younger breed of businessmen who do not put much stake in meetings with government officials. Nor do they pin their success on government grants, privileges, incentives, or tariff protection. Rather, they do business by the rules that apply in a market economy: they assess the market, then produce competitively for it, and obtain the best financial package available from the banking system. They do not seek to create waves, only to make money in the process of providing jobs and income opportunities for the people. The more their numbers can be multiplied, the better for the Philippine economy, which has been in dire need of individuals with a simple vision amplified by the specifics necessary to make it operational.

The challenge of public service lies in a combination of the human touch and the capacity to produce results. In a people's democracy, there are an ample number of politicians who show a flair for identifying with the common people and causing the latter to feel rapport with them. The ease and warmth with which they deal with the stream of ordinary citizens approaching them shows a great deal of heart, which is reciprocated by the good feeling towards them and by the sympathetic press they get. Increasingly, however, among the younger politicians now vying for office, warmth is accompanied by a cold calculation of the means to get to meaningful results, and heart comes with a mind committed to constructive activities that leave positive economic benefits behind. The politics of giving and dispensing favors is thus tempered by the resource constraints and by the unceasing requirement of viable economic activity for the society as a whole.

Economic recovery that must follow the political stability now in place can be fostered if the Philippines passes the multiple tests of creating thousands of institution-builders, market-disciplined entrepreneurs, and a new breed of heart-cum-mind politicians. These are the people who can deliver the goods for democracy. They are the ones who can help win the fight for peace and progress, and together with the military, against insurgency and succession.

It is far from clear if the Philippines can pass this supreme test, even under the fortunate leadership of President Aquino. Failure can mean continuing drift, greater confusion, and a slide into ungovernability. The 1986 revolution can quickly lose steam, and old feudal power politics can easily return: the many flamboyant personalities, of which the Philippines has an excess, can play to the galleries, seeking applause and support mainly for their own power, prestige, and peso accounts even as the country's real interests go begging.

Such a gloomy prospect is likely to be realized if Filipinos trade the gains of their peaceful February 1986 revolution for the glitter of a continuing political fiesta. If they forget that their revolution cannot be successfully completed unless they put their enormous talents to rebuilding the social and economic institutions that had been seriously weakened or totally destroyed, then the likelihood is for the democratic ideal to lose much of its luster and for the commitment to a middle-of-the-road alternative to communism to weaken. If they persist in clinging to the vain hope that the rules of the economic process can once again serve to accommodate primarily the interests of the more visible segments of big business, then economic recovery will fall far short of the targets set, and the resulting disillusionment can destroy the apparent consensus that had been built up for market discipline and economic liberalization. If the new politics that President Aquino has introduced gives way to the old politics, then the common welfare is likely to be sacrificed too often at the altar of political convenience and personal grandstanding.

However, it can be the Philippines's good fortune if the men and women in the government working closely with President Aquino realize the precarious straits in which the nation finds itself. Our new leaders must put their act together, seizing the unique opportunity before them. They can work as a team together with the new Congress so that the cultural reorientation demanded by the times is assiduously undertaken, thereby enabling the continuous restructuring of Philippine society.

People power must now be used to engage Filipinos through their hundreds of nongovernment organizations to help congress translate the visions and dreams enshrined in their newly-approved Constitution into specific workable laws that are then quickly made operative. The restructuring of the executive branch must be decisively carried out in view of the experience within the past year and of new realities that have emerged. Not only must the various departments of government work in harmony with each other, but all the sectors and regions of society must also work for a common purpose and be encouraged to assume a deeper sense of responsibility. The reforms that have been crying for attention can then be addressed with the sense of urgency that the total transformation of an entire society in a short time requires. These are the imperatives for getting out of our crisis. These are the challenges Filipinos must meet if they are going to project the current good fortune into the future.

There is more than an even chance that President Aquino and her government will succeed in the task of reorientation and reform. To tip the balance further in the positive direction, she and the Filipino people cannot rely merely upon prayers for further miracles. They will have to work for them.

NOTES

1. Philippine National Census and Statistics Office. Special Release: Office of the Executive Director, No. 586; December 19, 1986.
2. Florante B. Solomon, "Business May Need More than Dirt-Cheap Credit to Perk Up." *CRC Staff Memos*, No. 24, December 1986.
3. Center for Research and Communication (CRC). *Trends in Industrial Performance Series: 2nd Semester 1986*. Manila: CRC, 1987.
4. Securities and Exchange Commission (SEC), personal communication.
5. National Economic Development Authority (NEDA), *The National Income Accounts of the Philippines, 1984 to 1986* (December 1986).
6. Bernardo M. Villegas, *The Philippines: The Coming Boom* (Manila: CRC, 1987).
7. Central Bank of the Philippines (CB), personal communication.
8. Aarne B. Dimanlig, "Real Interest Rates Are Attracting High; So How Come Savers Aren't Biting?" *The Economy in 1987: One Year after EDSA* (Manila: CB), personal communication.
9. National Census and Statistics Office (NCSO), personal communication.
10. CRC, *Trends*.
11. Bureau of Agricultural Economics (BAECON), personal communication.

9

ASEAN and the Kampuchean Conflict:
A Study of a Regional Organization's Responses to External Security Challenges

by M. R. Sukhumbhand Paribatra

This chapter is a brief attempt to analyze systematically the efforts of the Association of Southeast Asian Nations (ASEAN)[1] to respond to the challenges and to resolve the problems emanating directly or indirectly from Vietnam's invasion of Kampuchea. From this analysis it is hoped that more can be learned about the use of regional organizations as means of promoting security and order.

It will, however, be useful to start by clarifying some of the concepts and to make explicit the analytical framework of discussion.

SECURITY, ORDER, AND REGIONAL ORGANIZATIONS

Of central importance to analyses such as this are the concepts of security and order, both immensely difficult, perhaps impossible, to define with precision or full satisfaction. For the purpose of this discussion, *security* at the international or regional level can be taken to mean a condition whereby the main actors in a defined system or geographical area are free from violence, actual or threatened, which endangers core values and normal processes of interaction with one another.

In a system or subsystem of sovereign states, security, as defined here, cannot be absolute. The international environment at present is essentially one of anarchy, or of semi-anarchy, where no common political culture, value, or definition of legitimacy prevails, and where states are required to rely only upon themselves for their protection, survival, and progress. As Robert Jervis points out in a brilliant essay, such an environment encourages not only noncooperative behavior but also mutual suspicions and individual quests for security against threats, real or imagined, quests which decrease the security of others and provoke often violent counter-vailing responses. Thus, conflict becomes part and parcel of the environment and international politics stands in a constant state of "insecurity" or "potential war."[2]

In such a context, only varying degrees of international or regional security are attainable. Often the quest is for some sort of order or framework in which conflict is confined "within tolerable limits" and "the risk of large-scale irreversible violence occurring in the relations among principal states" is minimized.[3] Hopefully, however, an element of positive cooperation is also present and encouraged.[4]

There seem to be three sets of variables governing such a framework. One is the structure and distribution of power. The second is the extent of mutual interests or interdependence. And the third is the efficacy of the "rules of the game" which govern the behavior of the actors within the system or subsystem.[5]

Though analytically distinct, these three sets of variables are closely interrelated. Rules of the game reflect the pattern of power distribution and the extent of mutuality of prevailing interests and are susceptible to change once they no longer reflect them. They also serve to signal, clarify, sustain, and/or reinforce the power distribution and mutuality of interests.[6]

Over the last two decades, regional organizations have gained increasing recognition as instruments of security and order in a world perceived to be troubled by growing disorder. The underlying assumptions seem to be firstly that both "peace" and "progress" are "divisible" and secondly that smaller associations of countries with similar resources, cultures, problems, and requirements are more realistic and efficient frameworks for maintaining peace and progress than individual state efforts.

References to regional organizations need, of course, to be tempered by an awareness of their diversity. However, for the purpose of the present discussion, the question which must be addressed is: broadly speaking, what are the scope and limitations of regional organizations as a means of bringing about a greater degree of security and order as defined above? Especially where weaker states are concerned, when faced with conflicts both among themselves and with others, such organizations might perform one or more of the following different, but by no means mutually exclusive, functions.

First of all, regional organizations can provide a means of managing relations with nonmember states. Grouping regional states together can alter the distribution of power between member states and nonmember states, which in turn can serve to deter, restrain, or eliminate threats from the latter. This is particularly true of organizations which take the form of military alliances providing for consultations, exchanges, and assistance in security questions. Furthermore, the redistribution of power in favor of member states creates a greater opportunity to sustain advantageous rules of the game, which can guide relations with nonmember states and thereby prevent, or at the very least mitigate, conflict and facilitate cooperation. Even where regional organizations fail to alter the real distribution of power, they can often provide psychological assurances that permit member states to deal with the outside environment in a more confident and effective manner; conversely, they can induce nonmember states to treat member states with greater consideration, thus providing opportunities for more orderly relationships between them.

Second, regional organizations can act as a means of managing or resolving conflicts and of promoting cooperation among members. By their very nature they emphasize commonalities rather than differences; embody norms of behavior, explicitly or implicitly, in order to identify and pursue established goals; and provide educational processes through which member states can become more familiar with each other, learn to mask or reduce differences, cultivate habits or cooperation, and build up what may ultimately turn out to be a sense of community. Supranationalism may not eventuate, but these functions are still crucial, given the fact that conflicts between neighbors usually involve domestic dimensions that defy conventional methods of interstate management or resolution.

Third, regional organizations can promote ideals as norms of behavior. Ideals of peace, prosperity, and progress usually provide points of convergence for regional cooperation, and the organizations often become channels for articulating them. In the short and medium term, these ideals are rarely if ever translated into practice in any sustained or concrete manner, but in the long run, repetition can make them progressively more binding on member states or at least more difficult to deny, reject, or transgress. Ideals can thus be gradually transformed into rules of the game that eventually may have to be taken into consideration when dealing individually or collectively with the member states. Furthermore, if these expressions of idealism strike the right chord, they can also act as mechanisms for mobilizing support in the international arena for regional organizations and their members.

And lastly, regional organizations can also promote member states' domestic stability. A more secure external environment, the prestige and legitimacy gained from membership, and other benefits, real or psychological, arising from regional cooperation may facilitate internal consolidation and enhance individual and collective strength and resilience. This, in turn, can help reduce temptations to use external conflicts as means of achieving internal order, and create greater degrees of commitment on the part of individual member states to regional organizations as means of promoting national interests.

At the same time, it must be pointed out that regional organizations face a number of limitations and, indeed, may serve to diminish rather than to enhance security and order. First, they are often set up and promoted as responses to external threats; thus, their successful development may in fact *accentuate* conflicts with the sources of those threats. Especially when ideology or idealism is a primary source of differentiation and the mobilizing force for regional cooperation, or when "regional" organizations are not fully regional and exclude some regional states that are in conflict with member states, greater security for one group of states means greater insecurity for another and may lead to countervailing responses, escalation, and polarization. In this sense Robert Jervis's security dilemma[7] is not resolved but merely transposed from one level of political organization to another.

Second, as previously intimated, idealism is a double-edged weapon. Where a set of ideals is deemed acceptable and appropriate, they can serve as a force supportive of unity and help to guide the conduct of relations both among member states and between them and nonmembers. But when those ideals are regarded as undesirable, counterproductive, or dangerous, they can be the cause of fragmentation and polarization. Conflicts may arise or escalate not only between member states and nonmember states, but also between member states that are "true believers" and member states that are not. Should security and order be realized through principles or expedience, through idealism or *realpolitik*? The dilemma is not new, but it has assumed an added dimension in this context.

Third, in the last resort there may be an inherent contradiction in the desire to develop *regional* cooperation as a means of promoting *national* security: where they conflict, there is a tendency for considerations of national security to prevail. To this extent there is what may be termed built-in centrifugalism in regional organizations. Crucial here are dilemmas concerning the norms of behavior that guide relationships among members. Regional organizations embody certain rules that reflect prevailing patterns of power, influence, and/or security concerns. But patterns are apt to change and may call for corresponding changes in the rules of the game. The appropriate responses may not be forthcoming from those member states that see their interests to be ill-served by such changes. This puts other member states in a dilemma: should the rules be maintained until they can be changed by consensus, or should gentle and not-so-gentle persuasion be used to bring about changes, because once the rules of the game cease to reflect the prevailing "realities" they must be changed? No matter what decisions are ultimately made, the costs arising may turn out to be considerable. On the one hand, preserving "unrealistic" rules of the game may only serve to postpone the day of reckoning and ensure that when that day comes, the conflict may be all the more intense; on the other, changing *some* rules of the game without one's partners' full consent may undermine confidence in *all* other rules of the game guiding the conduct of member states and thus jeopardize *all* aspects of regional cooperation.

This leads to the last and perhaps the most important limitation: the existence of centrifugal tendencies means that regional cooperation is apt to be an inefficient and unwieldy means of organizing and augmenting power. Thus, regional organizations may ultimately fail to bring about a more favorable distribution of power between member and nonmember states; to persuade or coerce adversaries to accede to their wishes; or to prevent externally supported interventions or subversions from taking place. The failure to bring about a more secure external environment may induce member states to augment their power through means other than regional cooperation. One such means is a return to greater self-reliance and unilateralism. Another is alliance with one or more extra-regional powers. If the means of augmenting individual member states' power violates the letter or spirit of regional cooperation, then centrifugal tendencies are likely to become exacerbated, thus completing the vicious circle.

In the light of the foregoing discussion of the concepts of security and order and of the possible role of regional organizations in preserving and enhancing them, a systematic examination can now be made of ASEAN's responses to the security challenges raised by Vietnam's invasion of Kampuchea in 1978–1979.

THE CHALLENGES—1978 to 1980

Vietnam's invasion of Kampuchea and the cluster of developments directly related to it, namely the growing Soviet–Vietnamese security ties that ultimately led to the Soviet presence at the former U.S. base at Cam Ranh Bay, to the Sino–Vietnamese border war, and to the Vietnamese efforts to wipe out Khmer resistance forces both in 1979 and 1980, presented security challenges to ASEAN at three related levels.

At one level, the presence in Kampuchea and Laos of up to 250,000 Vietnamese troops, generally thought to be battle-hardened and well-armed, posed threats of intervention and subversion, most notably to Thailand, which for geopolitical and historical reasons considers the trans-

Mekong region, comprising most of the land areas of those two countries, crucial for its security.[8] Furthermore, the invasion and the subsequent Vietnamese campaign to wipe out the resistance forces sent droves of refugees overland into Thailand,[9] whose early attempts to manage the security dimension of the problem merely served to provoke a major incident with the Vietnamese at Non Mark Moon in June 1980.[10]

At another level, the Vietnamese invasion nullified ASEAN's efforts to find a region-wide order based on consensus. Between 1967 and 1975, although its achievements were modest and recognized to be so, ASEAN made progress toward order in two ways. One was intra-organizational conflict management; the other was the development of the common notion, as evident in the Zone of Peace, Freedom, and Neutrality (ZOPFAN) declaration in Kuala Lumpur, Malaysia, in 1971, that relations with great powers should be conducted in such ways as ultimately to reduce their roles and at the same time to confer benefit on regional states.[11]

Between 1975 and the end of 1978, ASEAN attempted to extend this fledgling order to encompass the three Indochinese countries. Immediately after the fall of Saigon, there was a great deal of uncertainty and alarm among ASEAN members concerning the possibility of Vietnam's becoming, as termed by one veteran observer of regional affairs, "a twentieth-century Prussia in Southeast Asia."[12] This concern became exacerbated by Vietnam's declaration of support for armed insurgencies in noncommunist Southeast Asian countries and its refusal to accept or deal with ASEAN as a collective entity, thus rejecting more or less explicitly all the premises contained in ASEAN's quest for regional order. However, after a long and laborious process a semblance of order was established between ASEAN and Vietnam, as most evident in the joint communiqués issued during Vietnamese Premier Pham Van Dong's tour of ASEAN in September through October 1978. The rules agreed upon were coexistence based on respect for one another's rights, non-interference in internal affairs, and pacific settlement of disputes; an understanding that further cooperation can and should be developed through dialogues and expanded trade, economic, and various functional relationships; and an implicit "promise" to consider further "the desirability of Southeast Asia being an area of peace, independence, freedom and neutrality."[13] No one in ASEAN believed that such rules would be binding or sacrosanct, but compared to the relations prevailing in the immediate aftermath of the fall of Saigon, the improvement was substantive and significant. Consequently, there was a good deal of justifiable optimism about the future prospects for a regionwide order based on consensus.[14]

The invasion shattered these prospects. Instead, there seemed to be every possibility that a militarily-induced redistribution of power in Indochina might lead ultimately, via military intervention, political subversion or other forms of pressure, to a Southeast Asian regional order based more or less exclusively on Vietnamese *diktat*.[15]

Furthermore, the Sino-Vietnamese border war and the growing Soviet presence in Vietnam following the war meant that the trend was toward more and not less great power involvement in the region. This in turn raised the specter of Southeast Asia being embroiled once more in the geopolitics of extra-regional rivalry, especially that between China and the Soviet Union, which not only made any resolution of the Kampuchean problem immensely more difficult, but also rendered somewhat redundant the notion that somehow a regional order could and should be constructed in isolation from such a rivalry.[16]

At the third level, the expansion of Vietnam and the increasing roles of the two great communist powers, China and the Soviet Union, posed what might be termed a psychological challenge. It was not simply fear of communism, although, as Jorgensen-Dahl among others has pointed out, fear of communism has always been a crucial factor in the organization and development of ASEAN.[17] It was also uncertain as to whether the recently found sense of common purpose, evident during and after the Bali Summit in February 1976, could survive this new storm over Indochina.

Between 1967 and 1975 regional cooperation was an aspiration rather than an operational reality for ASEAN, whose members were divided by a number of differences and conflicts and strove unsuccessfully to forge a common political will to transcend them. As a result of the communist victories in Indochina, a new sense of identity and purpose emerged in the organization but was still largely fragile and untested.

After Vietnam invaded Kampuchea, which precipitated a chain of developments transforming the region's security environment, the ASEAN countries were at one in their refusal to legitimize Vietnam's attempted fait accompli, but were still divided as to how, how far, and at what price they should deny this fait accompli. As evident from the meeting of ASEAN foreign ministers in Bangkok in January 1979 and from the debate surrounding the "Kuantan Principle" announced in March 1980, ASEAN was far from being firmly united. Significant differences could be discerned within its ranks between the "hawks," who wished to pursue relentlessly a policy of attrition to end Vietnam's dominance over Kampuchea, and the "doves," who contended that Vietnam was not an intrinsically hostile state, has legitimate security concerns in Kampuchea, and, if truly independent and "satisfied," has an indispensable part to play in the containment of China and in the fulfillment of the ZOPFAN ideal. Given that the sense of common purpose within ASEAN was still unproven, clearly at question was not only the policy toward Vietnam and the Kampuchean problem, but also the future of regional cooperation as a whole.[18]

In addition, the Vietnamese invasion was also a psychological challenge to Thailand. Though recovered somewhat from the traumas from 1975 to

1977, when in its external relations it "lost" an ally-protector and in its internal politics met with unprecedented instability and bloodshed, in 1978 through 1980 Thailand's self-confidence and sense of internal unity were still somewhat weak and fragile. This was reflected in the domestic debates about the appropriate Thai responses to Vietnam's occupation of Kampuchea and also in the fact that some of these debates were publicized and involved high-ranking members of the armed forces, particularly the so-called "Democratic Soldiers." Considering that, except for the "democratic period" between 1973 and 1975, the conduct of Thailand's foreign relations is rarely if ever so debated, these developments were indeed a significant indication of the prevailing state of mind in the country at that juncture.[19]

THE RESPONSES—1980 to 1985

The Vietnamese incursion into Thailand at Non Mark Moon in June 1980 was a crucial turning point in that it served to dampen, if not to eliminate, debates in ASEAN as well as within Thailand and brought about a concerted set of responses, the substance of which, though modified and adapted in parts over time, still largely endures.[20]

Broadly speaking, ASEAN's overall objectives in the Kampuchean problem are threefold. First of all, it seeks to enhance Thailand's security against direct or indirect threats from Vietnam; secondly, to promote a balance of presence and interests among great powers, seen to entail ultimately a curtailment and reduction of Soviet and Chinese influence in Southeast Asia; thirdly, to bring about more order in its relations with Vietnam.

A settlement of the Kampuchean problem is seen as a sine qua non of the achievement of these objectives. While the ASEAN countries have modified their stance concerning the identity of those who have the right to participate in the governance of Kampuchea, they continue to insist that the final settlement contain the following elements: Vietnam's withdrawal from Kampuchea; the establishment of a free neutral, independent, and democratic Kampuchea; and some sort of international guarantees to preserve such an arrangement in that troubled land.

To realize these objectives, ASEAN employs a strategy that, again despite modifications and adaptations to suit prevailing exigencies, has remained substantively unchanged since 1980. This strategy is one that assumes political, diplomatic, military, and economic dimensions and that contains three interlocking components. The first of these components is political, diplomatic, and economic isolation of Vietnam. ASEAN has striven to forge and sustain three overlapping international coalitions to isolate and put pressure on Vietnam. One is what might be termed a security coalition—comprising the United States, China, and Khmer resistance forces—as central players and Australia and New Zealand as secondary or fringe ones. Another is an economic coalition comprising mainly ASEAN's "dialogue partners" of Australia, Canada, the EEC, Japan, New Zealand, and the United States. The third is a political-cum-moral coalition comprising all those in various international forums that disapprove or can be persuaded to disapprove of Vietnam's occupation of Kampuchea. The maintenance of these three coalitions in turn requires that ASEAN develop and utilize considerable political and diplomatic finesse, as evident during the negotiations leading to the formulation of the Coalition Government of Democratic Kampuchea (CGDK) in June 1982 and the "proximity talks" proposal in July 1985.

The second component is application of military pressure on Vietnam, as a means of both persuasion and deterrence, without ASEAN becoming directly involved if possible. One way of applying such pressure is to forge a working relationship with China, sometimes to the point of close coordination. Another way is to encourage, explicitly or otherwise, the U.S. military presence in the region and U.S. material support where necessary and appropriate. The third way is to provide assistance to the Khmer resistance forces either directly (Singapore's arms supplies to the noncommunists; Thailand's training of the same as well as frequent but unacknowledged provision of sanctuaries and other forms of aid and succor) or indirectly (transit through Thailand of China's matériel bound for the Khmer Rouge in particular). Related to these methods of applying military pressure on Vietnam are the improvement of the ASEAN countries' respective armed forces, which has continued apace since 1979, and increasing bilateral military cooperation among the members: these measures, apart from enhancing defense capabilities, are probably intended to communicate to Vietnam the ASEAN countries' collective and individual will to persevere with the present strategy.

The third component is the formulation of modalities seen as necessary for negotiation and settlement with Vietnam. These include decisions concerning the forum, participants, preconditions, and terms of negotiation and settlement. Partly as responses to Vietnam's initiatives, ASEAN has modified its collective stand. The so-called "Joint Appeal" of September 1983 and the "proximity talks" proposal of July 1985 demonstrate that, unlike at previous times, it is willing to agree to a regional, as opposed to international, framework of discussion; to the participation in some form of the Heng Samrin group in the processes of negotiation and settlement; and to a phased rather than a total withdrawal of Vietnamese troops as a precondition. At the same time, however, the "non-negotiable" terms have not been changed: that is, the right of the Khmer Rouge to remain a player in the processes of negotiation and settlement; a total withdrawal of foreign forces from Kampuchea as a part of the solution package; and a self-determined and neutral Kampuchea whose status is backed by international supervision and guarantees. Underlying this strategy is the assumption that a policy of attrition will work, that time is on ASEAN's side and that when sufficient pressure has been applied, Vietnam can be forced to leave Kampuchea on ASEAN's terms.[21]

Any evaluation of ASEAN's responses to Vietnam's invasion and occupation of Kampuchea has to start with the fact that Vietnam still remains in that country and that if there is a breaking point for Hanoi, it has evidently not been reached. But to confine evaluation to this fact would be too simplistic. What is needed is a more rigorous and thorough examination of ASEAN's achievements based on the analytical framework presented above. Such an examination is likely to lead to the conclusion that, at least in the short run, ASEAN's record has indeed been a successful one.

In the first place, Vietnam's occupation of Kampuchea was perceived, especially after the June 1980 incursion, to pose a common threat and thus heightened the ASEAN countries' awareness of the extent to which their security interests are intertwined. This, in turn, induced them to draw together and achieve a degree of solidarity in words and deeds which could not have been predicted even by the most optimistic of observers in 1967 or indeed in 1979.

In the process they have introduced, or developed to a high level of efficacy, certain rules of the game for the management of relations among them which continue to operate up to this date. One is the principle that, no matter what each individual member state's predispositions may be, the ASEAN countries are committed to securing a political settlement in Kampuchea that acknowledges Vietnam's violation of the latter's sovereignty and integrity and contains adequate measures to redress this violation. Another is the understanding that, again no matter what each individual member state's aspirations or reservations may be, the security interests and requirements of Thailand, the frontline state, receive first priority and give it a "veto power" in all questions related to the Kampuchean problem. The third is the norm that consensus is valuable in itself and must be preserved at all costs, that the process of decisionmaking must necessarily involve discussion, consultation and unanimous resolution or, where unanimity is impossible to achieve, synthesis of differing view points, as perhaps is the case with the proximity talks proposal.[22] And the fourth is the understanding that all security-related activities which conform to, or at least do not violate, the spirit of the foregoing rules are permissible, particularly if they serve to enhance cooperation. Notable in this respect are Thailand's informal security links with China, the members' upgrading of their conventional military capabilities, and, perhaps most important for ASEAN in the long run, the bilateral military cooperation—taking place within but is not formally related to the ASEAN framework—which has increased considerably since Vietnam's invasion of Kampuchea.[23] Conversely, any behavior which violates the spirit of these rules, such as some of the actions and words of the Commander of the Indonesian Armed Forces, General Benny Murdani, is strongly discouraged and, were it to become too publicized to make convincing retractions possible, is quickly modified or "synthesized" into a new "ASEAN policy," as evident in the ASEAN foreign ministers' call during their July 1984 meeting for Indonesia to act as a bridge towards Vietnam.

ASEAN's solidarity and commitment to the principles of sovereignty, territorial integrity, and non-interference have enabled the regional organization to function with a fair amount of success as an instrument for managing relations with nonmember states: the organization's solidarity has made both friends and foes recognize that they have to treat the ASEAN countries not individually but collectively, and its commitment has made the indifferent pay attention and give support. The two together have allowed ASEAN to develop bargaining power and self-assurance.

These attributes are reflected in a number of developments. One is the ability of ASEAN, after the International Conference on Kampuchea (ICK) in July 1981, to persuade China to give consideration and agree, at least in part, to its initiatives, as evident during the negotiations leading to the formation of the CGDK as well as the formulation of the Joint Appeal and Proximity Talks proposal. Another is the degree of confidence the United States seems to have in ASEAN's diplomacy, as evident from the fact that it has many a time reiterated its willingness to follow and support ASEAN's policy and, most recently in the case of the proximity talks proposal, actually done so despite private and not-so-private misgivings. Yet another development reflecting ASEAN's bargaining power and self-assurance is the fact that despite opposition, especially from France, the Kampuchean conflict has been placed high on the agenda of discussions with dialogue partners. The fourth is ASEAN's success in mobilizing international support in most international forums, especially the UN General Assembly, where the number of votes in favor of ASEAN-sponsored resolutions calling for Vietnam's withdrawal from Kampuchea has increased almost every year.[24]

ASEAN's record of solidarity and success has given Thailand a good deal of self-confidence and sense of security.[25] This is reflected in the Thai elite's present consensus concerning Kampuchea and in the degree of commitment they feel towards ASEAN and its ideals,[26] which is highly significant given the fact that Thais by nature are pragmatists and do not usually attach themselves to any one or any cause without calculating the real costs and benefits of that attachment. It is also partly reflected in Thailand's willingness to explore new directions[27] in its foreign policy, which are not all directly related to security questions, and its ability to preserve, however tenuously at times, internal stability and the democratic system of government, at the very moment that it is facing a "clear and present danger."

It is of course impossible to gauge with any measure of accuracy the degree to which ASEAN has influenced Vietnam's behavior; even to hazard a guess may require a great deal of knowledge concerning the extent of Vietnam's ambitions and its decisionmaking process, which is simply not available. Perhaps the question which should be asked is: what would have happened if ASEAN had not existed or maintained such solidarity and commitment? It is probable, first of all, that Vietnam would have asserted on an effective and sustained basis its mastery over Kampuchea; second, that rather than being isolated and asked to justify its actions to the international community, it would by now have launched itself into the tasks of economic reconstruction and put itself into a position more or less to dictate the pattern of power distribution within the region; and third, that Vietnam would have greatly accentuated Thailand's sense of insecurity, with adverse repercussions on Thai internal stability and cohesion. If the foregoing is correct, then ASEAN has succeeded to a degree in containing Vietnam, in preserving the *option* of bringing about a regional order through consensus, and in cushioning Thailand from the full physical and psychological impact of Vietnam's invasion of Kampuchea.

However, it is not at all certain that, especially in the longer run, ASEAN is likely to succeed in achieving what it has set out to accomplish. Indeed one can even argue that its apparent successes in the short term may only serve either to accentuate some of the existing problems or to postpone to a future date a sustained search for solutions to them, so that they may become more difficult to resolve in time.[28]

Where management of relations with nonmembers is concerned, a case could be made that ASEAN over the long run has contributed to an increasing polarization of Southeast Asia's international politics. One reason is that ASEAN has made the Kampuchean conflict an issue of *principle*. While this may have been necessary as a means of mobilizing international support and a device for managing the member states' relations with one another, adherence to principle has reduced flexibility on the part of both proponents and adversaries and made compromise that much more difficult to achieve. The inflexibility inherent in the Kampuchean conflict is encapsulated in the annual UN General Assemblies, where on one hand ASEAN is committed to propagating its principle and to increasing the number of votes in favor of that principle every year, while on the other hand Vietnam is committed to denying that a violation of principle has taken place.

Another reason is that ASEAN is bound by the rules of the game which require both consensus in its decisionmaking and the giving of priority to the interests and demands of Thailand, the frontline state. While probably essential for maintaining unity among the ASEAN members over the short run, these rules have also served to reduce the scope of choice available to ASEAN. More specifically, it has made ASEAN's policy toward Vietnam a function of Thailand's policy towards the same, which in turn is deeply influenced by the Thais' perceptions, suspicions, and fears of their traditional rival; at the same time, it has also discouraged or prevented individual members' initiatives to find a more orderly framework of relations with Vietnam. This predicament is encapsulated in the record of Indonesia's and Malaysia's diplomacy that, perhaps with exaggeration, has been characterized by a "one step forward, two steps backward" approach.

The third and most important reason is ASEAN's extra-regional affiliations. Given the various differences and conflicts among its members, ASEAN is not and, for the foreseeable future, is unlikely to be a military pact. This means that it cannot mobilize sufficient power to achieve its purpose where the Kampuchean problem is concerned. Thus, despite expressed desires to lessen the degree of involvement of external powers, its members collectively and individually have to seek extra-regional affiliations, especially with the United States and China. This serves to create a level of dependence which gives scope for the latter's priorities, threat perceptions, and strategies to become increasingly embedded in the structures of regional states' decisionmaking and interactions with each other. Particularly significant in this respect is the Sino–Thai alignment, which serves to sustain and enhance not only the strength of the Khmer Rouge but also Thailand's uncompromising posture towards Vietnam. ASEAN's external affiliations encourage Vietnam, in turn, to reinforce its ties with the Soviet Union, whose presence in Indochina has markedly increased since 1980. Thus, Southeast Asia's politics have become once more a microcosm of global rivalry between great powers as different blocs of nations peer at each other "eyeball-to-eyeball" across the Thai–Kampuchean border.

Nor is this state of affairs as safe as many observers and practitioners consider it to be. ASEAN's solidarity and external affiliations have frustrated and contained Vietnam up to a point, but are still insufficient to allow ASEAN to impose its will on Vietnam or to bring about the desired pattern of power distribution in Indochina. On the contrary, as the developments of the 1984–1985 dry season have shown, the pressures ASEAN has brought to bear on Vietnam have provoked the latter to more aggression, which neither China, the United States, nor ASEAN is capable of preventing and which is unlikely to diminish in the dry seasons to come.[29] What one specialist in Southeast Asian affairs wrote not long after the Vietnamese invasion of Kampuchea is probably now more true than ever before:[30]

The situation in Southeast Asia in fact has come increasingly to resemble that which has prevailed in Europe for much of the postwar period. But whereas in Europe the two antagonistic camps have arrived at a set of tacit rules which, with traditional diplomatic rules and procedures, govern their interaction, no such rules have emerged to serve a similar function in Southeast Asia. . . . ASEAN is an organizational expression of a regional polarization process which has as its other principal pole the communist states of Indochina.

The prolongation of the Kampuchean conflict and the increasing polarization of the region that this is likely to entail may have adverse consequences on the efficacy of ASEAN as a mechanism for managing relations among member states. In particular, intramural tensions and with them a greater propensity towards centrifugalism may arise in a number of forms.

First of all, the prolongation may enhance conflicts of interests within ASEAN. One consequence of the Kampuchean conflict has been qualitative and quantitative improvements in individual ASEAN countries' defense capabilities, and this trend may reactivate or accentuate the competitive element in their relations with one another; this may be already beginning to take place as a result of the decision by Thailand and Singapore to buy F-16A fighters from the United States. Moreover, tension can also emanate from the fact that Vietnam does not pose equal threats to all the ASEAN countries. In particular, over the long run, a conflict may arise between Thailand's and Indonesia's conceptions of their security interests.

For geopolitical reasons the Thais have always been highly sensitive to land-based threats coming from the west and east. From their perspective, whenever such a threat exists in an immediate and concrete form and is coped with unsatisfactorily, as now in the case of the presence in Laos and Kampuchea of a militarily strong and ideologically hostile Vietnam, other issues or requirements—especially long-term ones—are apt to be considered of lesser priority, and the main thrust of policy is usually directed at mobilizing all available forces in the international and regional environment to support the Thai position vis-à-vis that threat. In the face of a land-based threat, the Thais have a propensity to conceive their interests in a single-emphasis, short-term, minimalist manner, envisaging nothing more than the removal of such a threat by all possible means.

On the other hand, Indonesia's geopolitical security from an immediate external threat affords an opportunity to take a more multidirectional, long-term, and maximalist view of the world and the region, as evident from its continuing commitment to and promotion of the ZOPFAN concept. Moreover, since its history of anti-colonial struggle helps it to identify itself to a great degree with Vietnam, and since from its perceived internal security requirements it sees China as the greatest threat to the region in the long run, Indonesia has a propensity to see Vietnam not as an intrinsically hostile state to be contained at all costs, but as one with a potentially indispensable part to play in the containment of China and in the final fulfillment of the ZOPFAN ideal.

The conflict between these two conceptions of security interests is still largely dormant, and both parties are careful to mask their differences. However, if the various Indonesian dialogues with Hanoi, as well as Jakarta's refusal to come out with stronger condemnations of Vietnam for many Thai–Vietnamese border incidents, can be taken as indications of Indonesia's unhappiness with the Thais' "impositions" of their security requirements upon the rest of ASEAN and of Indonesia's greater willingness to assert its own strongly held viewpoints, then there is a possibility that the prolongation of the Kampuchean problem will bring this conflict out in the open. This is likely to be the case if (1) Thailand's growing self-confidence, which ironically ASEAN regional cooperation has helped to forge, leads to an even more uncompromising posture vis-à-vis its enemy and a corresponding failure to acknowledge what are perceived to be the legitimate requirements of its regional partners; (2) Thailand's insecurity, caused by intensification of the border conflict with Vietnam, against which ASEAN cannot offer protection, leads it to closer cooperation with extra-regional powers, particularly China, that have the requisite strength to offer Thailand protection; or (3) there is a new leadership in Indonesia that feels less committed to ASEAN or less sensitive to Thailand's security requirements.[31]

Second, there may be a conflict between ideals and expedience. As seen above, the Kampuchean problem has led to a significant degree of dependence on and policy coordination with extra-regional powers, particularly China, as a matter of expedience. This has created some dissatisfaction where Indonesia and Malaysia are concerned; for various reasons, they are more committed to the ideals underlying the ZOPFAN concept and a reduction of great power involvement over the long run than to immediate questions regarding Kampuchea. Since the prolongation of the Kampuchean conflict is likely to increase this involvement, the differences between Thailand and Singapore on the one hand and Indonesia and Malaysia on the other may become more pronounced, leading to stresses and strains within the organization.

More importantly, the Kampuchean conflict has also served to divert ASEAN's collective resources and energy from other fields of endeavor, again as a matter of expedience, as indicated by the fact that it takes up a high proportion of the agenda of the ASEAN foreign ministers' meetings;[32] this has created some dissatisfaction among those, especially in Indonesia, who wish to see regional cooperation expand and strengthen in other, "more desirable" directions. This conflict remains muted and, were it only a straightforward conflict between expedience and ideals, would be likely to remain muted, for nations have a propensity toward favoring the former over the latter. But in the long run the conflict may become critical because much more is involved. At stake may be the future of ASEAN itself.

Coping with the Kampuchean problem requires short-term, incremental and issue-specific responses, while the future progress of ASEAN, in terms of both intra-organizational conflict management and intra-organizational cooperation, demands the institutionalization over the long haul of measures designed to deal systematically with a wide range of actual and potential issues. Of particular significance in this respect are economic tensions and conflicts, not only between ASEAN and the industrialized countries but also among the ASEAN members themselves. The problem lies in the fact that the institutionalization of such measures, in turn, requires a much greater degree of vision, political will, idealism, altruism, and stamina than currently is the case, as the ASEAN Task Force Report has implied.[33] What the Kampuchean conflict does is to allow the ASEAN members to disguise their shortcomings in the short run by dramatic demonstrations of regional solidarity and to postpone to the morrow the more mundane but at the same time more critical tasks of long-term organizational development. The longer the Kampuchean conflict drags on, the greater the temptation of ASEAN to evade the reality of these tasks. The eventual costs of this *sine die* postponement may be high, especially if (1) the Kampuchean problem itself accentuates intra-ASEAN stresses and strains, or (2) other problems, particularly intra-ASEAN economic competition, are exacerbated.

These intramural tensions may lead to greater unilateralism within ASEAN that, in turn, would affect the efficacy of the rules of the game guiding the members' conduct of relations with one another and accentuate the differences between them. These differences are not likely to become formal, but it does not follow that they are unlikely to become serious and far-reaching in their implications. The essence of ASEAN cooperation is *process*—process of dialogue, consultation, and consensus-building—and it is through such processes that ASEAN has attained its progress and solidarity. Were these processes to be impeded or reversed, directly or indirectly, by the Kampuchean issue, the damage to regional cooperation may turn out to be irreparable.

If the foregoing analysis is correct, what can one learn about the scope and limitations of regional organizations in general and in particular of their usefulness as a means of promoting order and security as previously defined?

First of all, regional organizations may help to enhance order and security in the short run, particularly in members' relations with one another. But in the long run their efficacy is questionable, especially in cases where regional organizations serve to accentuate conflict with nonmembers.

Second, for regional organizations that do not take the form of military alliances, power, or rather the lack of it, may be the most critical and enduring constraint. This, in turn, leads to dilemmas concerning external affiliations which are not easily resolved.

Third, idealism and the existence of common external threats are forces of both unity and fragmentation. Their impact in each particular instance depends on the actions and behavior of member states themselves. These, in turn, are functions of their security interests and degree of commitment to the regional organizations concerned.

Last, and perhaps most important, the existence of regional organizations does not obviate the need to conduct real dialogues with adversaries. In fact, if tension and conflict with nonmembers constitute factors that impede the development of intra-organizational cooperation *in the long run*, then diplomacy with nonmembers may be one of the most essential instruments for promoting cooperation among member states. This, in the last resort, may prove to be ASEAN's most significant and enduring failure.

ASEAN'S PERFORMANCE IN PERSPECTIVE

The foregoing discussion suggests that the possible consequences of the current situation may be adverse for ASEAN, especially in the long term, and that in order to avoid them a new policy direction may be called for. This in the last resort may have to entail an acceptance over the short and medium term of Vietnam's predominant influence over, but not military occupation of, Laos and Kampuchea as a price for bringing about region-wide peace and order in the long term.[34]

The process of adjustment will not, however, be easy, even if such a new policy direction is seriously mooted and pursued by the ASEAN countries. For, where ASEAN itself is concerned, a great amount of individual and collective prestige and resources has already been committed to the present policy. Great powers, particularly China, are likely to exert strong countervailing pressures. And, most important of all, perhaps, there is no certainty that the present policy is incorrect.

The final appraisal of ASEAN's performance in responding to the challenges generated by the Vietnamese invasion and occupation of Kampuchea must await the unfolding of history. To put it another way, at this juncture it is well-nigh impossible to pass judgment, without a degree of equivocality, on a number of critical questions.

The first is: Whose side is time on? There is no doubt whatsoever that Vietnam is undergoing many political and socioeconomic strains and stresses and that this dire predicament has been brought about in part by ASEAN orchestrated pressures, which have severely restricted Vietnam's access to noncommunist markets and sources of aid, technology and investment. At present, Sweden is the only major noncommunist aid donor and Hanoi's relations with it have not been without friction.[35] Thus, it is not inconceivable that under duress Vietnam may be induced to become more accommodating in time and that ASEAN's present policy will turn out to be fully vindicated.

The second question is: Does ASEAN have any choice but to pursue the present policy direction? It can be argued that even though there may be many adverse implications arising from the present policy—and this is not absolutely certain—the consequences are likely to be more acceptable from ASEAN's point of view than if Vietnam is allowed to consolidate in peace its rule over Indochina and its power vis-à-vis noncommunist Southeast Asia; as many Thais are keen to point out, this consolidation process is dangerous, for no one can be absolutely certain that Vietnamese designs do not include hegemony oover the whole or parts of Thailand.

The third question is: Are some of the adverse consequences said to have been brouught aboout by tthe present policy inevitable in any case? It can be argued that given the ASEAN countries' past histories and differing security requirements, centrifugal tendencies are likely to assert themselves sooner or later; that given their respective economic structures, economic cooperation is difficult, or perhaps impossible to develop to any greater extent over the short and medium term; and that the trends toward increased military spending are global and, in the case of ASEAN, have been likely since the early 1970s, when the United States and Britain began to scale down their security commitments in the region. Thus, it may be misleading to attribute these developments to the prolongation of the Kampuchean conflict, the existence of which has so far served the cause of ASEAN solidarity.

However, while these considerations are important and cannot be ignored, certain realities need to be pointed out. One is that, although Vietnam is undergoing considerable stresses and strains, it still endures: its economy has improved to a degree; the much talked about and predicted divisions within the leadership over the Kampuchean policy have failed to materialize in any significant way;[36] the Soviet–Vietnamese alliance has proved its strength;[37] and, on the evidence of the 1984–1985 dry season campaigns, it is short of neither the firepower nor the willpower needed to continue pursuing its security interests in Kampuchea.[38] Another reality is that, as a result of the 1984–1985 dry season Vietnamese offensive, there are many exposed Khmer population concentrations straddled on both sides of the Thai–Kampuchean border, which the Vietnamese see as staging posts for guerilla operations and hence as legitimate military targets.[39] And the third is that, again on the evidence of 1984–1985, Thai forces are far from being well prepared for the task of defending their territory against major Vietnamese attacks.[40]

The juxtaposition of these realities makes for a highly volatile and dangerous situation for Thailand. A major Vietnamese incursion can take place at any time against a Thai or a Khmer resistance target on any point of the border. Responsibility cannot be solely attributed to ASEAN, but the harsh reality is that after seven years of diplomatic maneuvering on its part, the security of its front-line member has sharply deteriorated, and because by both structure and inclination ASEAN is not and cannot be a military alliance, it can do very little directly or immediately to reverse this trend. If it is accepted that where the Kampuchean conflict is concerned, the litmus test of ASEAN's effectiveness as a regional organization is Thailand's security, then it cannot but be argued that ASEAN's past performance leaves a good deal to be desired and that its future performance must be anticipated with a good deal of skepticism and concern. Ultimately it is within this context that the option of formulating a new policy toward Kampuchea should be considered and pursued.

NOTES

1. ASEAN comprises Indonesia, Malaysia, the Philippines, Singapore, Thailand and, as of January 1984, Brunei.
2. Robert Jervis, "Cooperation Under the Security Dilemma," *World Politics*, 30 (January 1978): 167.
3. Richard A. Falk, "Zone II as a World Order Construct," in James N. Rosenau, Vincent Davis and M. A. East, eds., *The Analysis of International Politics* (New York: Free Press, 1972), p. 191.
4. See Jervis, "Security Dilemmas," especially p. 171, and also Raymond Cohen, *International Politics: The Rules of the Game* (New York: Longman, 1981), particularly p. 3.
5. Cohen in *Rules of the Game*, pp. v and 6, explains that rules of the game "include general norms of behavior, aspects of international law, and rules which are created by formal and informal understanding, or are contained in the 'spirit' of agreements, verbal 'gentlemen's' agreements and different kinds of tacit understanding" (p. v.) and serve to "indicate the limits on permissible conduct, thereby permitting conflict to be contained, and act as guidelines for desirable behavior, thereby facilitating active cooperation" (p. 6).
6. See Cohen, ibid., passim.
7. Jervis, "Security Dilemmas."
8. See Sukhumbhand Paribatra,"Strategic Implications of the Indochina Conflict: Thai Perspectives," *Asian Affairs: An American Review* (Fall 1984): 28–46.
9. One estimate was that 188,114 land refugees arrived in Thailand from Indochina in 1979 and 92,318 in 1980. See K. K. Nair, *ASEAN–Indochina Relations Since 1975: The Politics of Accommodation* (Canberra: The Strategic and Defense Studies Center, The Research School of Pacific Studies, The Australian National University, 1984), p. 108.
10. See an interesting account in William Shawcross, *The Quality of Mercy: Cambodia Holocaust and Modern Conscience* (London: André Deutsch, 1984), pp. 302–27.
11. The most comprehensive overview of ASEAN's development, especially in the earlier years, can be found in Arnfinn Jorgensen-Dahl, *Regional Organization and Order in Southeast Asia* (London: Macmillan, 1982).
12. Guy J. Pauker in Guy J. Pauker, Frank H. Golay, and Cynthia H. Enloe, *Diversity and Development in Southeast Asia: The Coming Decade* (New York: McGraw-Hill, 1977), p. 65.
13. See Joint Statement by H. E. General Kriangsak Chomanan and H. E. Mr. Pham Van Dong, Prime Minister of the Socialist Republic of Vietnam, Bangkok, 10 September 1978. Text in *Documents of Thailand's Foreign Relations 1976–1981* (Bangkok: Department of Political Affairs, Ministry of Foreign Affairs, 1982), pp. 63–65.
14. For an overview of the diplomacy between ASEAN and Vietnam in the 1975–1978 period, see Nair, *Politics of Accommodation*, pp. 25–111, and Nayan Chanda, "Trends in ASEAN–Vietnam Relations," a paper prepared for the Conference on "Moving in to the Pacific Century: The Changing Regional Order in the Asia-Pacific," organized by the National University of Singapore and the Singapore Institute of International Affairs, 5–6 November 1983, in Singapore, pp. 1–10.
15. In his *Conflict and Regional Order in Southeast Asia* (London: The International Institute for Strategic Studies, Adelphi Papers, No. 162, 1980), Michael Leifer wrote: "It is by no means clear whether or not dominance in Indochina may be regarded as the logical limit to Vietnam's strategic bounds and political ambitions. It may be expected that, if in time the government of Vietnam effectively incorporates Kampuchea as well as Laos within a sphere of exclusive

influence, she would assume a different kind of interest in the political fortunes of Thailand than if Kampuchea and Laos had assumed the role of genuine buffer states . . . . Should Vietnam succeed in establishing a major concentration of power within Indochina, the government in Hanoi would find it difficult not to be especially concerned about the political priorities and external affiliations of governments in Bangkok. In such circumstances one would expect it to seek to fashion a structure of regional relations which would ensure that special account be taken of its interests."

16. For a good indication of ASEAN's perspectives during the first year of the Vietnamese occupation of Kampuchea, see Jusuf Wanandi, "Dimensions of Southeast Asian Security," *Contemporary Southeast Asia* (March 1980): 340–47.

17. Jorgensen-Dahl, *Regional Organization and Order*, passim.

18. For a detailed account of the diplomacy in this period, see Nair, *Politics of Accommodation*, pp. 111–156.

19. For surveys of these debates and some discussions of Thailand's collective state of mind, see Sarasin Viraphol, "Thailand's Perspectives on its Rivalry with Vietnam," Chai-Anan Samudavanija, "Implications of A Prolonged Conflict on Internal Thai Politics," and Alan Dawson, "Implications of A Long-Term Conflict on Thai–Vietnamese Relations," in William S. Turley, ed., *Confrontation or Coexistence: The Future of ASEAN–Vietnam Relations* (Bangkok: The Institute of Security and International Studies, 1985), pp. 19–30, 83–88, and 153–55, respectively.

20. For excellent, brief and more or less up-to-date discussions of ASEAN's policy towards the Kampuchea conflict, see Larry A. Niksch, "Vietnam and ASEAN: Conflict and Negotiation over Cambodia," a paper prepared for the Conference in "Southeast Asia: Problems and Prospects," sponsored by the Defense Intelligence College and the Georgetown Center for Strategic and International Studies, 4–5 December 1984, and Donald E. Weatherbee, "The Diplomacy of Stalemate," Chapter 1 of Donald E. Weatherbee, ed., *Southeast Asia Divided: The ASEAN–Indochina Crisis* (Boulder, Colo.: Westview Press, 1985). See also Sukhumbhand Paribatra, "Irreversible History? ASEAN, Vietnam and the Polarization of Southeast Asia," in Karl D. Jackson, Sukhumbhand Paribatra, and J. Soedjati Djiwandono (eds.), *ASEAN in the Regional and International Context* (Berkeley: Institute of East Asian Studies, University of California, 1986).

21. As one official of an ASEAN state eloquently wrote: "Conventional wisdom in the west has tended to say that Vietnam will stay the course in Kampuchea. It would be foolish to deny the Vietnamese record for tenacity. Yet even the best long-distance runner eventually gets exhausted. He may be prepared to run the extra mile if the end is in sight. This is what kept North Vietnam going, especially after 1968, when its leaders saw the clear erosion of domestic support for the war in the United States. This time, as Indochinese history produces yet another irony, the Vietnamese leaders have to ask themselves: Is there light at the end of the tunnel?" Kishore Mahbubani, "The Kampuchean Problem: A Southeast Asian Perception," *Foreign Affairs* (Winter 1983/84), p. 408.

22. For a discussion of ASEAN's consensus approach to decisionmaking see Pushpa Thambipillai, "ASEAN Negotiating Styles: Asset or Hindrance?," in Pushpa Thambipillai and J. Saravanamuttu, *ASEAN Negotiations: Two Insights* (Singapore: Institute of Southeast Asian Studies, 1985), pp. 3–28.

23. See Donald E. Weatherbee, "ASEAN Security Cooperation and Resource Protection," in Kusuma Snitwongse and Sukhumbhand Paribatra, eds., *The Invisible Nexus: Energy and ASEAN's Security* (Singapore: Executive Publications Pte, 1984), pp. 116–21, and "Southeast Asia in 1982: Marking Time," in Pushpa Thambipillai, ed., *Southeast Asian Affairs 1983* (Singapore: Institute of Southeast Asian Studies, 1983), pp. 14–15; also B. A. Hamzah, "ASEAN Military Cooperation: Neither a Pact Nor Threat," *Asia Pacific Community*, 22 (Fall 1983): 33–47.

24. In 1979 it was 91 for, 21 against; in 1980, 97:23, in 1981, 100:25; in 1982, 105:23; in 1983, 105:23; in 1984, 110:22; and in 1985, 114:21.

25. See Viraphol, *Thailand's Perspective*.

26. Kramol Tongdhammachart, Kusuma Snitwongse, Sarasin Viraphol, Arong Suthasasna, Wiwat Mungkandi & Sukhumbhand Paribatra, *The Thai Elite's National Security Perspectives: Implications for Southeast Asia* (Bangkok: Institute of Security and International Studies, Chulalongkorn University, 1985). The findings concerning ASEAN were confirmed by the author's own interviews with some 50 high-ranking officials and individuals throughout 1984 and 1985. See also Suchit Bunbongkarn and Sukhumbhand Paribatra, "Thai Politics and Foreign Policy

1980's: *Plus Ça Change, Plus C'est la Meme Chose?*," a paper prepared for the Third U.S.–ASEAN Conference on "ASEAN in the Regional and International Context," 1985.

27. See the Institute of International Affairs, Ministry of Foreign Affairs, ed., *The Role of the Ministry of Foreign Affairs in National Security and Economic Development* (Bangkok: Policy and Planning Division, Ministry of Foreign Affairs, 1983).

28. A fuller version of the argument made in the passages below is to be found in Paribatra, "Irreversible History?" See also Donald E. Weatherbee, "The Kampuchean Crisis: Year 'N'," a paper prepared for the Conference on "Southeast Asia 1985–1995; A Strategy for Growth, Prosperity and Security," organized by the Pacific Forum and the Institute of Foreign Affairs, Thailand, in Bangkok, 16–18 January 1985.

29. Sukhumbhand Paribatra, "Compromise, or the Slide Towards War," *Far Eastern Economic Review* (hereafter cited as *FEER*))July 18, 1985): 44–45.

30. Jorgensen-Dahl, *Regional Organization and Order*, pp. 237–238.

31. See Michael Leifer, "ASEAN under Stress over Cambodia," *FEER* (June 14, 1984): 34–36.

32. For example, the joint communiqué after the fifteenth Annual ASEAN Foreign Ministers' Conference in Singapore in June 1982 has 55 substantive paragraphs, 19 of which were on Kampuchea and related questions; the one after the sixteenth conference, in Bangkok in June 1983, has 22 out of 55; the one after the seventeenth conference in Jakarta in July 1984, has 28 out of 69; and, most recently, the 1985 communique, after the July Kuala Lumpur conference, has 25 out of 68.

33. *Sixteenth ASEAN Ministerial Meeting and Post-Ministerial Meeting with the Dialogue Countries, Bangkok, June 24–28, 1983.* Jakarta, Indonesia: ASEAN Secretariat, 1983. See also the statement of its chairman, Mr Anand Panyarachun.

34. One possible approach to finding a solution to the Kampuchean conflict is suggested in Paribatra, "Irreversible History?"

35. Jose Katigbak, "Bai Bang Controversy," *The Bangkok Post* (September 9, 1985), p. 5. For more or less up-to-date overviews of Vietnam's economy and politics, see Paul Quinn-Judge, "Hanoi's Bitter Victory," *FEER* (May 2, 1985), pp. 30–34 and K. W. Taylor, "Vietnam in 1984: Confidence Amidst Adversity," in Lim Joo-Jock, ed., *Southeast Asian Affairs 1985* (Singapore: Institute of Southeast Asian Studies, 1985), pp. 349–363.

36. See Taylor, *Vietnam in 1984*, passim.

37. See Robert C. Horn, "The USSR and the Region," in Lim. ed., *Southeast Asian Affairs*, pp. 67–77.

38. See Paribatra, "Compromise, or the Slide to War."

39. Rodney Tasker, "Variations on a Theme," *FEER* (December 12, 1985): 26–27.

40. See John McBeth and Rodney Tasker, "Slack in the Line," *FEER* (July 4, 1985): 36–37, and John McBeth, "Bangkok's High Risk," *FEER* (August 8, 1985): 12–13.

FOUR

Prospects for Cooperation

10

Southeast Asia: Prospects for Regional Cooperation

by Evelyn Colbert

INTRODUCTION

In the years since 1945, Southeast Asia has been transformed from an amorphous geographic expression (one that came into currency only during the Pacific War) to a well-defined region. Not very long ago, it was unclear even what countries should be included in Southeast Asia, an area defined only by its spatial relation to others—south of China, east of India. Today, however, Southeast Asia's identity is well-established. Ten countries claim themselves and only themselves as making up the region; their right to do so is universally acknowledged. The region, itself, however, is divided into two separate blocs, the noncommunist Association of Southeast Asian Nations (ASEAN) and the communist Indochinese "Special Relationship" or "Strategic Alliance." Not only are these two subregions divided by ideology, political and economic organization, and external orientation; they are also in a state of confrontation brought about by the Vietnamese invasion of Cambodia in 1978.

ASEAN, which celebrated its twentieth birthday in 1987, is a voluntary community of equals. It includes all the noncommunist states of Southeast Asia except Burma. Its members account for four-fifths of the region's population and five-sixths of its land area. The alliance among the three Communist states of Indochina is an imposed system, dominated by Hanoi. Its transformation from a party-to-party to a state-to-state relationship began with the Communist victories in Vietnam and Laos in 1975.

The resistance of Pol Pot's Democratic Kampuchea to incorporation in the alliance helped to prompt the Vietnamese invasion. Only after Hanoi had installed the Heng Samrin regime in power in Phnom Penh could the alliance become complete.

Neither grouping is highly organized in the NATO sense. Of the two, ASEAN possesses much the more elaborate structure, having acquired over time a small secretariat, numerous joint committees, and an increasingly elaborate substructure in the private sector. The Indochinese Special Relationship barely exists in organizational form, and Hanoi is at pains to deny that it is or will become a federation. Vietnam's military power is, in fact, the glue that holds Indochina together; its troop presence ensures that Cambodia and Laos will remain Hanoi's client states..No such dominant power exists in ASEAN, whose cohesion and capacity for common action stem from two decades of broadening consensus and thickening ties in both the public and private sectors.

The Vietnamese occupation of Cambodia not only brought Indochina and ASEAN into confrontation; it also sharpened the differences in the external orientation of the two subregions and expanded the great power presence. ASEAN has not abandoned its formal nonalignment. However, identified with the West and tightly linked to the Western trading system, it has moved toward closer political links with the Pacific democracies and more open reliance on the military power of the United States and its allies. At the same time, common interests with respect to Cambodia have brought China and the ASEAN states, especially Thailand, into a much closer relationship than might have resulted merely from Chinese adherence to peaceful coexistence policies. Meanwhile, such trends toward normal Indochinese relations with Japan and the West as existed up to the end of 1978 have withered away. By Hanoi's designation and in fact, China has become Vietnam's main enemy; and a close Hanoi–Moscow partnership has brought Soviet air and naval power into Southeast Asian territory for the first time ever.

In addition to conflict over Cambodia, deep-seated differences in ideology, national goals, and international orientation keep the two subregions apart. Nevertheless, they have been careful to hold their differences below explosive levels. Both have accepted the principle of peaceful coexistence of different social systems. Disputes over such matters as border demarcation and rival claims in the South China Sea create intermittent tensions between ASEAN and Indochinese countries, but those involved have shown little inclination to pursue their quarrels to the point of real danger.

Confrontation over Cambodia has also been kept within bounds. Vietnam has levied bitter propaganda attacks against Thailand—frequently portrayed as Beijing's tool—and has mounted forays into Thai territory as part of its effort to destroy the Khmer resistance. But its incursions into Thailand, although varying over the years in number and scope, have been essentially small-scale, and the Thai response, although determined, has not been escalatory. ASEAN supports the Khmer resistance and was largely responsible for the organization of the anti-Vietnamese coalition government. But officially it acknowledges only its political and diplomatic role; military assistance, where provided to noncommunist Khmer by individual ASEAN countries, is not publicized. ASEAN has also made a point of recognizing Vietnam's special interest in Cambodia and has sought to disassociate itself from Beijing's more rigid and punitive attitude. Both sides, not without a careful eye to tactical advantage, have been assiduous in maintaining their dialogue and both seem to want to leave open for the longer run the possibility of some regional entente.

Meanwhile, however, the two sides remain far apart on the Cambodian issue. Although both have moved away from some of their earlier negotiating positions, these changes have been peripheral to the central issues— ASEAN's requirements for a Vietnamese troop withdrawal and self-determination for Cambodia, Vietnam's for recognized dominance in that country. Each side sees its security as inextricably bound up with the achievement of its objectives. Intermittent differences within ASEAN over how to deal with Hanoi have attracted a good deal of attention; if there are similar disagreements in Hanoi, they have been well-concealed. Neither side, however, shows any signs of yielding. And, at this time, both can count on continued support from their respective great power associates.

However, while Cambodia contributes heavily to the current division of Southeast Asia into two essentially antagonistic blocs, a solution of the Cambodian problem would not automatically result in the broader Southeast Asian community that both sides profess to support. Rather, the division between communist and noncommunist Southeast Asia seems likely to persist well into the future. Meanwhile, although the strains of prolonged stalemate may come to have a negative impact on ASEAN, the ties that bind the ASEAN countries together have become much stronger, the organization's capacity for common action has grown, its international standing is high, and its contribution to progress and stability in the Western Pacific is substantial.

THE INDOCHINA SPECIAL RELATIONSHIP

Unlike the members of ASEAN, geographically connected less by land than by sea, the three states of Indochina together constitute a compact geographic unit. Even so, the diversity among them is great, rooted in centuries of Southeast Asian history. Of Southeast Asia's traditional kingdoms, only Vietnam was colonized by China and deeply influenced by Chinese culture and institutions. As in much of the rest of Southeast Asia, the strongest external political and cultural influences on Laos and Cambodia came from India. Reflecting these different cultural traditions, the Buddhism common to all three is of two varieties—Theravada in Cambodia and Laos and Mahayana in Vietnam, which is also the only mainland Southeast Asian state with a substantial Roman Catholic population. In the precolonial period, Thai and Vietnamese kingdoms—frequently in conflict with one another—expanded into Laos and Cambodia; the latter two often sought protection from one enemy by allying with the other. Then and later, links between Thai and Lao elites were facilitated by their common Tai origin; anti-Vietnamese sentiment, while it exists in Laos, has not been virulent. In contrast, Khmer enmity toward the Thais is surpassed only by an even more passionate enmity toward the Vietnamese.

Out of this ill-assorted trio, France created the jurisdictional unit Indochina. Post-Pacific War nationalism and the drive for independence destroyed the jurisdictional links, and Laos and Cambodia, for a time, were permitted to go their separate ways. Hanoi has now brought the three together again in what it sometimes terms a special relationship and sometimes a strategic alliance, which is held together both by superior Vietnamese power and by leadership ties stemming from long revolutionary association and common ideology. Hanoi's two junior partners, while remaining nominally independent and in possession of all the surface attributes of sovereignty, can be counted on to respond to Vietnamese requirements for common positions or actions.

The origins of this special relationship lie in the links between Indochinese Communists that were first established during the period of French control. It was, in fact, at Comintern behest that the effort merely to unify three competing Vietnamese Communist factions was transformed into the establishment in 1930 of a single Communist Party for all of Indochina (ICP), the membership of which remained largely Vietnamese. It was then on Vietnamese initiative that the single party was dissolved in 1951 and replaced by three separate parties, with the Vietnamese (Lao Dong) party reserving to itself the right to oversee the development of the other two. Thereafter, the Vietnamese party's relationship with its Lao and Cambodian counterparts, while contributing to their growth, was nevertheless heavily shaped by the primacy of Lao Dong interests. This became even more the case after the 1954 Geneva settlement consolidated communist control of North Vietnam but left the South still to be liberated and the two newly independent states of Laos and Cambodia under noncommunist leadership. In Laos, the local Communist Party was a force to be reckoned with; in Cambodia, it was of no particular consequence.

The war with the French had significantly affected Lao Dong attitudes toward Laos and Cambodia, demonstrating as it did their strategic utility to enemies or potential enemies, or as General Giap put it in 1950:

Indochina is a single strategic unit, a single battlefield, and here we have the mission of helping the movement to liberate all of Indochina. This is because, militarily, Indochina is one bloc, one unit, in both the invasion and defense plans of the enemy. For this reason, and especially because of the strategic terrain, we cannot consider Vietnam to be independent so long as Cambodia and Laos are under imperialist domination, just as we cannot consider Cambodia and Laos to be independent so long as Vietnam is under imperialist rule.[1]

Victory in the South, however, was by far the highest priority and its achievement was thus the prime consideration in North Vietnamese relations with Laos and Cambodia, mostly to the advantage of the local Communists in Laos, to their detriment in Cambodia. Hanoi's subordination of fraternal party interests to its own was to become a major element in the quarrel with Pol Pot. As officially portrayed, however, no such subordination occurred. Thus in 1951, a month after the dissolution of the Indochinese Communist Party, a conference of the national fronts of the three countries in the resolution establishing a "Vietnamese-Khmer-Lao people's alliance" emphasized that the alliance would be based "on the principle of free choice, equality, and mutual assistance."[2]

The organization of the peoples' alliance having "created a tremendous force that dramatically changed the balance of forces on all battlefields in Indochina," its victory in 1975 then "strengthened the strategic and militant alliance between the three nations and led to the formation of an interconnected bloc of the three fraternal countries together advancing to socialism and closely bound to the Soviet Union and other members of the socialist community."[3] First, however, it was necessary to dispose of a recalcitrant and provocative Pol Pot. This accomplished, a Vietnamese publication tells us, the formal basis for the alliance was provided in 1979 when Vietnam and Cambodia signed a treaty of peace, friendship, and cooperation, matching one signed between Vietnam and Laos in 1977.

With these treaties the special relations among the three countries had a firm legal basis, and the three countries became closely united in the struggle against the common enemy.[4]

It remains to be seen whether, in due course, Hanoi will see the need to supplement the two bilateral agreements with other formal pacts defining the alliance more fully. Up to the present, the Vietnamese have seemed less concerned with explaining what the alliance is and how it functions and more intent on denying that it is a federation. In April 1978, an official statement, in some historic detail, rebutted Khmer charges that Vietnam was seeking to enslave Cambodia by forcing it into a federation. The statement conceded that resolutions of the Indochinese Communist Party adopted in 1935 had indeed looked toward a federal structure as the outcome of Communist victory. But, according to the statement, even then other provisions left each Indochinese state free to join the federation, remain outside, or leave. Moreover, the 1978 statement claims that the whole idea of federation was abandoned when the ICP was disbanded and "the question of an Indochinese federation was never raised again."[5] Returning to this theme, the communiqué of the first Indochinese Foreign

Ministers' Conference in January 1980 explicitly denied that the meeting was a step toward an Indochina federation.

Since this first meeting in 1980, the semi-annual Foreign Ministers' Meeting has become the principal medium through which the Indochina alliance has addressed the world and outlined variations on Hanoi's position on Cambodian issues. The role of the foreign ministers was formalized in February 1983 at the first, and thus far only, Indochina Summit Meeting. According to the summit's final declaration, the foreign ministers would continue to meet twice a year. These meetings would deal with "all problems concerning relations among the three countries" and constitute a mechanism through which leaders of the three countries could consult with each other between summit meetings. In addition, the final declaration called upon each country to establish a committee to promote economic cooperation and coordination of economic development plans; these committees were to meet together twice a year. Commissions were also to be established "whenever feasible" to promote cooperation in specific sectors of the economy and in culture, science, technology, sports, and physical education.[6]

The coordinating committees have since been established, each headed by a fairly important Central Committee member. In addition to the coordinating committee meetings, since 1984 there have been what appear to be annual meetings of economic and trade ministers and planning ministers. Health ministers, finance ministers, trade union leaders, and bank presidents have also met periodically.

Expectations of what might be accomplished by cooperation among three very weak economies have seemed appropriately modest. In March 1985, for example, a Vietnamese journal stressed the many obstacles in the way—low levels of economic development, shortages of capital and technology, and enemy destruction and sabotage. While the article defines economic cooperation as "simultaneously an inevitable development of the traditional relationships and a requirement for rapidly boosting each country's economy," it concludes that "cooperation in the immediate future must be selective so as to overcome difficulties systematically and generate the impetus for more vigorous development in subsequent years."[7] Nevertheless, a number of achievements have been ascribed to trilateral cooperation. Agriculture, forestry, and fisheries appear to be the focal areas, with accomplishments claimed in water conservation projects, seed development, and aquaculture, as well as in road and river transportation. In August 1985, an action plan for trade cooperation was adopted for the following five years and other plans for cooperation have also been described. However, despite periodic applause for the accomplishments of tripartite cooperation, the most active Indochinese economic interchange seems to be outside the trilateral relationship, between Vietnam and each of its smaller clients.

While Indochina as a subregion, like ASEAN, gives considerable emphasis, at least in principle, to economic cooperation as a major objective, in contrast to ASEAN it is openly committed to advancing military security as its preeminent role. The final declaration of the February 1983 summit meeting defines the "militant alliance" among the three countries as "a fundamental factor in defeating all enemies."[8] Among these, China looms largest. "The Indochinese countries are far from their strategic allies but next door to their direct and most dangerous enemy—Chinese expansionism and hegemonism. This situation attests to the urgency of the need to strengthen and consolidate the special relations among the three Indochinese countries as a regional and strategic alliance."[9]

Security concerns have also been dominant in Indochina's external orientation, enmity with China and the hostilities in Cambodia being largely responsible for dependence on the USSR for economic as well as military support. The importance of the Soviet deterrent role aside, the value of the military assistance the USSR has provided since 1975 probably runs into several billions of dollars. Thanks to Soviet support, Vietnamese forces on the border with China are better armed than their Chinese counterparts. The Soviets also supply military assistance to Laos and, in lesser amounts, to Cambodia, while earlier in the war, Soviet aircraft ferried men and arms within Vietnam and from Vietnam to Cambodia and Laos. Soviet military advisers, present in very large numbers in Vietnam down to regimental level, provide technical assistance and guidance for the modernization of the Vietnamese army along Soviet lines. There are some 300 Soviet advisers in Laos and a very small Soviet military presence in Cambodia (but none serving with military units), and reports (mostly from Thai sources) that the Soviets are constructing a naval base at Kompong Som seem to be without foundation.

The USSR and Eastern Europe have become virtually the only outside sources of support—whether through aid or trade—for the backward, inefficient, and war-burdened Vietnamese economy, with aid from the USSR alone estimated at about $1 billion a year. The USSR also provides considerable economic assistance to Laos and some to Cambodia. Aid to Laos is provided directly and some Russian technicians are stationed there. However, in a 1982 tripartite accord, Vietnam, Laos, and the USSR agreed to principles governing economic and trade cooperation. Soviet aid to Cambodia is provided for the most part through Vietnam and is, in effect, controlled by Vietnamese advisers to the Cambodian ministries involved.

In exchange for this very substantial assistance, Vietnam has given the Soviets access to its territory and waters for stationing aircraft, surface vessels, and submarines in increasing numbers and for establishing or expanding accompanying facilities for repair, refueling, and intelligence collection. This access constitutes a very substantial return on Moscow's heavy investment in Indochina, contributing to the USSR's encirclement of China, strengthening its intelligence and surveillance capabilities against both China and the United States and its Pacific allies, contributing to the enhancement of Soviet competitive standing in the Western Pacific, and facilitating the passage to the Indian Ocean of ships from the Soviet Pacific fleet.

The relationship is not wholly satisfactory to either side. The Soviet–Vietnamese economic relationship has been a source of dissatisfaction: on the Soviet side, dissatisfaction with Vietnamese mismanagement and demands for a greater role in Soviet-supported economic projects; on the Vietnamese side, dissatisfaction with the amount of aid and terms of trade, overbearing Soviet behavior, and the large size of the Soviet advisory presence. There have also been reports of friction over alleged Soviet efforts to use aid to Laos and Cambodia as a basis for building up independent positions of influence there. With ample historic reasons for distrusting each other, the Vietnamese have been intermittently uncomfortable over the Sino–Soviet dialogue, the Russians over problems that might stem from an overly aggressive Vietnamese policy toward Thailand. These frictions and concerns, however, remain outweighed by far by the benefits each side gains from the relationship.

By comparison with ties to the USSR and Eastern Europe, Indochinese relations with other countries pale into insignificance. Formal relations, diplomatic and aid-related, between Laos and Western countries are more extensive than those of Vietnam and Cambodia, but are still far too limited to provide Vientiane with any relief from its dependence on Hanoi and, through Hanoi, on Moscow. Of noncommunist countries only France, Sweden, and India have aid programs in Vietnam. Not only have relations between Vietnam and the West been blighted by Cambodia, but Vietnam's formerly very high status in the Third World has also declined drastically. Although in the Non-Aligned Movement (NAM) itself, Vietnam has at least managed to win a consensus for leaving the Cambodian seat empty, in the United Nations NAM members have contributed substantially to votes retaining the Cambodian seat in the General Assembly for the Coalition Government of Democratic Kampuchea and to the passage by very large majorities of resolutions calling upon Vietnam to withdraw its troops.

ASSOCIATION OF SOUTHEAST ASIAN NATIONS (ASEAN)

Even more than Indochina, the ASEAN region is characterized by great diversity among its members and a historic record of conflict and competition. Like Indochina, ASEAN has not relied heavily on detailed charters, elaborate organization, and a large bureaucracy. Both groupings are alike in seeking through the unity of their members to exclude foreign interference in their respective subregions. Each has developed considerable capacity for independent pursuit of its own objectives but each requires also the assistance and support of outside powers. There, however, similarities end. The Indochina alliance has little standing regionally or internationally as other than a euphemism for Hanoi's control over its smaller neighbors. ASEAN, on the other hand, has won increasing recognition, respect, and influence in the international community, ranking high for cohesion and effectiveness among the world's regional and subregional organizations.

Shared perceptions and action by an increasingly enlarging consensus have been the key elements of the ASEAN relationship. A shared conviction that internal disorder, not military aggression, is the principal threat to national survival has encouraged a common commitment to economic growth and development, as the key to what is called national resilience. This shared perception and a common desire to avoid confrontational postures have precluded ASEAN's transformation into a security organization. A shared perception that opportunities for external intervention are provided by intra-regional conflict as well as by internal disorder has reinforced commitment both to economic growth and to regional peace and the subordination of national rivalry and conflict to ASEAN unity.

Its formal objectives regarding economic cooperation notwithstanding, ASEAN has not advanced very far in this direction. Competitive rather than complementary economics have been a factor in this regard as have different stages of economic development. ASEAN leaders, however, see no important contradiction between ASEAN's doctrinal commitment to the advancement of regional economic well-being and the first priority their governments have given to national development and competition for markets and foreign investment. The peace and stability the ASEAN relationship has brought to the subregion, they argue, have been central to the ability of the ASEAN countries to devote themselves to the tasks of economic development, to achieve their characteristically high levels of economic growth, to concentrate their budgetary investments in the civilian sector, and to attract foreign investment and trade. Moreover, even if economic cooperation has not progressed very far within ASEAN, the common positions on economic issues taken by ASEAN members internationally and in the dialogue relationship with major trading partners have brought both tangible and intangible benefits. Increasingly important also in encouraging a regional outlook and common action on sectoral issues is the network of ASEAN-wide private sector associations stimulated by the existence of the organization.

More recently, declines in economic growth rates, reflecting unfavorable trends in the global market, have focused attention on possibilities for enhanced economic cooperation within ASEAN as one way of coping with protectionist and other threats to ASEAN well-being. As ways are sought to enable ASEAN members to benefit more than they do now from a regional market estimated as worth $70 million annually, proponents of enhanced cooperation have offered proposals ranging from free trade in selected manufactures to a customs union or common market. The approach of a third ASEAN summit by the end of 1987 has stimulated a good deal of discussion both in official and business circles, but in this area, as in others, it can be expected that ASEAN will proceed slowly, cautiously, and by consensus.

Concern with internal security has contributed significantly to ASEAN concentration on national economic development; it has also been a stimulus to bilateral security cooperation. Communist and ethnic insurgencies and other sources of disorder spilling across common borders motivated such cooperation—first between Malaysia and Indonesia, then, in addition, between Malaysia and Thailand. More recently, while the insurgent threat has declined everywhere but in the Philippines, concern with external military threats has increased somewhat in reaction to the Communist victory in Indochina, Vietnam's armed presence on the Thai border, and the new Soviet military lodgement in the region. Military cooperation between ASEAN states outside the organization itself has thus extended beyond the continuing effort to maintain security on common borders. Bilateral military exercises of various kinds have become more frequent, as has the exchange of intelligence, professional experience, and military students, while some steps are being taken toward standardizing equipment. Although all of these developments have taken place outside the ASEAN framework—and this will probably continue—cooperation in security matters, as in other areas, has reinforced the confidence of ASEAN members in each other, multiplied their contacts among themselves, and reinforced habits of cooperation on matters of common concern.

Just as ASEAN's rejection of a military security role has not precluded strengthened military ties among its members, so the organization's official nonalignment has not precluded increasingly close ties of all kinds with the Pacific democracies. Committed as they have been to pragmatic economic policies and export-led growth, the ASEAN countries have become inextricably linked to the Western trading system and especially to the U.S. and Japanese economies. In 1983 and 1984, according to IMF figures, the ASEAN–OECD trading relationship accounted for $84.23 billion of total ASEAN trade of $133.6 billion; within the OECD, Japan accounted for $29.14 billion and the United States for $23.61 billion. The other Pacific members of the OECD—Australia, New Zealand, and Canada—while they too are ASEAN dialogue partners, fall well behind not only Japan and the United States but also the European Community, with only Australia of the three consistently included among ASEAN's top trading partners.

By contrast to trade with the West and even to the Third World (predominantly OPEC), ASEAN trade with the socialist countries as a whole is insignificant. Despite absolute growth, mirroring the growth of overall ASEAN trade, it has remained a tiny percentage of the total since the early 1970s. ASEAN countries are now actively seeking to expand this trade, especially as they anticipate shrinking Western markets. However, a significant increase in the Soviet/Eastern Europe share seems unlikely, although more can probably be expected from trade with China.

ASEAN security concerns as well as its economic interests link the organization to the West in fact if not in principle. Of ASEAN's members, only Indonesia is without some formal Western security tie. The Philippines and Thailand are allied with the United States; Malaysia and Singapore—although, like Indonesia, NAM members—are linked with Britain, Australia, and New Zealand under the Five-Power Defense Arrangement (FPDA); Britain has retained some rather ambiguous responsibilities for the defense of Brunei; and even Indonesia depends mainly on the United States and Australia for military assistance and training.

Even though these security relationships are not ASEAN-wide, they are seen by its members as forming part of the loose web of Pacific security arrangements of which the United States is the center, in which all ASEAN countries are explicitly or tacitly engaged and from which all derive some degree of protection. Even though it resists being drawn into the Cold War and is at times critical of what it regards as Washington's overemphasis on the Soviet military threat, ASEAN looks to the United States to maintain a favorable military balance with the USSR, both globally and, especially, in the Pacific. It looks to Japan and to the United States—although not very optimistically of late—for economic policies that will help the ASEAN countries to help themselves. From the ASEAN perspective, U.S. bases in the Philippines help guarantee the desired American "over the horizon" military presence in the region. The U.S. security commitment to Thailand, even though viewed with some skepticism, is also valued as another deterrent against a major Vietnamese military assault on Thailand, as encouraging a willing American response to requests for military assistance not only from Thailand but also from its ASEAN partners, and as a counterbalance to the Thai–Chinese connection. The U.S. strategic relationship with Japan and China, despite reservations about some of its aspects, is seen as contributing to the favorable balance in the Pacific, constituting something of a check on the prospect that either of these two still-distrusted neighbors will revert to policies that threaten ASEAN interests, and encouraging each to contribute to Southeast Asian well-being—China through continued and strengthened policies of peaceful coexistence and non-intervention and Japan through helpful trade policies, generous aid, and appropriate political support.

The ANZUS relationship has been important to the ASEAN countries as supporting a continued American presence in the Western Pacific, contributin; to the maintenance of peace and stability on their southern flank, and reinforcing Australian and New Zealand interest in ASEAN's welfare. Accordingly, the suspension of ANZUS military cooperation as a result of New Zealand's ship visit policy has caused some apprehension. However, the ANZUS problem is unlikely to affect ANZAC–ASEAN security links, bilaterai or FPDA. To be sure, the ANZAC military presence under FPDA is very small. It is soon to become even smaller. In 1988, the Australian Air Squadron now stationed in Malaysia will be withdrawn to Austi alia and only periodically rotated to Butterworth. In 1989, New Zealand will terminate its long-standing deployment of an infantry battalion and supporting units in Singapore. Even so, the FPDA connection is of more than symbolic importance: joint military exercises of various kinds are held under its auspices—more actively so in recent years—and it supports an integrated air defense system for its two Asian members. The commitment under FPDA also plays a part in encouraging ANZAC military assistance to other ASEAN countries.

RELATIONS BETWEEN THE BLOCS

Despite their current confrontation, ASEAN and Indochina share at least a rhetorical commitment to a broader Southeast Asian community, encompassing all of the regional states without regard to ideology. This concept played some part even in ASEAN's founding; Hanoi, as the leader of the Indochina bloc, has come to espouse it only recently, having been more inclined in the past to link the achievement of Southeast Asian unity with the expansion of communism in the region. In practice, however, war in Indochina has made the development of regionalism on a Southeast Asia-wide basis as impracticable now as in the past.

When ASEAN was organized in 1967, two of its five members were directly involved in the Indochina hostilities. Thailand was an active military participant, providing facilities for the U.S. bombing campaign and ground troops of its own as well. Although the Philippines itself was only marginally involved, American bases there constituted an important link in the U.S. logistical chain. Even Malaysia and Singapore, although non-participants, demonstrated their sympathy for South Vietnam and the American effort in various ways. Only Indonesia, of the founding five, maintained diplomatic relations with North Vietnam and even permitted the National Liberation Front to maintain an office in Jakarta.

The sympathies of their governments aside, the founders of the new organization, anticipating an ultimate Indochina settlement, sought to avoid obstacles to future region-wide cooperation as well as any implication that ASEAN was merely another instrument of the American campaign against Hanoi. This desire to avoid any appearance of confrontation was important among the reasons for ASEAN's strong emphasis on nonalignment, disavowal of a security role, and insistence that its mission was confined to promoting economic and social cooperation.

As the war continued into the 1970s, it seemed reasonable, if not necessarily realistic, for ASEAN to lay some claim to a role in its settlement. Ghazali Shafie in 1971, urging that Southeast Asians, including both Vietnams, meet to seek a peace settlement, called also for excluding outside powers:

For too long the diplomatic fate of Southeast Asia has been in the hands of powers external to the region. Even the venue of these international conferences, whether Paris, or Geneva, or elsewhere, is symptomatic of this tendency. It is time surely that Southeast Asian countries must be the primary actors in what is after all their own future.[10]

In line with this Malaysian view, Kuala Lumpur's original proposal for the Zone of Peace, Freedom, and Neutrality (ZOPFAN) called for a Southeast Asian-initiated peace settlement in Indochina as the first step in the establishment of the Zone. The final ZOPFAN Declaration included no such proposal, but its invitation to "all of the nations of Southeast Asia" to broaden their cooperation was clearly aimed at Hanoi. In 1972 in a more specific statement, the ASEAN foreign ministers called for a cease-fire in Indochina, the withdrawal of foreign troops, release of political prisoners, a political solution, and free general elections, only to have their proposal rejected by both Saigon and Hanoi. In February 1973, the foreign ministers, welcoming the Paris Peace Accords as an opportunity to move forward on the road to regional cooperation, pointed to "the desirability of convening a conference of all Southeast Asian nations to serve as an Asian forum." They agreed also "that every effort should be made towards establishing contacts and promoting interlocking relations amongst these countries" and that it would be desirable to expand "the membership of ASEAN at the appropriate time to cover all the countries in Southeast Asia." Meanwhile "the neighboring countries of Southeast Asia should participate in whatever way possible toward rehabilitation and reconstruction throughout Vietnam and the rest of Indochina."[11]

When the war ended in 1975, ASEAN was uncertain of Hanoi's future course and divided over how to deal with it. Malaysia argued in favor of inviting Hanoi to join, with Prime Minister Tun Razak announcing that "the moment has come for that community of Southeast Asia, which has been our dream, to be realized."[12] Others, notably Indonesia and Singapore, were less optimistic and the communiqué issued by the foreign ministers in May, although noting Tun Razak's hopes for a new era of cooperation, made no mention of membership for Indochina.

By the time of the first ASEAN Summit meeting in Bali in February 1976, consensus had developed against soliciting Vietnamese membership, especially since Hanoi's comments on ASEAN made it quite clear that such an invitation would be rejected. Also dismissed, however, was the proposition that ASEAN, facing a victorious, heavily-armed, and possibly belligerent Vietnam, should now take steps to transform itself into a security organization. Instead, the hand of friendship was to be offered; the ASEAN countries, it was agreed, should seek friendly bilateral relations, Hanoi should be encouraged to identify its interests with Southeast Asia rather than with the PRC or the USSR, and tendencies toward solidifying Southeast Asia into two separate blocs should be resisted. A year later, the communiqué of the second ASEAN Summit at Kuala Lumpur again emphasized ASEAN desires "to develop peaceful and mutually beneficial relations with all countries in the region" while Philippine Foreign Secretary Carlos Romulo declared that ASEAN would "continue extending the hand of friendship to Indochina regardless of what the three communist states say."[13]

Hanoi's hostility to ASEAN at this time was, of course, by no means new. Understandably enough, during the war with the United States, Hanoi had not been impressed by ASEAN's effort to distinguish its own policies from those of its members. It consistently rejected ASEAN overtures, dismissing the organization as a tool of American imperialism and a SEATO in disguise. Matching Thailand's role in the hostilities, it joined the PRC in providing training and material and propaganda support for the insurgent Thai Communist Party. When the war ended it still had scores to settle with Thailand, and its posture toward ASEAN remained basically hostile.

In this early period, the ASEAN countries seemed to have good grounds for their fears that the Communist victory would be followed by an upsurge of Vietnamese-supported communist activity within ASEAN. Hanoi's official media referred to the victory as changing the balance in Southeast Asia "completely in favor of the revolutionary forces and against the counterrevolutionary forces."[14] Vietnamese and Lao Communist leaders joined together in pledging their support for the "revolutionary struggle of the peoples of the Southeast Asian nations."[15] And Le Duan himself described one of the basic principles of Vietnamese foreign policy as full support "for the just struggle of the peoples of Southeast Asia for national independence, democracy, and social progress."[16] References to ASEAN were also predominantly hostile, continuing to emphasize its role as an instrument of U.S. "neo-colonialist" policy to "oppose the patriotic and progressive movements in Southeast Asia."[17]

In mid-1976, however, signs emerged of a more conciliatory attitude, at least toward individual ASEAN countries. By August, with the establishment of relations between Hanoi and Bangkok, normal, although not necessarily cordial, diplomatic relations existed between the now unified Socialist Republic of Vietnam (SRV) and all of the ASEAN five. In July, visiting all of the ASEAN countries except Thailand, Vice Minister of Foreign Affairs Phan Hien emphasized "friendly and good-neighborly relations, economic cooperation, and cultural exchanges on the basis of equality and mutual benefit." To a question about support for insurgent movements in neighboring countries, he replied, "The path taken by each country should be decided by the people of each country." In Singapore, he declared that the Vietnamese had "taken note" of assurances that ASEAN is neither a military alliance nor under the influence of any foreign country.[18]

This mildly encouraging remark notwithstanding, in August the NAM summit at Colombo, Sri Lanka, became the occasion for an attack on ASEAN, spearheaded by Laos, naming the organization as an instrument of American imperialism. Because of the ensuing controversy over the demand that the NAM substitute for its 1973 endorsement of ZOPFAN support for the "legitimate struggle of the peoples of Southeast Asia against neocolonialism," the final communiqué omitted any mention of Southeast Asia. In December, when the Lao Dong Party held its Fourth Congress, its foreign policy statement included a commitment to peaceful coexistence. The credibility of this commitment, however, was somewhat undermined in ASEAN eyes by the accompanying pledge of full support for the "just struggle of the peoples in Southeast Asia for national independence, democracy and genuine neutrality . . . without military bases and troops of the imperialists." That this "just struggle" was viewed by Hanoi as a struggle against ASEAN governments was made evident in other Vietnamese statements. For example, denouncing Thai–Malaysian joint operations on their common border early in 1977, Hanoi described these as "military collusion between the present Thai power holders and Malaysia designed to suppress the patriotic struggle movement of the peoples of the two countries."[19]

By mid-1978, however, escalating conflict with Cambodia and the PRC had prompted a significant alteration in Hanoi's ASEAN policy. As Vietnam moved simultaneously toward the invasion of Cambodia, the new alliance with the USSR, and the final rupture with the PRC, it began to move toward rapprochement with ASEAN (and normalization with the United States). In July, Phan Hien embarked on another voyage to ASEAN, this time visiting all its members and, in the course of his travels, taking a much more accommodating position toward ZOPFAN, dismissing previous differences with ASEAN over terminology as semantic problems of no great importance. In September, Prime Minister Pham Van Dong himself toured ASEAN, reiterating Phan Hien's assurances of cooperation, peaceful coexistence, and respect for national boundaries and sovereignty. To the ASEAN countries, however, it was quite clear that the courtship they were now experiencing, not only from Hanoi but also from Moscow and Beijing, was linked to the gathering storm in Cambodia. As Singapore's Rajaratnam observed: "Everybody wants to win the friendship of ASEAN. That is a good thing. At the same time, the ASEAN members are very cautious. They know exactly what the game is."[20]

The Vietnamese occupation of Cambodia inaugurated a new phase in the relations between the two subregions, one that was both more active and more confrontational. On the one hand, their dialogue has quickened as each has sought to bring about some real alteration in the other's basic terms: ASEAN's for the withdrawal of Vietnamese troops from Cambodia and Khmer self-determination; Vietnam's for recognition of the legitimacy of Heng Samrin's government and of its own military presence in Cambodia. But on the other hand, as neither has yielded in any major way, ASEAN has continued to lead an international campaign that has imposed heavy costs on Hanoi, and Vietnam persists in policies that ASEAN regards as a direct threat to its security and an assault on the principles for which it stands.

Public exchanges between ASEAN and Indochina are not infrequently heated. ASEAN condemns Vietnamese aggression, its "blatant violation" of Thailand's territorial integrity, and its attacks on refugee camps. Indochinese media accuse ASEAN of acting as the instrument of the Chinese hegemonists and the American imperialists, and they condemn Thailand in particular for support of the Khmer resistance.

Despite the heat of some of these public exchanges, private contacts remain almost continuous and each side shows some concern for the preoccupations of the other. Hanoi now declares its willingness to accept ZOPFAN as the basis for discussions about establishing a Southeast Asian zone of peace and stability, applauds the Declaration of ASEAN Concord adopted at Bali, and tries to establish a link with ASEAN on the basis of common suspicions of the PRC whose "dark designs" are directed not only toward "sabotaging the Indochinese revolution" but are also a danger to the ASEAN countries, "threatening the independence and sovereignty of these countries and peace and security in the region."[21] Indochina and ASEAN, Hanoi argues, have a common cause in defending their sovereignty and territorial integrity. Confrontation between them has been instigated from outside, but Indochina has "persisted in its friendly attitude rather than fall into the instigators' trap."[22] ASEAN, meanwhile, has reiterated its own continued allegiance to ZOPFAN, for which, it argues, a settlement in Cambodia is a prerequisite. It has made clear its recognition that such a settlement must reflect Vietnamese security interests and ensure that Vietnamese withdrawal does not precipitate a takeover by forces hostile to Hanoi. Moreover, it has been largely in response to ASEAN pressures that the PRC has modified some of the more rigidly punitive aspects of its own position.

PROBLEMS AND PROSPECTS

The campaign in Cambodia has imposed heavy costs on Vietnam, both materially and politically. By contrast, the material costs of ASEAN's Cambodia policy have been very low indeed. For ASEAN members other than Thailand they are confined largely to supplying the Khmer resistance. For Thailand, they include the damage, casualties, and requirements for military response resulting from Vietnamese military incursions, with the international community meeting most of the expenses involved in sheltering displaced Khmer. The gains for each side have been somewhat less disproportionate. Vietnam's control over Cambodia has fulfilled its aspirations for dominance in Indochina and eliminated what was a continuous and quite serious threat to the security of sensitive border areas. ASEAN's role has raised the organization's international status, strengthened its self-confidence, and reinforced its links with other noncommunist Pacific countries.

Despite intermittent suggestions of some imminent breakthrough, the stalemate seems unlikely to be broken any time soon. ASEAN continues to place its faith in the ultimate efficacy of the pressures it continues to orchestrate so effectively. Hanoi is convinced that time, as in the past, is on its side. And, the Southeast Asian contenders aside, it is hard to see how any compromise solution could be reached without some change—not yet visible on the horizon—in Chinese policy.

Continued stalemate in Cambodia will postpone any prospects there might otherwise be for regional cooperation on a Southeast Asia-wide basis. It could also, over time, do some damage to ASEAN and its interests. Already, ASEAN's ZOPFAN aspirations have been significantly undermined, not only by the new Soviet presence in the region, but also by the revived American and more active Chinese roles, and the heightened possibility of Southeast Asia's emergence as a major theater in U.S.–Soviet or Sino–Soviet conflict. Similarly, the shift in ASEAN security preoccupations toward more concern with external threats has led to rising military budgets and greater interest in military assistance from the United States—to the distress of those who see correspondingly reduced attention to ASEAN's priority tasks of economic development and social betterment—and increasing possibilities that ASEAN might be precipitated into the quarrels of outside powers.

An even more pressing question is whether ASEAN unity will continue to be more important to its members than their differences over how to deal with Hanoi and implicitly with Beijing. This is not a new question. However, it has recently attracted more anxious attention with the involvement of the Cambodian issue in Jakarta politics, the possibility of some decline in Indonesia's allegiance to ASEAN when President Suharto relinquishes power, and the evident restlessness in some elite circles over what is regarded as Thailand's undue preeminence in ASEAN decisions about Cambodia. Even within Thailand, concern has risen over the possible national implications of prolonged stalemate: interruption of Thai progress toward political pluralism, as Cambodia exigencies reinforce military predominance; opportunities for excessive Chinese influence; and heightening Vietnamese reprisals, both on the border and in the form of clandestine support to the Thai Communists.

ASEAN leaders, however, seem to believe that their organization has become strong enough to accommodate national differences and that its unity has brought benefits much too substantial to abandon on behalf of what is, after all, only one of ASEAN's many interests. Thus far, certainly, this optimism is supported by the record.

The future of a broader Southeast Asian regionalism remains very much in doubt. Even in the event of some settlement in Cambodia, there will still be much that divides the two subregions ideologically, in terms of political and economic organization and external ties, in unsettled territorial disputes, and perhaps in competition for preeminence between Indonesia and Vietnam. Even so, there are factors that will keep interest alive in at least some level of Southeast Asian cooperation; among these factors are common concerns over the growing power of a nearby, united, and modernizing China and a common interest in reducing the influence of outside powers over the region's fate.

NOTES

1. William S. Turley, "Vietnam's Challenge to Southeast Asia Regional Order," in Young Whon Kihl and Laurence E. Grinter, eds., *Asian-Pacific Security: Emerging Challenges and Responses* (Boulder, Colo: Lynne Reinner Publishers, 1986).

2. Foreign Broadcast Information Service, *Daily Report: Asia and Pacific* (FBIS, *AP*) (April 7, 1978).

3. FBIS, *AP* (April 7, 1978, May 1, 1985).

4. *Tap Chi Cong San* (January 1982).

5. FBIS, *AP* (April 7, 1978).

6. Ibid. (February 23, 1983).

7. Ibid. (March 19, 1985).

8. Ibid. (February 23, 1983).

9. *Tap Chi Cong San* (January 1982).

10. Ghazali bin Shafie, "The Neutralization of Southeast Asia," *Pacific Community*, III (October 1971): 116.

11. Jae Kyu Park and Melvin Gurtov, eds., *Southeast Asia in Transition* (Seoul: Institute for Far Eastern Studies, Kyungnam University, 1977), p. 167.

12. Alison Broinowski, ed., *Understanding ASEAN* (New York: St. Martin's Press, 1982), pp. 31–32.

13. Institute of Southeast Asian Studies, *Southeast Asia Affairs 1978* (Singapore: Heineman Educational Books, Ltd., 1978), p. 320.

14. *Quan Doi Nhan Dan* (May 28, 1975).

15. *Southeast Asian Affairs, 1977* (Singapore: Heinemann Educational Books, Ltd., 1978) p. 14.

16. William J. Duiker, *Vietnam Since the Fall of Saigon* (Athens, Ohio: Ohio University Press, 1981), pp. 18, 19.

17. *Southeast Asian Affairs, 1977,* p. 18.

18. Nayan Chanda, "Vietnam Breaks the Ice," *Far Eastern Economic Review (FEER)* (July 23, 1976): 8.

19. Joseph J. Zasloff and MacAlister Brown, *Communist Indochina and U.S. Foreign Policy* (Boulder, Colo: Westview Press, 1978), p. 60.

20. Rodney Tasker, "Rivals for ASEAN's Hand," *FEER* (September 15, 1978): 20.

21. FBIS, *AP* (January 16, 1980).

22. Ibid. (November 19, 1984).

11

Regionalism in East Asia

by Richard L. Sneider

HISTORY OF THE REGION

East Asia is distinctive as the only large region in the world that lacks a broadly structured regional institution. Yet to emerge is an intergovernmental organization comparable to the Organization of American States, the Organization for African Unity, or the North Atlantic Treaty Organization (NATO) and European Community. Efforts to organize such an institution have foundered in the past. These efforts were largely security-oriented. The first was built around the Manila Pact and the Southeast Asia Treaty Organization (SEATO) was set up to implement it. Membership was very limited, and though the pact remains in force, the organization was disbanded following the end of the Vietnam War for the lack of common bonds sufficient to hold the membership together in an organizational arrangement. The second effort was the Asian Pacific Council (ASPAC), which also collapsed due to the failure to reconcile the interests of the Southeast Asian members and the nonaligned countries with those of such front-line countries as South Korea. Unlike the circumstances that led to NATO, there was no overwhelming or urgent security threat to bring the region together.

The failure to develop a broad regional institution in East Asia is understandable. In essence, Pacific regionalism has lacked a common thread of mutual interest between countries sufficiently strong to overcome their inherent diversity. The region is characterized by its heterogeneity rather than any commonality. Represented there is every major religious grouping, with great differences of national experience, culture, ethnic composition, and ideological affiliation. Countries are divided also by very different perceptions of their security interests and by wide disparities in their levels of economic development.

In the past, the Pacific Basin was characterized by an absence of any sense of regional identity. During much of the postwar period, relationships were largely bilateral and the United States often provided the common reference point. Lines of communication often led to Washington rather than between the countries of the region. A recognition of regional interests has only begun to emerge in recent years, and only in the last decade have there been the beginnings of regional interaction and communication. The introverted focus on national concerns has gradually begun to break down under the pressures of increased economic interaction and the process of understanding the growing interrelationships between countries. Yet the pattern of the past—inhibited against coalescing in a regional institution dealing with regional problems—still dominates.

REGIONAL INSTITUTIONS TODAY

Despite the absence of a broad umbrella regional institution, a surprisingly large number of organizations in East Asia and the Pacific Basin have been established, perhaps well over a hundred. They are largely nongovernmental, but there are a number of governmental institutions of a more specialized nature or subregional structure.

The closest approximation to any form of broad regional organization is the annual meeting of the ASEAN foreign ministers with their counterparts, or their representatives, from five developed countries of the region—the United States, Japan, Australia, New Zealand, and Canada.[1] These meetings have covered a diversity of problems, but more importantly they provide a means for private communication on common political and security issues. They are informal and largely unstructured, providing a good deal of flexibility and a minimum of commitment. At the 1984 meeting of the so-called "Six and Five," a further step was taken in agreement to have an interim study of human resources for discussion at the 1985 meeting. The annual meetings of the Six and Five are still a far distance from a more formal regional structure. They do, however, form a basis for continuing broader communication and cooperation in the future.

More effective institutions have developed at the subregional level. Most noteworthy of these is ASEAN, which, following the Vietnam War, developed a more cohesive and cooperative framework, providing an interesting example of an institution evolving and responding to changing circumstances. Originally organized with the objectives of economic and cultural cooperation, its real cohesiveness was attained on political and security issues. It has developed machinery for settling or ameliorating the intraregional disputes that have plagued the region. It has been the focal point for developing a common strategy to respond to the Vietnamese takeover of Cambodia (Kampuchea), demonstrating a capacity for compromise— illustrated by the willingness of Malaysia and Indonesia to submerge their own national viewpoints for the sake of supporting Thailand in its confrontation with Vietnam. While efforts at economic integration and intra-regional trade preference have not been too successful, the ASEAN countries have had some success in forming a negotiating group to deal with the European Community, Japan, and the United States on economic and trade issues. Perhaps the most successful aspect of ASEAN has been the emergence of a continuous dialogue and far closer communications within the region. As a result, a sense of common interest has emerged, facilitating compromise and concession both at the official and nonofficial levels. The relatively unstructured, pragmatic, and flexible process characterizing ASEAN could provide a model for any expanded regional institution.

A second less-known subregional grouping is in the South Pacific. The South Pacific Commission was formed after World War II by the former colonial powers as a means of providing technical assistance and training to the island countries of the South Pacific. By the 1970s, the indigenous representatives had come to dominate the commission's work and structure; even before that time, they formed their own organization—the South Pacific Forum—which excluded the nonregional countries. The latter organization has become increasingly important as a means of dealing with some of the political issues in the region and developing some sense of cohesiveness in dealing with outside powers. For the very small states, most with low per capita incomes, the South Pacific Forum has served a useful and limited purpose. It has probably been less successful in dealing with intra-regional problems than it has in presenting a common front to the former colonial powers and in coordinating positions in the United Nations and other multilateral organizations.

At the governmental level, there are other regional institutions with special purposes and functions. The two largest are the Asian Development Bank and the United Nations Economic and Social Commission for Asia and the Pacific. Both of these institutions embrace countries outside the more limited Pacific Basin community. Both have carefully defined functions of an economic nature, and neither has become a focus for an active regional program beyond this limited scope. Even more specialized are such subregional organizations as the Southeast Asian Fisheries Development Center, the Association of Tin Producing Countries, and the like. They function with minimal structure and secretariats but provide a means of communication and, to some extent, training and research, though with no real "bite" or commitment to action.

At the nongovernmental level, there has been an even greater proliferation of regional activity and institutions, designed in essence to broaden common understanding and communication, and generally built around a process of research studies and periodic meetings. The three most important of these is the Pacific Basin Economic Council (PBEC), representing business interests; the Pacific Trade and Development Conference (PAFTAD), which is limited to academic economists from the major free-market trading nations of the Pacific rim; and, more recently, the Pacific Economic Cooperation Conference (PECC), with representation from government officials in their private capacity, businessmen, and academics. PBEC has focused its efforts principally on trade and investment problems of concern to the business interests of the region, and, through its national committees, regularly provides advice to governments on regional economic and business problems. PAFTAD has had a long history since 1968 of studying a wide variety of regional economic issues, such studies generating other regional activities as well as government responses. PECC is a broader effort, begun on the initiative of the Japanese and Australian governments in 1980, to discuss systematically closer regional economic ties. The membership permits interaction with government officials while avoiding governmental commitments to its recommendations. Since its initial meeting in Canberra in 1980, the commission has had three subsequent conferences at Bangkok, Bali, and in 1985 in Seoul. Studies conducted by task forces have been increasingly focused on problems of a very specific nature, of concern to the whole economic community in the region. A key decision reached at Seoul, as always by consensus, was to take a strong stance against protectionism and to provide a forum for regional discussions of trade issues, particularly with reference to the forthcoming round of GATT multilateral trade negotiations. PECC is less an institution and far more a part of a dynamic process of developing communication and understanding on areas of common economic concern. It is not an international organization, but rather a carefully prepared international conference structure. Importantly, it provides a testing ground for a broader and more formalized institution at the governmental level while at the same time avoiding any commitments by the governments of the region to such an institution. To the ASEAN nations, PECC is particularly useful in experimenting with a broader form of regional cooperation and determining whether a Pacific community institution would benefit, rather than damage, ASEAN interests, as at least some of them fear.

Regionalism in the Asian-Pacific region is still in a formative stage, nowhere near as highly developed as in other regions but still very active in a variety of specialized sectors. It can be characterized as experimental, pragmatic, and essentially unstructured, with very small institutional secretariats and no charter or constitution. It is responding not to any broad conceptual approach but to the process of economic growth and interaction, and it has achieved far more extensive understanding of common regional problems. At this stage it would be a mistake to judge Asian–Pacific regionalism by the standards of European regionalism, but it would likewise be a mistake to underestimate the progress that has been made in groping toward some form of broader regional institutions of an umbrella nature.

Disincentives

The slow progress toward a formal regional organization in East Asia and the Pacific is not surprising, and is a logical consequence of a number of factors. The constraints are formidable and the progress toward more informal or limited organizations is therefore striking. The major inhibitions are as follows.

The Character of the Region

The very geography of the East Asian region argues against any sort of cohesive organizational structure. It embraces everything from a divided Korea; an island chain; small countries on the land mass adjacent to China; a large archipelago; two large island groups, the Philippines and Indonesia; Australia and New Zealand; and finally, reaching out eastward, the South Pacific islands. The geography and resource bases have very little, if anything, in common. Unlike Latin America, Europe, and Africa, the cultural, ethnic, and religious origins of the regions are diverse and divided. There is no common base, and historically there have been conflicts between religious and ethnic groups.

The Historical Base

The history of the region also provides little foundation for a strong institutional base. The region has been largely separated historically on a subregional basis, with little relationship between Northeast and Southeast Asia, let alone with Australia and New Zealand. Up to World War II, the role of the United States and Canada in the region was very limited. Most of the countries of the region had very little intercourse, or understanding, or knowledge of each other. The one common thread throughout the region was the fear or actuality of domination by the two largest regional powers, China and Japan. In the postwar period, independence and freedom from colonial rule by the Western powers and Japan made the newly independent nations of Southeast Asia even more introverted and zealous in protecting their sovereignty and freedom from external domination. This factor alone was sufficient to raise suspicions and doubts about any broader regional institution linking the smaller nations with larger and much more powerful powers.

Limited Common Security Interests

The countries of the region share no common perception of their security interests. While all sense the growing Soviet military presence, none has the keen perception and concern about the Soviet threat within the region that is held by the United States. Even Japan, which is probably more keenly conscious of the Soviet threat than the others, sees this in more localized and less urgent terms than does the United States. South Korea and Thailand have probably the deepest sense of insecurity as a result of the North Korean threat and the Vietnamese occupation of Cambodia. But again, they see these threats in a more localized, limited sense, and their concerns are not broadly shared to the same acute degree.

While other ASEAN countries have supported Thailand and meet regularly on security problems despite Soviet protests, they have shown little willingness to make any form of military commitment. And ASEAN and Japan are certainly unprepared to provide more than moral and, in the case of Japan, economic support for the Republic of Korea. From the security point of view, perhaps the strongest common thread in Southeast Asia is a residual fear of China, a fear harking back to past history rather than any current apprehension. Fears of Japan are far from dissipated. Any sign of resurgence of Japanese militarism immediately awakens concern, particularly in the Philippines and Indonesia. Thus the countries of the region are far away from American perceptions of a security threat, whether related to the Soviet Union, China, or Japan. These factors are a formidable barrier to any political or security-oriented institution.

Diverse Political Systems

There is no common political thread in the region. Japan and Malaysia share with Australia, New Zealand, the United States, and Canada a common dedication to democracy. The other regional states have varying forms of authoritarian rule, with the trappings, if not the reality, of democracy. Thus, a common dedication to political ideology does not bind the region. In fact, there is concern about American efforts in the so-called human rights area to force the American system down their throats.

Mixed Economic Base

Disparity between the economies of the region is so patently obvious that it hardly needs underlining. Economic intercourse, particularly trade, has greatly expanded within the region over the past decade as demonstrated by trade between the countries of East Asia and by the fact that American trade with East Asia is now far greater than with Western Europe. Yet coordination of economic policy has so far foundered, even within ASEAN. The very expansion of trade has left a residue of concern among the poorer countries of the region, about overdependence and potential domination of their economies by the two economic super-powers, the United States and Japan. Foreign investment is still impeded by fears that investment will bring a revival of the former colonial domination of the economies and infringe upon the independence of the countries.

In this psychological dimension, a regional institution tends to be seen, particularly by ASEAN, more as a means for the larger, dominant powers to exert pressures on the smaller economies, particularly those of ASEAN nations. These countries instinctively feel that their economic interests are shared much more with the Group of 77 and other developing countries, rather than in combination with the highly developed or even the newly industrialized economies of the region.

Fear of Big Power Domination and Loss of Independence

By definition, any regional institution will force some degree of commitment to the broader regional consensus and some loss of independence of action. Even the loosest of charters and organizational structures involves some limited commitment, as demonstrated by ASEAN. In all the countries within the East Asian Pacific region, there is concern about accepting such a commitment.

The ASEAN nations fear that they will be dominated in their policies by the interests of the United States and Japan, and that ASEAN, still in the growing phase, will lose its identity. There is concern that regional institutional actions will tend to respond to American pressures—whether economic, political, or security-oriented. There are also concerns about a formal tie with Japan, which stem from the wartime experience, the power imbalance between Japan and ASEAN, and a record of Japanese unresponsiveness to ASEAN trading interests. The dichotomy of internal Japanese views on regionalism—between those who see it as a vehicle for regional cooperation and those who see it as a means of expanding Japan's economic and trade interests—leads to further suspicion of Japan. The United States is seen as overly concerned with security problems and less so by economic problems, and as being active only in support of its own policy initiatives while passive to those of other regional countries. Another barrier, from the viewpoint of ASEAN states, is the implicit commitment to a Western orientation that would set them apart from their affiliation with the neutral Third World countries and blur their nonaligned image.

At root, there is a fear that a regional institution will impinge too deeply on the sovereignty of these newly independent countries and will involve commitments that would limit the scope of independent action. At the present stage, few countries in the region are prepared to sacrifice what may be a more hypothetical than real loss of independent scope by adherence to any sort of regional institution.

Global versus Regional

For the United States particularly, another barrier to a regional institution is its fear that regionalism will somehow impede its global economic policies. There has been concern until recently that any Asian regional trading group, even of the most informal nature, would run counter to American pressures for a global liberal trading environment.

The Membership Issue

A problem that will continually make organizing a regional institution difficult is that of its membership. An economically oriented regional grouping would probably best be built around the market economies of the ASEAN nations, the Republic of Korea, and the five outside powers (the United States, Japan, Canada, Australia, and New Zealand) with possibly some representation from Papua New Guinea and the other small South Pacific island countries. This leaves open the whole question of representation from the People's Republic of China (PRC) and Taiwan. From this viewpoint, Chinese membership in an economic grouping would be difficult to conjure with. Yet can China or Taiwan be excluded from an economically oriented regional institution? There is, further, the very complex issue of how both could be included.

On the other hand, a regional institution that is more political and security-oriented is likely to exclude Chinese membership and be built around the noncommunist powers. The inclusion of China in any sort of regional institution, on the other hand, is likely to arouse serious Soviet concerns. The Soviet Union is already watching regionalism in East Asia very closely, concerned that it will strengthen the American role and position in the region. Of lesser concern, but still evident, is ASEAN's fear that any sort of formal association with the Republic of Korea, even of an economic nature, will in some manner involve a commitment to its defense. These worries about membership and its implications need not be decisive, but they certainly add another serious impediment to progress toward establishing a regional institution.

An additional membership issue is the desire of some Latin American countries, particularly Chile, to belong to the Pacific Community grouping. Pressures are already manifest in the PECC, where these countries have observer status but participate very little in the substantive work of the task forces. A drive for membership in any formal institution by the Latin Americans would enormously complicate and most probably undermine the regional movement.

Lack of Compelling Pressures

For most of the countries of the region, the inhibitions, constraints, suspicions, and uncertainties about launching a new regional organization comprise a formidable obstacle to making a commitment to move in this direction in the near future. While there is interest in probing the potential benefits without making any commitments, the general viewpoint, particularly in ASEAN but shared by most of the other countries, is that the present system is working relatively satisfactorily and that any radical change will involve considerable risk. Even under the best of circumstances and with the best of will, the diversity of the region and the limited commonality or the lack of broad common economic and security interests impose considerable restraint.

The critical factor is that inhibitions could only be overcome by a recognition of the need to unify under compelling external pressures, particularly on the ASEAN nations. As to security concerns, there are no such pressures now or are any foreseen in the near term. In the economic sector, there are external problems arising from a fear of protectionism, particularly from the highly protected European market. But they are not of a crisis nature or sufficiently strong to force a reevaluation of a regional institution in thwarting protectionism both from outside the region and from countries within it, principally Japan and the United States. It would require a sense of crisis to overcome the pressures to protect sovereignty and independence in a pluralistic region.

THE CASE FOR REGIONAL INSTITUTIONS

Although the prevailing attitudes in all the countries of the Pacific Basin argue against an early commitment to regional institutions, there are compelling arguments that they ought not. In the first place, objections to and fears of a regional institution are largely overdrawn; a commitment to such an institution need not be as limiting on the sovereignty and independence of the smaller nations as is now imagined. Secondly, while the area of common interest and commonality is clearly less extensive than is found in Western Europe or Latin America, the interests of the nations of the Pacific have drawn more closely together with each year. A clear-cut interest is to maintain the constructive involvement and commitment of the United States and Japan in the region, both of which have global interests that tend to keep their priorities and attention focused on areas other than East Asia and the Pacific.

A regional institution will force these two major powers to place greater policy priority and emphasis upon a region where they share a common interest. The symbolism of drawing together the ASEAN nations, South Korea, and the outside powers within a formal governmental organization should not be underestimated. A formal structure in the Pacific area will give more positive recognition to the emergence of the region as a major force in international politics, while the absence of one inevitably weakens the impact of the region on the global economic and political sphere. For the United States, a regional institution will mark a new level of involvement and dampen down the recurrent nightmare of American disengagement from East Asia. An institution would provide a means for exercising leadership outside the purely bilateral area. With Japan, it will provide an avenue for finally dampening the latent suspicions of resurgent Japanese efforts to control the region, whether by military or economic means. These symbolic and psychological advantages should not be ignored or even minimized.

Clearly, any development of a formal regional institution must be along the path of an economic structure. The regional countries are unwilling to enter into any broader political or security organization, even though, like ASEAN, an economic organization can have political and security undertones. In fact, there is a strong rational and logical case to be made for a regional economic organization, based upon constantly increasing intra-regional trade and other economic activity. There would be benefits of both a positive and negative kind.

On the negative side, it would give the countries of the region a further means to protect themselves, first against arbitrary unilateral actions by the larger powers, such as the American export embargo on soybeans and the Japanese import barriers on processed goods. Both countries have a strong tendency to act unilaterally in their economic policies, responding to perceived national interests while ignoring both the global and regional implications of their actions. An institutional framework may not force them to consult before taking action but can act as an increasing restraint upon unilateral economic policies. It can be argued that countries in the region would have greater leverage within such a framework to constrain protectionist tendencies in the United States and Japan than they have had in dealing bilaterally.

ASEAN leverage in dealing with protectionist pressures from the European Community is likewise limited, and both the ASEAN nations and South Korea, let alone Australia and New Zealand, have been at a distinct disadvantage in negotiating with the Community. A regional institution would provide a much stronger negotiating base in dealing with Brussels, as well as additional leverage against protectionist actions by members within the Pacific grouping. It may also be of some real advantage in dealing with what has become an excessively bilateral negotiating framework between the United States and Japan on trade and other economic problems. It could soften the sharp edge and emotional quality of these negotiations, although bilateral negotiations will still be required.

From the positive point of view, the advantages of a regional institution as a forum for consultation have been well described by Krause and Sekiguchi.

If any of these goals are to be reached, a regular and continuous procedure for consultation among governments of the Pacific basin must be created. International cooperation will help to broaden and lengthen policy horizons of national governments. International consultations can help resolve economic problems in the Pacific basin if they encompass all of the interacting and overlapping aspects of economic issues and bring together both developed and developing countries.[2]

A regional institution will thus provide a framework for management of disputes, reconciliation of conflicting economic policies and developmental plans, consensus against protectionism and unilateral economic actions, expansion of trade, and accelerated development processes in both the less-developed countries and the newly industrialized ones.

Finally, the discipline of an institution is in itself an advantage in that it would make the United States focus on East Asia, since policymakers in Washington tend to ignore regional problems unless a crisis arises. Periodic ministerial meetings and summit meetings of a more occasional nature will force the leadership of countries in the region to develop a broader understanding of the problems faced by the region, as well as providing a forum for consulting outside the economic framework on common political and security problems without getting involved in a regional security system.

FUTURE SCENARIOS

The many obstacles to establishing a regional institution in the Pacific Basin at an early date and the track record so far dictate a strong degree of caution regarding the future. There is at present no strong momentum for pushing ahead with a regional institution soon, nor is there any crisis or overriding pressure to do so. Furthermore, none of the major players in the community, the United States, Japan, or ASEAN, is inclined to take strong leadership to promote a formal institution. No country senses an overriding national interest in moving ahead rapidly with this process.

As a consequence, the most likely scenario is a continuation of present trends. There will be fuller communications between the countries of the region, a broadening effort to understand the problems they face, increased discussion of cooperative actions, and the larger use of non-official regional structures as well as specialized regional organizations. The movement toward Pacific regionalism is likely to be much more of a process of communication and meetings rather than of structural change.

It is likely to be pragmatic in approach, involving a continuing testing process to see whether broader regionalism of a more formal nature will have benefits that outweigh the risks, and whether such a construct can avoid binding commitments that could infringe upon what are conceived of as national sovereign rights. The movement toward regionalism is likely to be incremental and not linked to a specific charter or institution until the final stages.

More specifically, the two key groupings likely to advance the pragmatic, de facto movement toward regional institutionalization are the annual meetings of the Six and Five and the Pacific Economic Cooperation Conference. Both of these groups have made progress in recent years in expanding their dialogue and increasing mutual understanding, trust, and confidence regarding regional cooperation among the leadership of the countries of the region. For the first time, the Six and Five have agreed to a continuing study program between meetings, and there is a more formal commitment of ministers to attend the annual sessions. The PECC has gradually expanded its dialogue and become more specific in terms of its projects, as noted above. The 1985 Seoul meeting was highlighted by a relative absence of rhetoric and set speeches, and an increasing discussion on key issues of importance to the region. It also agreed upon specific projects of real concern: a continuing dialogue on trade aimed at the next round of multilateral trade negotiations, a forum to be developed on energy, a fishery training program, aimed particularly at the smaller countries of the South Pacific, and a major investment conference.

One outcome of the present tendencies may be the development of a more formal relationship between Six and Five and PECC. An ASEAN study group has already proposed that PECC become a resource for research and study on economic affairs for the Six and Five. This relationship would exploit the nonofficial character of PECC and, in particular, its inclusion of the business sector, but still permit a degree of separation from formal governmental cooperative activity and an advisory role which commits none of the governments, although officials participate in an unofficial capacity.

Other possible scenarios would involve more rapid movement to a formal umbrella structure or, less likely, a diminution of the present level of regional interaction. An even more remote possibility is some form of security-oriented organization. This last would only arise from a combination of direct Vietnamese pressure on Thailand and heightened security concerns of the other ASEAN nations.

The prospects for a formal regional institution in the near future are likely to hinge on an evaluation of the economic pressures and benefits accruing particularly to the developing sector of the Pacific Basin. Should a major economic crisis occur, particularly in the trade sector or in a diminution of commercial credit available to the countries of the region, the impetus for an organization which would combat protectionist pressures from the developed countries would be likely to increase. Such a crisis is not at present in the offing, but could occur through a combination of a slowdown or a recession in the United States economy and a build-up of protectionist measures by the United States and the European Community, unaccompanied by any compensating liberalization from Japan. At that stage, the ASEAN nations and Korea might see significant advantage in bringing the United States and Japan into an organizational framework to counteract trade and investment restraints.

Should a regional institution emerge, its structure is likely to resemble closely the look and flexible style of ASEAN rather than the more formalized, elaborate European models. Such an organization would provide a forum for discussion on foreign trade, investment, and economic issues, as well as a means for consultation on national economic policies so as to avoid conflicting development programs. It would also provide a means for discussing longer range and broader issues, such as exploitation of the sea bed, energy resources, and conflicting claims to waterways in the Pacific. It would certainly not serve as a formal negotiating mechanism, nor deal formally or directly with political or security issues. It might well have some sort of cultural adjunct to bridge the cultural gaps in the region.

A regional organization of this nature could operate essentially at three levels. At the top would be a ministerial meeting, perhaps on economic matters, to coincide with the annual ASEAN Six and Five meeting. Periodic summit meetings would be a possibility, perhaps every two years. At the second level, there would be sub-cabinet economic officials, more technically oriented, who would meet on a more regular basis than the annual ministerial meeting, to prepare for the ministerial meeting as well as to provide the means for continuing dialogue. At the third level would be a small secretariat staffed primarily by professionals with economic backgrounds. The professional level could be supported by PECC-type task forces drawn from the business and academic communities and a nucleus of governmental officials on a less-than-official basis. There are a number of possible blueprints, but any such regional organization is bound to begin only on a very informal basis, with its activities gradually expanding as the structure and support grows and suspicion diminishes.

NOTES

1. ASEAN has five founding members: Indonesia, Malaysia, the Philippines, Singapore and Thailand; Brunei joined in January 1984.
2. Lawrence B. Krause and Sueo Sekiguchi, *Economic Interaction in the Pacific Basin* (Washington, D.C.: The Brookings Institution, 1980) pp. 260–261.

Glossary of Acronyms

ACC	ASEAN customs code
ACU	Asian Clearing Union
ADB	Asian Development Bank
AFC	ASEAN Finance Corporation
AIC	ASEAN industrial complementation programmes
AIJV	ASEAN industrial joint ventures
AIP	ASEAN industrial projects
AMU	Asian Monetary Units
ANRPC	Association of Natural Rubber Producing Countries
ANZUS	Australia, New Zealand, and United States Security Treaty Organization
APCC	Asian and Pacific Coconut Community
APDC	Asian and Pacific Development Centre
ARC	Asian Reinsurance Corporation
ASA	ASEAN swap arrangements
ASEAN	Association of Southeast Asian Nations
ASPAC	Asian Pacific Council
AUS	Australia–United States Treaty Organization
BAECON	Bureau of Agricultural Economics
CB	Central Bank of the Philippines
CCOP	Standing committee of ESCAP, for the coordination of joint prospecting for mineral resources in the East Asian subregion
CCOP/SOPAC	Standing committee of ESCAP, for the coordination of joint prospecting for mineral resources in the South Pacific
CGDK	Coalition Government of Democratic Kampuchea
CIA	Central Intelligence Agency
CMEA	Council of Mutual Economic Assistance
COMECON	East European–Soviet economic orbit
CPC	Communist Party of China
CPP	Communist Party of the Philippines
CPSU	Communist Party of the Soviet Union
CPT	Communist Party of Thailand
CSCD	Cooperation in Development in South Asia

DMZ	Demilitarized Zone
DPRK	Democratic People's Republic of Korea
EC	European Community
ECAFE	United Nations Economic Commission for Asia and the Far East
ECDC/TCDC	Economic and technical cooperation among developing countries of the ESCAP region
EDSA	European Distribution System Aircraft
EEC	European Economic Community
ESCAP	United Nations Economic and Social Commission for Asia and the Pacific
FAO	Food and Agricultural Organization
FBIS	Foreign Broadcast Information Service
FEER	*Far Eastern Economic Review*
FPDA	Five-Power Defense Arrangement
FSR	Food Security Reserve
GATT	General Agreement on Tariffs and Trade
GDP	Gross Domestic Product
GNP	Gross National Product
GRU	Soviet military intelligence
ICK	International Conference on Kampuchea
ICP	Communist Party for all of Indonesia
IDA	International Development Association
IME	Industrial Market Economy Country
IMF	International Monetary Fund
IS	Import-substitution
LDC	Less-developed country
LDP	Liberal Democratic Party of Japan
LIBOR	London Interbank Offered Rate
MIA	(Servicemen) Missing in action
MIC	Middle-income developing countries
NAM	Non-Aligned Movement
NATO	North Atlantic Treaty Organization
NCSO	National Census and Statistics Office
NEDA	National Economic Development Authority
NIC	Newly industrialized country
NPA	New People's Army (Philippines)
OAS	Organization of American States
OAU	Organization of African Unity
OECD	Organization for Economic Cooperation and Development
PAFTAD	Pacific Trade and Development Conference
PBEC	Pacific Basin Economic Council
PEC	Pacific Economic Community

PECC	Pacific Economic Cooperation Council
PLA	People's Liberation Army (Communist China)
PRC	People's Republic of China
PTA	Preferential trading arrangement
RCTT	Regional Centre for Technology Transfer
RMRDC	Regional Mineral Resources Development Centre
RNAM	Regional Network for Agricultural Machinery
ROK	Republic of Korea
RPR	Revolutionary Party of Reunification
SAARC	South-Asian Association for Regional Cooperation
SDI	Strategic Defense Initiative
SEALPA	Southeast Asia Lumber Producers Association
SEATO	Southeast Asia Treaty Organization
SEATRADC	Southeast Asian Tin Research and Development Centre
SEC	Securities and Exchange Commission
SGS	Société Generale Surveillance
SPARTECA	South Pacific Regional Trade and Economic Cooperation Agreement
SPEC	South Pacific Bureau for Economic Cooperation
SPF	South Pacific Forum
SRV	Socialist Republic of Vietnam
UN	United Nations
UNESCO	United Nations Educational, Scientific and Cultural Organization
ZOPFAN	Zone of Peace, Freedom, and Neutrality (ASEAN-sponsored)

SeCAP Publications

How the West Should Protect Persian Gulf Oil: And Insure Against Its Loss,
by Henry S. Rowen (August 1982).

The U.S.–Japan Relationship in the 1980s: Achievements, Challenges, and Opportunities (January 1983)

Soviet Expansionism in Asia and the Sino–Soviet–U.S. Triangle, by Harry Gelman (March 1983)

U.S.–Japan Economic Problems, by Shinichi Ichimura (April 1983).

Power Balance and Security in Indochina, by Evelyn Colbert (April 1983).

Richard H. Solomon and Masataka Kosaka, eds., *The Soviet Far East Military Buildup—Nuclear Dilemmas and Asian Security.* Dover, Massachusetts: Auburn House Publishing Company, 1986.

Specimen copies and general inquiries should be addressed to Publications, Security Conference on Asia and the Pacific (SeCAP), Post Office Box 9844, Marina del Rey, California 90295, USA.

SeCAP Directors

About the Contributors

Evelyn Colbert is a professorial lecturer at the Reischauer Institute, School of Advanced International Studies, Johns Hopkins University in Washington, D.C. She received her MA and PhD from Columbia University and has spent much of her professional career in government service, primarily with the State Department. For more than 30 years, she held numerous posts in the Department of State. From 1962 to 1968 she was chief of the Southeast Asia Division, Office of Research and Analysis for East Asia and Pacific (REA), in the Bureau of Intelligence and Research (INR). She served as deputy director of REA for the next six years and then spent three years as National Intelligence Officer for East Asia and the Pacific for the Central Intelligence Agency. Dr. Colbert retired from the State Department as deputy assistant secretary in the Bureau of East Asian and Pacific Affairs in 1980 and since then has been associated with the Foreign Service Institute, the Carnegie Endowment for International Peace, and SAIS at Johns Hopkins. She serves on the advisory boards of several organizations dealing with Asia and the Pacific, including the Asia Society and the Committee on Government Relations of the U.S. National Committee for Pacific Economic Cooperation.

Dr. Colbert's publications include "ASEAN as a Regional Organization" in *ASEAN in the Regional and International Context*; "Regional Cooperation and the Tilt to the West" in *The Challenge of the Pacific Basin*; "The Great Powers and Cambodia" in *Southeast Asia: Problems and Prospects*; "Southeast Asia: Stand Pat" in *Foreign Policy*; *Southeast Asia in International Politics, 1942–1956*; and *Issues of Power Balance and Security in Indochina*.

Jesus P. Estanislao is chairman of the Development Bank of the Philippines. He received his PhD from Harvard University. From 1981 to 1983 he served as a director of the Institute of Industrial Economics and its Center for Research and Communications, and from 1983 to 1986 as president of the Associated Bank, Manila. His major publications include: *Industry: Forecasting for Corporate Planning*; *Regional Economic Development of the Philippines*; and *Rising Prices versus Personal Savings*.

William H. Gleysteen, Jr. is a former ambassador to Korea and State Department specialist on Northeast Asia. At the State Department, Ambassador Gleysteen was a career Foreign Service officer, serving in

Taipei, Tokyo, Hong Kong, Seoul, and Washington. From 1974 to 1976 and again from 1977 to 1978, Ambassador Gleysteen was deputy assistant secretary of state for East Asian and Pacific Affairs. He was also detailed to the National Security Council as a senior staff officer in 1976 and 1977. During this period of service in Washington, he made many trips to China because of his involvement with normalization of U.S.–China relations. His last Foreign Service posting was as U.S. ambassador to the Republic of Korea from 1978 to 1981. Ambassador Gleysteen is a member of the Council on Foreign Relations and serves on the board of a number of organizations and companies focused on Asia.

Ryokichi Hirono is a professor of economics at Seikei University, Tokyo. He was educated at the University of Chicago and has been a visiting professor at the University of Malaya, the University of Singapore, and Sussex University. From 1974 to 1976, he served as chief of the Research Planning Division of ECAFE. He edited *ASEAN–Japan Industrial Cooperation: An Overview* (Singapore, Institute of Southeast Asian Studies, 1984) and has contributed numerous articles to journals and books published in Japan and in Southeast Asian countries.

Masataka Kosaka has been a professor of International Relations at Kyoto University since 1972. From 1983 to 1984 he was Chairman of Prime Minister Nakasone's Peace Problems Study Group, which in December 1984 produced a report on Japan's national security problems. Previously, in 1979 and 1980, he had served as rapporteur in Prime Minister Ohira's Comprehensive National Security Study Group. Dr. Kosaka's major publications include *Saishō Yoshida Shigeru* [Chancellor Shigeru Yoshida], Chūō Kōron Sha, 1968; *Koten gaikō no seijuku to hōkai* [Rise and Collapse of Classic Diplomacy], Chūō Kōron Sha, 1978; *Bunmei ga suibōsuru toki* [When Civilizations Decline], Shinchō Sha, 1981; and *Gaikō kankaku* [Diplomatic Senses], Chūō Kōron Sha, 1985.

Lawrence B. Krause is currently a professor at the Graduate School of International Relations and Pacific Studies, University of California at San Diego. From 1958 to 1963, Dr. Krause was assistant professor at Yale University; from 1967 to 1969, senior staff member for the Council of Economic Advisers; and from 1963 to 1967 and then again from 1969 to 1986, senior fellow at The Brookings Institution. He also served as a consultant for the State Department from 1961 to 1962 and consultant and special representative for trade negotiations (Christian Herter) from 1963 to 1964. Currently Dr. Krause is an active member of the International Steering Committee, Pacific Trade and Development Conference, and the Editorial Advisory Board of the *Political Science Quarterly*. He is also a member of the Advisory Board for the Institute for International Economics, the Academic Board of the National Institute of Economics and Industry Research (Australia), and the executive committee of the U.S. National Committee for Pacific Economic Cooperation.

Some of Dr. Krause's most recent major publications include *The Singapore Economy Reconsidered*, Institute of Southeast Asian Studies, 1987; *The Australian Economy, A View from the North*, The Brookings Institution, 1984; *The Economic Interaction in the Pacific Basin*, The Brookings Institution, 1980; and *The Mineral Resources in the Pacific Area*, Federal Reserve Bank of San Francisco, 1978. Dr. Krause received his PhD from Harvard University.

Hongkoo Lee has been a professor of International Relations at Seoul National University since 1968. He received his MA and PhD from Yale University and was a visiting fellow at the Woodrow Wilson International Center and Harvard Law School. His major publications include *Social Conservation and Political Development*, 1968; *Modernization*, 1978; and *One Hundred Years of Marxism*, 1984. Dr. Lee has contributed numerous articles to journals and books published in Korea and the United States.

Masashi Nishihara has been a professor of International Relations at the National Defense Academy, Japan, since 1977. He received his MA and PhD in political science from the University of Michigan. From 1981 to 1982, he served as a visiting research fellow at The Rockefeller Foundation. His major publications include *The Japanese and Sukarno's Indonesia*, University Press of Hawaii, 1976; "Promoting Partnership: Japan and Europe," *The Washington Quarterly* (Winter, 1983); "Expanding Japan's Credible Defense Role," *International Security* (Winter, 1983–1984); and *East Asian Security and the Trilateral Countries*, New York University Press, 1985.

Sukhumbhand Paribatra is an assistant professor of International Relations at Chulalongkorn University, Bangkok, and director of the Security Studies Programme, Institute of Security and International Studies at the same university. He graduated from Oxford University and Georgetown University. He has focused his research interest on Thai foreign and security policies and the Cambodian conflict. His publications on Cambodia include "Can ASEAN Break the Stalemate," *World Policy Journal* (Winter 1985–1986) and "Irreversible History? ASEAN, Vietnam and the Polarisation of Southeast Asia," in Karl Jackson, Soedjati Djiwandono and Sukhumbhand Paribatra (eds.), *ASEAN in the Regional and International Context*, Institute of East Asian Studies, University of California, in press.

Robert A. Scalapino is currently Robson Research Professor of Government at the University of California at Berkeley and also director of the university's Institute of East Asian Studies. He is also an editor of *Asian Survey*, a scholarly publication. Professor Scalapino has written over 200 articles and 15 books or monographs on Asian politics and U.S. Asian policy. His most recent works include *Asia and the Major Powers* (1972); *American–Japanese Relations in a Changing Era* (1972); *Communism in Korea* (two volumes, with Chong-Sik Lee, 1972, for which they received the Woodrow Wilson Award for the best book published in 1973 on government, politics or international affairs); *Asia and the Road Ahead* (1975); *The Foreign Policy of Modern Japan* (editor and contributor, 1977); *The United States and Korea—Looking Ahead* (1979); "Asia," in *The United States in the 1980s* (1980); "China and Northeast Asia," in *The China Factor* (1981); "The Political Influence of the USSR in Asia," in *Soviet Policy in East Asia* (1982); and *Modern China and its Revolutionary Process* (co-authored with George T. Yu, 1985).

Richard L. Sneider was an adjunct Professor for Columbia University after a long distinguished career with the Department of State. He received his M.I.A. from Columbia University.

Mr. Sneider served four years as U.S. ambassador to Korea, after having held other senior positions in government. For two years prior to becoming ambassador to Korea, he was deputy assistant secretary of state, Bureau of East Asian and Pacific Affairs. From 1969 to 1972, he served as minister and deputy chief of mission at the American Embassy in Tokyo. Concurrently, he served as principal negotiator for the Okinawan Reversion Negotiations, which resulted in the return of Okinawa to Japan. In the late 1960s, Mr. Sneider was the senior staff member for East Asia at the National Security Council.

Ambassador Sneider served on the advisory boards of many organizations devoted to U.S.–Asian and Pacific affairs. Both in government and outside of it, he dedicated himself to promoting the bilateral relationship between the United States and Japan.